Political Theory and Political Science

POLITICAL THEORY AND POLITICAL SCIENCE

Studies in the Methodology of Political Inquiry

MARTIN LANDAU
City University of New York—Brooklyn

THE MACMILLAN COMPANY
NEW YORK
Collier-Macmillan Limited · LONDON

COPYRIGHT © 1972, MARTIN LANDAU

PRINTED IN THE UNITED STATES OF AMERICA

All rights reserved. No part of this book may be reproduced or transmitted in any form or by any means, electronic or mechanical, including photocopying, recording, or any information storage and retrieval system, without permission in writing from the Publisher.

Portions of this material have been reprinted with modifications from articles by Martin Landau which originally appeared in *American Behavioral Scientist, Social Research, Political Science Quarterly, Political and Administrative Development,* and *Concepts of Issues in Administrative Development*. Specific acknowledgments appear at the beginnings of chapters.

THE MACMILLAN COMPANY
866 Third Avenue, New York, New York 10022
COLLIER-MACMILLAN CANADA, LTD., Toronto, Ontario

Library of Congress catalog card number: 77-176058

Printing: 1 2 3 4 5 6 7 8   Year: 2 3 4 5 6 7 8

To Bobby

Preface

THERE SEEMS to be little doubt that the proverbial man in the street operates on the basis of a set of decision rules that are variously referred to as "recipes," "codes," "maps," and "mazeways." These, generally, are *conventions* and accordingly tend to be taken for granted. They are trusted not because they have been tested or grounded but because they are familiar. It often turns out that these familiar modes of procedure, these trusted habits of mind, are nothing more than "dead metaphors" —giving rise to the nonsense, error, and even tragedy that can attend the use of stereotypes. If, however, we follow Alfred Schutz, the sign of the "well-informed citizen" is that he will not accept formulas until he understands them and he will not act under their guidance unless they are reasonably well founded. The well-informed citizen, therefore, is a methodologist; the moment anyone transforms the "givens" of his day into problematic questions, at that moment he has opened inquiry into the logic and procedure of analysis. If he continues to engage in this inquiry, extending it to the novel as well as the traditional, he displays the critical scrutiny, the rigorous intellectual effort, that is the hallmark of any knowledge-producing enterprise.

The growth of methodology courses in our discipline is, then, a happy circumstance. It is to be associated with a heightened awareness of the need for a tough-minded critical stance. Disciplines, like societies, also produce conventions, retained not because they are time-tested but because they are timeworn. Timeworn and unquestioned, they constitute implicit categories of thought that engender "schoolmen"; and when these abound, a discipline exhibits the organizational paradox (the displace-

Preface

ment of goals), thereby abandoning the commitment to knowledge and the principle of accountability of assertion. Hence it is that constant methodological inquiry, constant and searching criticism, is so refreshing a development. If anything, it protects against dogma. It also enables "well-informed" political scientists.

Chapters 1 and 2 were written at Berkeley, where I visited for two years, and constitute my attempt to cope with some of the major criticisms that have recently been lodged against the application of scientific methodologies to the study of politics. At Berkeley, I enjoyed a vital and stimulating intellectual environment and a most gracious hospitality. My debt to Carl G. Rosberg, Ernst Haas, and Eugene Lee is considerable. I also want to thank Jack Citrin, Giuseppe Di Palma, Todd La Porte, Dan Lev, Herbert McClosky, Nelson Polsby, Frank Rourke, John Ruggie, Aaron Wildavsky, and my daughter Madeline. They joined with the students in my course on methodology in providing a critical and constructive audience. Nor can I omit my daughter Claudia, who worked with her mother to help immeasurably in putting this book together.

The remaining six essays were written in association with the seminar in methodology that I was privileged to teach at Brooklyn College. The extent of my debt to such students (now colleagues) as George Balch, Henry Beck, Alan Dershowitz, James Farganis, Vincent Fuccillo, Joel Kassiola, Robert Kvavik, Jacob Landynski, Ellen Rosen, Allan and Marvin Schick, Edward Schneider, and David Schwartz is truly immense. Over this period, I profited greatly from discussions with Charles S. Ascher, Abraham Bargman, Morton Berkowitz, Bernard E. Brown, John Hope Franklin, Albert Gorvine, K. William Kapp, Martin Lean, Dennis Palumbo, Benjamin Rivlin, and Salvatore Cannavo. I have a special debt to two colleagues who are no longer with us, Gerald Henderson and Samuel J. Konefsky. The untimely death of these scholars robbed anthropology and po-

Preface

litical science of truly extraordinary teachers. And beyond those, I am indebted to every footnote in this volume, and to hosts of scholars who have contributed to my education in one way or another. All too often we restrict the concept of teaching to the classroom and fail to realize that the books, monographs, and articles that we read are, in their first estate, teaching materials. I will have paid back some of my debt if it can be said that the essays presented here do teach something of value.

I am very pleased that The Macmillan Company, under the initiative of James J. Carroll, Jr., has seen sufficient unity in these essays to publish them as a book. In the essays that have been reprinted, I have made both editorial and substantive changes in an effort to improve the story line. It runs as follows:

Strolling in Central Park one sunny day, a famous philosopher of science came upon a group of young people busily working to create a "happening." Somewhat bemused, he paused to observe. One young man in the group recognized him and sauntered over.

"Well, professor," said the young man, "How do you like it?"

"It looks fine to me," came the answer, "but I don't quite understand what is going on."

"Oh," said the young man, "you don't have to understand; you just have to do your own thing."

"Yes," the philosopher responded, "but the trouble is that understanding is my thing."

M. L.

Contents

1. Science and Political Science: Some Observations on Prevailing Complaints   3
2. Objectivity, Neutrality, and Kuhn's Paradigm   43
3. On the Use of Metaphor in Political Analysis   78
4. On the Use of Functional Analysis in American Political Science   103
5. The Myth of Hyperfactualism in the Study of American Politics   122
6. Development Theory: Some Methodological Problems   147
7. Political Science and Public Administration: "Field" and the Concept of Decision Making   177
8. Due Process of Inquiry   211

   Index   235

Political Theory and Political Science

CHAPTER I

Science and Political Science: Some Observations on Prevailing Complaints

> Experience has shown that—all enthusiastic ideas to the contrary—society must cultivate science on its own terms and for its own intrinsic purpose, if science is to make any progress at all.
>
> MICHAEL POLANYI

A DECADE ago, in a vigorous protest, Howard B. White denounced the manipulation of public opinion and decried the production of the "processed voter." White held the academy accountable; most particularly, the professors of political science. "They are responsible because they have indoctrinated their students with a political science that is either 'value-free' or guided by a 'value relativism.' "[1]

The following year, the Strauss group published its critique of the scientific study of politics. In the final epitome, Leo Strauss remarked that this movement placed a premium on observations which could be made with the greatest frequency "and therefore by people of the meanest capacities," often culminating "in observations made by people who are not intelligent about people who are not intelligent." He hastened to add that it was not diabolic—it had none of the attributes of fallen angels. Nor, he suggested, was it Machiavellian: "for Machiavelli's teaching was

[1] Howard B. White, "The Processed Voter and the New Political Science," *Social Research*, Vol. 28 (1961), p. 127. The statement by Polanyi is quoted from *The Republic of Science* (Chicago: Roosevelt University, 1962), p. 18.

graceful, subtle, and colorful." Nor was it Neronian: "one may say of it that it fiddles while Rome burns," but "it does not know that it fiddles, and it does not know that Rome burns."[2]

More recently, McCoy and Playford accused the "behavioralists" of having "concocted their own ivory tower out of jargon and scientism." They are apolitical, having failed to address those "genuinely significant problems" which concern us most. "By establishing methodology as the most relevant criterion for research they turn the students of politics into political eunuchs."[3]

And, finally, the scientific school, "methodism" as Wolin refers to it, has not only impoverished education but has restricted imagination and thereby trivialized theory.[4]

Covering a full decade, these are comments that reflect the tone of much of the criticism lodged against the scientific movement. What has been offered, however, appears more an indictment than a criticism. The full bill tells us that "science" is "characterized by conservatism, fear of popular democracy, and an avoidance of vital political issues"; states "it is presumptuous at best for [empirical social science] to claim to have solved the Mannheim Paradox"; charges that it is "opposed to any massive extension of democratic participation in the political process"; and, finally, asserts that the movement is "anti-political. In [its] attempt to turn politics into a value-free science, [it has] shown a marked tendency to throw out politics altogether."[5] Against this backdrop, the image which emerges is that of an intruder at once

[2] Leo Strauss, "An Epilogue," in Herbert J. Storing (ed.), *Essays on the Scientific Study of Politics* (New York: Holt, Rinehart & Winston, 1962), pp. 326–327. Strauss's use of "mean" is statistical.

[3] Charles A. McCoy and John Playford (eds.), *Apolitical Politics* (New York: Thomas Y. Crowell, 1967), pp. 8–9.

[4] Sheldon S. Wolin, "Politics As a Vocation," *American Political Science Review*, Vol. 63 (1969).

[5] These are taken from the Introduction to McCoy and Playford, *op. cit.* See also David Easton, "The New Revolution in Political Science," *American Political Science Review*, Vol. 63 (1969), where it is said that behavioral science "unwittingly purveys an ideology of social conservatism tempered by modest incremental change" (p. 1052).

Science and Political Science

foolish and menacing. But less a fool than a menace. And while we may in charity suffer fools, menaces must be put to an end.[6]

In this respect, it is instructive to consider Whorf's suggestion that the cue to a line of behavior "is often given by the analogies of the linguistic formula [by] which a situation is spoken of...." Metaphors, rhetorical flourishes, figures of speech generally, tell us something of how a phenomenon is to be treated—to be analyzed, evaluated, and allotted its place in the scheme of things.[7] In the case at hand, a science of politics, no more incendiary issue confronts the discipline. Nor has there ever been a period marked by such sustained warfare.

And "warfare" is the proper term. Consider, for example, the analogies contained in the following formulations of Schaar and Wolin—delivered, incidentally, on the occasion of their assault on the Straussians: "Not all the bastions of the older political science have fallen . . . the new political scientists continue to press the offensive . . . assuming a continuation of the present rate of advance . . . the ease and quickness with which the new forces have occupied large sectors of the field . . . without serious resistance from the older political science...."[8] On the other side, and immediately corroborative—though written before the "post-behavioral revolution" had been announced—Easton warned that "the battle . . . is by no means over," as he cautioned against "mistaking a series of continuous preliminary skirmishes for the main engagement."[9]

It now seems that we have reached this point. It is therefore

---

6 See Marvin Surkin and Alan Wolfe (eds.), *An End to Political Science: The Caucus Papers* (New York: Basic Books, 1970).

7 Benjamin Lee Whorf, *Language, Thought, and Reality* (New York: John Wiley & Sons, 1956), p. 137.

8 John H. Schaar and Sheldon S. Wolin, "Essays on the Scientific Study of Politics: A Critique," *American Political Science Review*, Vol. 57 (1963), p. 125.

9 David Easton, "The Current Meaning of Behavioralism," in James C. Charlesworth (ed.), *Contemporary Political Analysis* (New York: Free Press, 1967), p. 11.

understandable, though most unfortunate, that methodological discussion invariably occurs in a charged atmosphere; that exchanges are matters of combat, not communication; that epithet and invective explode; and that more is defended than clarified. In this circumstance, that honored enterprise, begun so long ago and at such great cost, devoted to "a specially firm determination not to persist in error if any exertion of hand or mind can deliver us from it"[10] becomes our first casualty. For what matters in warfare is victory, not knowledge.

But if it is the case that in the pursuit of enlightenment we must take the path of systematic doubt, then the enabling rule of the discipline stands as presented originally by Charles S. Peirce:

Upon this first, and in one sense this sole, rule of reason, that in order to learn you must desire to learn, and in so desiring not be satisfied with what you already incline to think, there follows one corollary which itself deserves to be inscribed upon every wall of the city of philosophy: Do not block the way of inquiry.[11]

Two Classes of Objections

I believe it was Bertrand Russell, in commenting on the scientific outlook, who observed that there are viewpoints that first describe certain goals as impossible and then denounce them if they are proven realizable.

McCoy and Playford tell us that there are two classes of objections to the application of scientific method to politics. The first, which they themselves hold, states that some things cannot be analyzed scientifically; the second, evidenced by the Straussians, argues that some things should not be analyzed. These positions often merge, as a reading of both the Storing and the McCoy-Playford volumes reveals. But there is a difference. The

---

10 Peter B. Medawar, *Induction and Intuition in Scientific Thought* (Philadelphia: American Philosophical Society, 1969), p. 59.

11 Charles S. Peirce, *Essays in the Philosophy of Science,* edited by Vincent Thomas (New York: Liberal Arts Press, 1957), pp. 229–230.

Science and Political Science

former states a hypothesis; the latter, a preference. Let us examine both in order.

Objection I: One Cannot

However we define science, it remains manifestly clear that some such "thing" exists. The name itself has been with us a long time and is a part of our common idiom. In the vernacular, it presents us with few problems and is assigned to certain spheres of life without too much difficulty—and by both layman and scientist alike. Astronomy, for example, is a science; so is physics, and so is chemistry. These are natural sciences. Where social science is concerned, there is a doubt. But there is none as to poetry. Evidently, there are some criteria of identification, implicit or otherwise, which are employed in a fairly stable manner. Thus, it would be curious if we observed people calling poetry a science and physics poetry. Curious indeed: for the obvious statistical property of common linguistic usage is that the opposite is invariant. Physics and poetry name two distinctive, mutually exclusive domains and the reversal of these terms is either ironic, quixotic, or purely metaphoric. The ordinary lexicon, thus, establishes some demarcation between pursuits that can be predicated as scientific, even potentially so, and those that cannot. Poetry lies in the latter context, whereas physics stands as our clearest instance of a science. Its successes are legendary, its demonstrations have been overwhelmingly powerful, and its history, increasingly publicized, tells us something of the manner in which it has proceeded. In contrast, the successes of social science are minimal, its demonstrations lack persuasive force, and its history is rather confusing. Yet we still say social *science*. Apparently it is deemed to possess some of the properties of this term, sufficient to enable the assignment, if only weakly. If we draw out the implication of this usage, the difference between physics and politics is not disjunctive: it is not either-or, but to what extent.

While there is a general acknowledgment that the study of

Political Theory and Political Science

politics is largely undeveloped along the dimensions that describe physics, the idea that the gap can be closed intrigues many scholars. That is, physics models science for much of the contemporary movement. Any reading of its literature permits one to say that the prevailing vision is of a politics that possesses the scientific properties of physics.

To assert now that there cannot be such a political science is simply to describe a future state of affairs. This assertion clearly belongs to the class of hypothetical propositions. It is literally hypothetical and cannot be accepted a priori. Insistence that the hypothesis is correct, that a science of politics is impossible, may perhaps be taken as a matter of preference. As a matter of fact, it possesses no warrant; the question of a political "science" remains problematical.

This situation is not altered in any way by a positive claim. Necessarily cast in the future tense, any such proposal constitutes only a possibility. But possibilities are not probabilities and they cannot be so transformed by mere acts of faith or expressions of hope. One may admire, even share, a spirit of optimism but those who offer the promise of a science bear the burden of proof. They must provide evidence, demonstrations of sufficient power to move this goal from the stage of plausibility to that of probability and, perhaps, even to certainty. Against this ideal, given any time span, it may also be that only a partial success can be attained; that the formal and precise character of physics is forever elusive. In that event, we may employ the term "science" but it will be a science of sorts—an inexact system of much lesser probability value. Or it may apply to very restricted and specific segments of our experience; or life may sustain a perpetual conspiracy to confound our explanations.

Yet it seems inevitable that once a domain of inquiry is set on the foundations of experience, the attempt will be made to treat it scientifically. If there are methods that allow us to gain a systematic knowledge of the field under scrutiny, it is a self-defeating strategy not to use them.

Science and Political Science

Methods, however—i.e., methods of science—are themselves objects of controversy. There is doubt as to whether there is a "methodology of science"—a well-conceived, tried and tested set of decision rules that can be taken as programmatic. Oftentimes, attention will be called to philosophers of science who continue to argue about the logic and procedure of scientific analysis and who have been unable to provide a universally accepted description of its properties. Nevertheless, any claim that there is not a "methodology of science" amounts to the proposition that scientific successes have been random events, sheer accidents, or the results of plain luck.[12] One can accept the notion that there will never be a complete methodology, that there are many unresolved problems, that, like science itself, methodology is all the time becoming—but this does not gainsay the fact that there is some powerful apparatus at work. Nor is this apparatus mysterious, for it has become, precisely because of its power, an object of inquiry in itself. Having been exposed, analyzed, and, to a considerable degree, clarified, its contributions to knowledge commend it. No surprise should therefore attend its extension into other, seemingly remote, domains. But in these, obviously, it will be results that count.

More immediately, it is *counting* that is at issue. In political science, critics have made methodology synonymous with quantification, which is itself taken as a "pathological condition"[13] that leads only to "pretentious collections of triviality."[14] Problems, it is said, are chosen on the basis of such methodological criteria, not because of their political significance, and the consequence is an impoverishment of the discipline.

What is interesting here is that we are all "counters"—and any suggestion to the contrary defies the logic of everyday experience.

[12] See Joseph Agassi, "Positive Evidence in Science and Technology," *Philosophy of Science,* Vol. 37 (1970).
[13] McCoy and Playford, op. cit., p. 10.
[14] Hans Morgenthau, "Reflections on the State of Political Science," *Review of Politics,* Vol. 17 (1955), p. 442.

Political Theory and Political Science

There is no human judgment that is not based upon "sampling": any observation, of any kind, is a count, and any conclusion must be based on a sample survey. When, for example, Strauss states that the scientific movement places a premium on observations which can be made with the greatest frequency, this is a quantitative statement. Presumably, he has "measured." If Morgenthau and Wolin have concluded that quantification has trivialized our work, have they not assigned a "grade?" There must be a scale involved in this judgement, probably unidimensional, ranging from trivia to importance—and by some count of some sample, they have plotted the "quantifiers" on this scale. If Christian Bay says that much of the current work on political behavior fails to articulate its real "value biases," he can only state this on the basis of a count. What is more, we often correlate the counts we make of different things, going so far as to produce causal connections—as when one says "the political impact of this supposedly neutral literature is generally conservative and . . . antipolitical."[15]

Now it is rather obvious that neither Strauss, nor Morgenthau, nor Wolin, nor Bay has examined the work of every "behavioral" political scientist. And it can be hypothesized that their findings of "central tendency" are based on rather crude sampling procedures and are quite prone to error. Yet it is a rare event to see such "findings" carry an estimate of the probable error involved. (Presently, I am worrying about the extent of error that accompanies the statements I am making.) It may, of course, be said that all they are doing is typifying or characterizing certain groups of political scientists. But even the act of identification is measurement for what we are obliged to do is to map the object under scrutiny to some set of class properties and if there is equivalence assign it to that class. A careful look at this type of "nominal scaling" reveals that the process of measurement is tantamount to the process of comparison: the mapping of some unknown X

---

[15] Christian Bay, "Politics and Pseudopolitics," in McCoy and Playford, op. cit., p. 13.

to some fixed, known standard. If, incidentally, this standard is vague, ambiguous, and imprecise, it is a safe bet that we are employing a metaphor—which is the way we usually begin when we search for precise connotations.[16]

In any case, the fundamental act of typification or identification is a form of measurement. We employ scales and scale types and we are required, always, to sample. There is no other way open to us if we want to reduce risk and uncertainty. We are forced to imagine more people than we can see; more actions, more events, more things. And we draw inferences; we go from sample to population, correlate our conclusions and even ascribe causation. We are "counters," and we cannot avoid it. Do we not, for example, assume that there is a known statistical property to our institutions, that they exhibit a definite probability structure? If we did not, we should never express surprise at an observed (counted) deviation from a norm. In fact, we should never use the latter term. Conservatism, power, apathy, alienation, behavioralism, methodism—these words name dimensions, and it is quite understandable that we think of them in terms of more or less: i.e., quantitatively. Perhaps this is the context within which Anatole France once remarked, "People who won't count, don't count."

Compare (measure), however, the way a scientist counts— the way he constructs his categories, establishes typical instances, draws inferences, and so on. At every step of the way he assumes error. If he does not pursue a policy of systematic doubt, he is a bad scientist. If his report does not state a probable error, it is bad science. His doubt begins with the act of observation itself, for even this can be considered a hypothesis, and it extends to his apparatus, to his procedures, and to the manner and substance of his descriptions and conclusions. To see how large this concern looms, all one need do is to turn the pages of a standard statistics

---

[16] See Chapter 3 of this book, "On the Use of Metaphor in Political Analysis."

text. But then, statistics is a theory of error reduction: its purpose is to lessen the risk that attaches to any presentation of fact.

There are, alas, dunces. There are "scientists" who rush into research thoughtlessly even as they talk of theoretically directed inquiry. Sometimes they do not even pose a question. There are those who do avoid theoretically interesting or socially compelling problems because such problems are resistant to our technical repertoire. Yet the measure of a science lies precisely in its ability to render messy, difficult, complex, and seemingly incorrigible problems capable of solution. And, on the contrary, there are some who plunge into these, unlimber a powerful apparatus, only to research poorly conceived variables. They have still to learn that "measuring efforts which undertake to render faulty concepts more precise are fore-ordained to be more precisely faulty."[17] Such "scholars" are not too different from those who, consumed by the urgency of the times, think that because words are said over a problem, it is thereby solved. There are, frankly, many people who are just dumb, or who ply fashion and ride bandwagons—or whatever. The theory of probability tells us that this will be so in any population, whether traditionalist, behavioralist, or post-behavioral revolutionary. Vitiating, then, scientific methods on this count is like invalidating baseball because there are lousy batters.

Moreover, it should be clear even to the most obdurate of opponents that whatever the pretension, extravagance, even foolishness, to be found in the last fifteen years of social scientific effort, it has produced results that warrant a substantial investment of our resources. Insofar as weaknesses are concerned, the antidote here is more and better work, more exacting accountability, and quality control—a task to be regulated by the measured cadence of analysis, constant criticism and a ruthless effort to expunge error. Such repair is more likely to come from those

[17] Harold Lasswell, "Measurement of Public Opinion," *American Political Science Review*, Vol. 25 (1931), p. 311.

Science and Political Science

who, in the interest of science, pursue the problems of science. One needs, for example, to contrast the treatment of "methodism" by Morgenthau, Wolin, Strauss, and McCoy and Playford with that of Paul Meehl. After painstaking analysis of psychological researches, Meehl offers a critique in the form of a paradox:

> In the physical sciences, the usual result of an improvem nt in experimental design, instrumentation, or numerical mass o data is to increase the difficulty of the "observational hurdle" hich the physical theory of interest must successfully surmount whereas, in psychology and some of the other social sciences, the usual effect of such improvement in experimental precision is to provide an easier hurdle for the theory to surmount.[18]

If Meehl is right, and I think he is, what we have been prone to take as improved research procedure turns out to weaken the rectitude of our findings and to impair our ability to refute them. In continuing to urge an abandonment of the methodologies of science, even temporarily, Strauss, McCoy and company invite us to return to a casual, implicit posture which insures error as it proclaims truth.

Objection II: One Should Not

There are, to be sure, a set of in-principle reasons which are said to foreclose a social science. These I should like to treat in later portions of this discussion. Now, I wish to turn to the caveat that we should not seek a science—which, in historic perspective, becomes an injunction against the liberation of man's mind.

It is sometimes suggested that the order in which our various sciences have appeared in human history is a function of their complexity. Astronomy, our oldest science, is taken to be far less complex than, say, psychology, one of our youngest. And, paren-

---

[18] Paul Meehl, "Theory-testing in Psychology and Physics: A Methodological Paradox," *Philosophy of Science*, Vol. 34 (1967).

thetically, it is frequently urged that it will be a very long time, if ever, before the extraordinary complexity of human behavior is systematically reduced.

The anthropologist Leslie White finds, on the contrary, that the chronology of science is more a function of man's ability to distinguish between subject and object (between self and nonself) than of complexity. This distinction, which constitutes a shift from philosophies of supernaturalism (of animism and anthropomorphism) to those of naturalism, is more easily made with phenomena that are distant and that "play an insignificant role as determinants of human behavior." The converse of this proposition is clear: such a separation is most difficult to make when phenomena are close at hand and taken to be powerful determinants of human behavior.

Historically, the differentiation of subject and object is first to be seen with respect to heavenly bodies. Before this occurred, the stars were held to be animistic spirits capable of exerting powerful controls over human behavior. Man worshiped stars then, or he feared them; he did not study them. It took ages before he learned that these remote bodies do not govern his daily life. When that happened, he made them "objects," separate and distinct objects of inquiry. Astrology is indicative of our primeval orientation, but astronomy constitutes our oldest science. It is often said that it is our most perfect science.

As to the order of appearance of the various sciences, astronomy precedes terrestrial physics as physics precedes chemistry—and their maturity varies accordingly. The older the science, the more developed it is; and the older the science, the less immediate its subject matter in determining our behavior. "Anatomical determinants being more remote and less influential than physiological processes, the science of anatomy precedes physiology." And physiology precedes psychology, with each predecessor a more developed science. The age of science and the maturity of science bear so close a correspondence to each other, White concludes, that they vary with the distance between their objects

Science and Political Science

of inquiry and man himself. In fact, the constancy of this relationship is described by the following law:

Science emerges first and matures fastest in fields where the determinants of human behavior are weakest and most remote: conversely, science appears latest and matures slowest in those portions of our experience where the most intimate and powerful determinants of our behavior are found.[19]

But as "science" approaches man, as it moves closer and closer to man as object, resistance increases. The story of scientific development is replete with episodes of unremitting hostility and "charred bones." Who does not know of the warfare against the Copernican system, the fate of Giordano Bruno, or Galileo's trial before the Inquisition and those words of legend as he rose from his knees: "Eppur si muove." Wherever we look we find "warfare" rising in intensity whenever science engaged a new domain of experience and waning only after countless demonstrations of its power. After several centuries of conflict, one would think that the legitimacy of this enterprise has finally been established—and so it has, in astronomy, in physics and chemistry, in biology, but not so decisively in the social sphere. It requires only a very short memory to recall the battles over evolution—and we cannot yet be sure that they are over. When the modes of science are extended to man, not man as particle or as tissue, but as a social being, any prediction of resistance is safe to make. Now, having reached "the most intimate portions of our experience," science threatens to transform "our very humanity" into just another "event in nature."

This extension violates deeply held, often theologically sanctioned feelings that man's essential character, "his very soul," lies beyond nature's realm and is and should be beyond the reach of science. The object of the social sciences, asserts Morgenthau,

---

[19] Leslie A. White, "The Expansion in the Scope of Science," in Morton Fried (ed.), *Anthropology* (New York: Thomas Y. Crowell, 1959), p. 20.

"is man, not as product of nature but as both the creature and the creator of history in and through which his individuality and freedom of choice manifest themselves."[20] These linguistic formulas are mellifluous; they do strike resonant chords. But they also place man beyond natural science by fiat. Where behavior is cued by such formulas, it is possible to see science, behavioral science, as an alien thrust which seeks to subvert man's special status. Hence it is that some have warned, as they raise the spectre of dire consequence, that this new science, this "new political science . . . is based on the fundamental premise that there are no essential or irreducible differences . . . between men and brutes and men and robots."[21] Man is to be subject only, never an object; to take him as an object, even as "object of inquiry," is to strip him of his humanity—to treat him as brute.

There is a curious reasoning here, bordering on the paradoxical. If we were to adopt this position, what is there for us to do? We cannot study man (probe, research, analyze his behavior) because to do so is to render him an event in nature, an object. But if we do not study him, how can we *know* that he is both creature and creator, that he possesses individuality and freedom of choice? Nor can we know that he is a brute: we can neither judge him, nor value him, nor respect him, nor teach him—for all of these behaviors require that we know something about him. The act of judgment always involves a knowledge claim; the act of evaluation requires that a person be measured (described) on some scale of values; and we cannot teach or correct him until we *find* that his behavior has violated some rule. If we do not study man, if we do not take him as an event in nature, the alternative open to us is to take ourselves as the stars were taken by primitive man.

The notion arises that those who see the extension of empirical knowledge as a threat to man's special status in the universe are

20 Morgenthau, op. cit., p. 441.
21 Strauss, op. cit., p. 311.

Science and Political Science

still waging theological warfare against science or—if one wishes—naturalistic philosophies. From this vantage point, the idea of a "science" of man must continue to offend, and deeply so. Theologies, and their equivalents, are systems of dogma which constitute closed sets that are by definition independent of experience. But science, or empirical methodologies generally, opens the set by transforming dogma into hypothesis. The tensions that arise are readily understandable.

Should one suggest now that the idea of a science of politics (or of man) is a recent aberration that debases the search for truth and depreciates man, he has lost the sense of English empiricism and the thrust of the Enlightenment. And he has yet to come to grips with the "enforcers" of the nineteenth century—those moral philosophers (pre-eminently concerned with "political things," as the phrase now goes) who built synoptic systems on "first and final causes" and drew their inspiration from "higher kinds of truth." From these heights they could readily extol a Teutonic genius for nation-building as having been endowed by Providence; they could worship at the Constitution and revere the Supreme Court as "the representative of God"—all the while rejecting any deviation from their "theory" as sinful. Where the Newtonians had taken for themselves the task of discovering the immutable laws of nature, these guardians of man's noble spirit commanded that their higher law was not to be tampered with.

It must, therefore, be emphasized that the present categorical framework of American social science represents a deliberate rejection of this injunction and a direct repudiation of its epistemological presuppositions. It is, to use a modern locution, an instance of "development." It was designed to destroy the "ascriptive" foundation of knowledge, to set aside the received and revered axioms of the past, and to eliminate, once and for all, those formulations that were protected from the independent checks of experience. Knowledge claims were now to be held accountable, and this was to be "achieved" by a system of close

Political Theory and Political Science

and sustained study of classes of behavior that fell into the natural domain. Hence it was that the "modern" disciplines of social science exhibited in their emergence the principle of structural differentiation and functional specificity.

The thrust was Darwinian, evolutionary: as Parrington tells us, "When the flood of light that came with the doctrine of biological evolution lay brilliant on the landscape [even] the dullest mind caught something of its reflection."[22] It shone, too, on the moral philosopher, who, after all, had learned his philosophy in the halls of German idealism. But it did not affect the Aristotelian cast of the concept of evolution that he expounded—that the essence of a thing, its character and form, were given. To the members of the Metaphysical Club, however, forms themselves were taken as subject to evolution and before their deliberations were over, they had dispatched what Chauncey Wright called German Darwinism, pierced the "thin abstraction" of the moral philosopher, and produced the American version of pragmatism under the inspiration of Peirce. And as pragmatism penetrated social science, its effect was to "open the set" so as to permit empirical variables to play a decisive role in the conduct of inquiry.[23]

Those who minimize the magnitude of this change by easy reference to an early "realism" might do well to recall that politics, the play and process of American politics, was not an object of inquiry in our university curricula until the last decade of the nineteenth century. Then, when the pragmatic realists had specialized inquiry and differentiated disciplines, when they had finally succeeded in placing knowledge on the foundation of experience, curricula changed and research began. Thereafter, in the case of politics, it was an easy task to create the American Political Science Association so as "to assemble on common ground those

---

[22] Vernon L. Parrington, *Main Currents in American Thought* (New York: Harcourt, Brace & Co., 1927), Vol. III, p. 402.

[23] A fuller discussion of these developments is to be found in Chapters 3 and 5 of this book.

persons whose main interests are connected with the scientific study of the organization and function of the state."[24]

The choice of the name *science* is not to be understood as deriving from any expressed desire to model politics on physics. It did not connote the rigor that comes to mind today, nor was it directed toward formal theoretical systems. On the contrary, the deductive method was frowned upon and a reliance on axiomatic nets was held to be the prime defect of the grand system builder. Yet the name was not simply a figure of speech. The pragmatic movement was a search for veridical knowledge, for fact and for cause-effect relations—goals which exhibit a cardinal property of the scientific situation. Moreover, this effort to transform the study of politics rested upon ontological and epistemological premises that lead logically to a science. One need only contrast Theodore Dwight Woolsey, who held "most firmly to a system of final causes," with Lord Bryce:

in calling Politics a Science we mean no more than this, that there is a constancy and uniformity in the tendencies of human nature which enable us to regard the acts of men at one time as due to the same causes which have governed their acts at previous times. Acts can be grouped and connected, can be arranged and studied, as being the results of the same generally operative tendencies.

The data of politics are the acts of men. The laws of political science are the tendencies of human nature and are embodied in the institutions men have created. These tendencies are in so far uniform and permanent that we can lay down general propositions about human nature and can form these propositions into a connected system of knowledge.

---

[24] This quotation is from the first presidential address delivered to the newly formed American Political Science Association. It is taken from Jesse S. Reeves, "Perspectives in Political Science, 1903–1928," *American Political Science Review*, Vol. 23 (1929), p. 2. And see W. W. Willoughby, "The American Political Science Association," *Political Science Quarterly*, Vol. 19 (1904).

Such propositions, Bryce added, "correspond to what in the sphere of inanimate nature we call natural laws."[25] Similarly A. Lawrence Lowell insisted, while acknowledging that the ultimate goal of politics is moral, that "the investigator may study [politics] as a science, as a series of phenomena of which he is seeking causes and effects."[26] Even where there was objection to the use of the name, these purposes were not challenged. "I do not like the term political science," Woodrow Wilson declared. "You must not classify men too symmetrically; you must not gaze dispassionately upon them with a scientific eye." But in that same statement Wilson also reveals his basic methodology: "I take the science of politics to be the accurate and detailed observation of those processes by which the lessons of experience are ... at last given determinate form in law."[27]

"Science," then, was neither an alien intruder nor a mere rhetorical flourish. It was seen as a necessary way of inquiry, a way that would break open the vise within which the moral philosopher had locked political inquiry. When one contemplates the history of the American discipline of political science, it may be said that the empiricism of its first generation of scholars laid the basis for the theoretical science that later generations were to strive for. Now, however, Easton tells us that we should not pursue this path because "behavioral research must lose touch with reality." And, in an extraordinary statement, he adds "The heart of behavioral inquiry is abstraction and analysis and this serves to conceal the brute realities of politics." Our task instead is to "break the barriers of silence that behavioral language necessarily has created and to help political science to reach out to the real needs of mankind in a time of crisis."[28]

25 James Bryce, "Relations of Political Science to History and to Practice," *American Political Science Review*, Vol. 3 (1909), p. 3.
26 A. Lawrence Lowell, "The Physiology of Politics," *American Political Science Review*, Vol. 4 (1910), p. 14.
27 Woodrow Wilson, "The Law and the Facts," *American Political Science Review*, Vol. 5 (1911), pp. 10, 2.
28 Easton, *"The New Revolution ...,"* op. cit., p. 1052.

Science and Political Science

Some Thoughts on Relevance

Were it not for the fact that the cry for relevance is so popular a slogan today, I should dispense with any discussion of this subject. And the reason that one may, in good conscience, make this statement derives from the fact that "relevance" can in no wise be legislated. When we address this concept, we are talking about relation, connection, bearing, association, correlation, correspondence, pertinence. It is, therefore, "discoverable": it cannot be established a priori. In addition, the discovery or finding of relevance is never unbounded; it is always *with respect to* some property, condition, or problem. If one proposes that X is relevant to Y, the statement is incomplete. X is relevant to Y only with respect to Z, and any such proposition remains hypothetical until warranted. Nonetheless, it often happens that an assumed certainty of relationship turns out to be quite irrelevant on further examination. The search for relevance, then, is the search for those facts that establish the bearing of X on Y with respect to Z; those which establish the character of the connection, the nature of the correlation, the type of association.

This situation does not change when the issue is posed in terms of the selection of a "relevant" problem. For we often do not *recognize* a relevant problem when we see it, and just as often the problem we think is relevant vanishes before our eyes. There are events and states of affairs that are disturbing. They are dislocating, even ominous, and assume threatening proportions. We are certain that something is dreadfully wrong. But what is it that is wrong? It is not unusual for us to be distressed and not *know* to what we can attribute our anxieties. We may not even know how to characterize this situation or what context to place it in, and we may be entirely confused as to its properties. In fact, our tendency to distrust the surface appearance of events prompts us to search for hidden meanings, and we assume that there must be a reason (a "because" or an "in order to") for what we see—

Political Theory and Political Science

a reason that will tell us what it is that we really see. The Premier of the Soviet Union is removed, and the Kremlinologists take to the airwaves to tell us what *really* happened, what the *relevant* problem *really* is, what the *relevant* forces *really* are—and there is a good chance that their choices, while plausible, are *really* irrelevant. When we observe someone who is regularly "stoned," what is the relevant problem here? Is it drugs, or alienation, or an inability to solve the oedipal problem? Are the recent campus episodes phenomena or epiphenomena—indicators of some rather fundamental, profound, basic dislocations which remain problematical to us? What, in short, is the relevant question to ask here?

Nature, Einstein once urged, is very kind. If you ask it the right (relevant) question, it will supply you with the right (relevant) answer. But it is not so easy. For any disturbance of magnitude, there are many suggestions as to the relevant question to be asked. And for any problematic issue, there are dozens of proposals as to what is relevant. Most are very familiar. They employ the language of everyday life, and we often think that because they are couched in ordinary language, they contain the wisdom of the ages. But they, too, are only possibilities and they are made no more probable because they are conventional. Some are esoteric, couched in strange languages, apparently distant from the proximate scene, and we often think that because they are remote and unfamiliar, they are thereby irrelevant. It may be an irony of history that man's record is replete with illustrations of seemingly irrelevant formulas, usually scientific, which have turned out to be directly relevant to the solution of our most difficult social problems.

Return now to Easton and the incredible notion that abstraction conceals the brute realities of politics. What can this admonition mean? Not to abstract, as C. I. Lewis has taught us, is not to think—and surely Easton is not proposing this as a guide to the post-behavioral movement. The fact is that we must abstract no

Science and Political Science

matter what language we use, whether the ordinary language of the common-sense world or the specially contrived technical languages of theoretical science. Is it necessary to point out that every noun, every verb, every adjective and adverb in the English language is an abstraction—a class term? Or that the syntax and dictionary of this language together constitute a theory that is not any the more correct because it is in widespread use? Assuming the existence of some "brute reality," what guarantee do we have that the way in which our linguistic maps direct our observations will be most relevant to the problems at hand? All languages *typify* and *categorize,* and we need no reminder that ordinary language does so in a crude, ambiguous, and often contradictory manner—and that the observations it directs are of a similar character. But even more importantly, we do not take such a language as a theory which is to be held accountable. It is simply there; we must learn it in order to get by, and we rarely, if ever, test out its adequacy. On the contrary, we take its category system and congeal it: we reify it, or we use it as a gigantic stereotype by means of which we socialize our young.

It is enough to point out that as science has developed, as it has extended its reach to areas of experience previously ordered only by the vernacular, it has frequently corrected and improved upon the common-sense theory. Scientific concepts have entered the ordinary language, displacing ineffective, inappropriate, and even destructive categories; and scientific findings have eliminated harmful superstitions and dangerous dogma. This is true even of the imperfect and underdeveloped social sciences. A good deal of its vocabulary is now a part of the common idiom, and with salutary and benign effects. Strange and bewildering behaviors once seen through categories that coerced condemnation and punishment are now taken as types of behavior that demand remedial therapies. The kleptomaniac is no longer a criminal, alcoholism is now classified as an illness, hysteria is no longer a female disorder, and poverty is not a sin. One could extend this list without difficulty. But it is more important to urge that to confine the concept of relevance to a reality that is described by the linguistic system in common use is to observe with the equipment of our ancestors.

None of this is to minimize the threat of thermonuclear warfare, the calamity that has befallen our cities, the atrocity of racism, and such hopeless and disastrous expeditions as we have undertaken in Indo-China. These are problems of magnitude and moment and their importance and urgency is beyond question. Mankind does seem to be working under the pressure of time—and demands for immediate solutions have built up.

It is, however, a strange counsel to lay aside our basic researches, to cease to cultivate science on its own terms and for its own intrinsic purposes. There has never been a time devoid of crisis and emergency, and the demand to set aside basic theoretical work has appeared in every decade of this century. Such theoretical work has always faced an opposition built on the foundation of a current crisis, and the refrain has not varied much over time: "The purer a science . . . the less will it be socially relevant."[29] This will be said by practical, applied social scientists who repeatedly fail to see that if there is to be an applied social science, this necessarily presupposes a theoretical science; in the attainment of the solution of a problem, it is the findings of a theoretical science that are *applied*.

It will be said in response, it has been said, that to halt basic theoretical work now will not cost us much, that such science as we do have is constituted of trivia—sheer trivia. Maybe so; at any rate, I do not propose to argue this. But if we take a page out of history, it has happened that findings taken as trivial opened the way to remarkable discoveries. Consider, for example, these trivialities and the changes they wrought: the attraction of chaff by amber, the twitching of a frog's legs, and the attraction of iron

[29] F. M. Marx, "A Closer View of Organization," *Public Administration Review*, Vol. 8 (1948).

filings by a "lodestone." It is a great marvel, Sir George Thomson has written, that such trivialities often lead to astounding results.[30] None of this, I hasten to add, is to be taken as a proposal to concentrate on trivia; it is, rather, that the trifles of today may be of great moment tomorrow. The discovery that the stereotype constitutes a self-fulfilling prophecy is, perhaps, trivial. But who can tell where it will take us?

There is the further allegation that a "behavioral science conceals an ideology of empirical conservatism," and that, unwittingly or otherwise, it "purveys an ideology of social conservatism."[31] I do not know what *empirical conservatism* means here, but it often happens that a social or political ideology is presented as a scientific thesis; that value judgments are disguised as fact. In the social sciences, this is an ever-present risk and should not be treated lightly.[32] It is bad science. But there are ways to cope with it, not the least of which are those procedures which permit us to uncover and correct errors of logic and of fact. If it is said, however—as Easton asserts—that an empirical science must lend its support to the very factual conditions it explores, this statement is incomprehensible. I do not understand how it is that I *must* support that factual condition known as racism if I study it. To make contact with any domain of experience is to assume that it exists; hypotheses do presuppose ontologies. But how this contributes to the maintenance of those factual conditions as a matter of logical necessity is baffling. On the contrary, studies of racism and poverty have in fact exposed the extent of their existence. Once exposed, once revealed in full implication, these conditions can be acted upon intelligently.

---

30 Sir George Thomson, "Some Thoughts on The Scientific Method," in Robert E. Cohen and Marx Wartofsky (eds.), *Boston Studies in the Philosophy of Science,* Vol. 2 (New York: Humanities Press, 1965).

31 Easton, "The New Revolution . . . ," op. cit. And see McCoy and Playford, op. cit.

32 See Chapter 6 of this book on the effects of "persuasive definitions."

Political Theory and Political Science

It is the *ignorance* of such factual conditions that supports their maintenance.

The main charge really turns on "pluralism." And while I have no desire to add to the debate on this issue, some things can be said. If pluralism is advanced as a value judgment, it is subject, at the very least, to axiological analysis. If it is an ideology disguised as an objective thesis, this must be demonstrated—not proclaimed. If it is a rule of efficient means, we can only judge it in relation to some stated end. And if it is presented as a descriptive thesis, it stands as a hypothesis.

There is little doubt that much of the writing on pluralism (pro and con) is faulty—at once a declaration of values and a hypothesis. As with a good deal of theoretical work, it is often a very arduous task to unravel this confusion, and analysis is consequently made all the more difficult because of this. But the central criticism of pluralism seems to turn on the notion that as a descriptive hypothesis, it features certain aspects of reality to the exclusion of others. And is thereby bad. Yet all hypotheses must do this; otherwise they are literally pointless. It is the function of a hypothesis to direct a search for (to point to) those facts which are relevant to the problem at hand. In this respect, to criticize the concept of pluralism is to criticize the concept of hypothesis.

Still, it may be said that the choice itself is at fault—that the trouble with the theory is that it selects out the "wrong" variables. What this amounts to is a claim that the "opportunity costs" are too high; that there is a better, stronger, more correct theory that zeroes in on the "right" variables and thereby provides a more powerful description. When the challenge is offered in this manner, the situation is salutary; there is now an alternative theory, a competitor, that can be brought into play to provide both a criticism and a check on pluralism. The appearance of a competitor tends to prevent a "leading theory" from degenerating into a dogma. And this is to say that all such competitors must be treated seriously if only to forestall the elimination of facts that may refute the leading theory.[33] But if the character of this competition is permitted to become ideological, then determinations of validity become hopeless efforts, and we easily descend to the battlefield—where, it must be stressed, might makes right.[34]

As a final note, it can be suggested that the contemporary version of the "credo of relevance" is associated with the notion that in a time of crisis the scientist who insists upon theoretical autonomy betrays a trust—that somehow he is violating a prime ethic of social responsibility. Again and again we can observe the damnation of the political scientist because his work does not engage the "immediacy" of critical problems. If we follow this logic, should we not condemn Darwin for failing to practice veterinary medicine in the face of all the suffering so apparent in the animal kingdom? And if we follow a logic that constrains abstraction and analysis, we will be obliged to follow the rule "Don't think—DO!"[35]

Free Will and Reflexive Prediction

I have noted that there are important in-principle arguments which are said to debar a political science. Let us turn to these now, taking first the problem of volition.

When the issue of a science of behavior is discussed, it is often the case that the doctrine of "free will" enters on a note of triumph. And it is a powerfully persuasive concept on many counts. It has been sustained and sanctioned to such an extent that in some quarters it is a sin to hold otherwise. Then too, freedom is an enshrined value for which mankind has shed much blood over many centuries. But even more compelling, we know

---

[33] Paul K. Feyerabend, "How to Be a Good Empiricist," in Bernard Baumrin (ed.), *Philosophy of Science—The Delaware Seminar,* Vol. 2 (New York: John Wiley & Sons, 1963).
[34] More will be said on this subject.
[35] With apologies to Morris R. Cohen.

ourselves to be actors who possess volition, who choose goals, who select alternatives, who have the power to do as we will. We take this power as the essence of our humanity and, accordingly, the notions of regularity, uniformity, causation, and lawful behavior become dehumanizing. They not only offend, however. They are incorrect—at least as far as human behavior is concerned. For we can confound regularity, upset predictions, and "violate," as it were, law. Clearly, free will is a doctrine that constitutes one of the many obstacles that a social science must overcome—or so it is asserted.

We should understand to begin with that to speak of violating a natural law is an inappropriate metaphorical license—on a par with formulas that tell us that a given phenomenon is governed by law. In a scientific situation, a law is not a command. It enjoins no one and nothing. It is neither a prescription nor a prohibition. It is, on the contrary, a description in the most fundamental sense—as, for example, for every action there is an equal and opposite reaction. If we have employed the metaphor "law" here, the point is to suggest a description so powerful that it applies to all bodies in motion at any time and at any place. It anticipates no exception. But if an exception occurs, it is senseless to say that a violation occurred or that the phenomenon in question failed to conform. Indeed, if anything failed here, it was the law itself. It failed to give a correct description, an appropriate account of those phenomena within its stated range of application. Phenomena do not conform to laws; laws, if they are adequate, conform to phenomena.

I emphasize this because those who postulate "free will" claim for their assertion exactly that kind of law-like status that a science seeks to establish. The doctrine purports to describe human behavior; its coverage is universal, and its formulations are unbounded by either space or time. Free will, thus, is not an obstacle to science; it is, instead, a matter to be investigated. When not presented as dogma, as an article of faith, it appears as a hypothesis and is, therefore, problematical.

Science and Political Science

Doubtful, really. "To expect," as G. K. Chesterton once put it, "that all men for all time will go on thinking different things, and yet doing the same things, is a doubtful speculation. It is not founding society on a communion, or even a convention, but rather a coincidence."[36] And if this construction is not sufficiently compelling, we might consider the "common-sense" of daily life which consists of a stockpile of typifications that permit us to make the predictions that we need to make in order to get by. Or reflect a moment on the use of such terms as *politics,* or *legislature,* or *power,* or *party.* These are classifications, and their continued use is presumptive of regularities or constancies of behavior—else we would not use them to group seemingly, even patently, diverse behaviors into the same class or seemingly, even patently, similar behaviors into different classes. But in either case, we can only do this on the basis of some principle, some criterion, some set of properties which the objects we group possess in common. They are, then, similar, uniform, even constant, *with respect to* those stated properties. With this procedure we have begun to "systematize." That is, the *common-sense world,* the world that is common to our senses, is a systematic world. It is built on those constancies and regularities which its class terms name. This is the cardinal assumption of those who proceed in terms of the methodology of "subjective understanding" (*Verstehen*)—which, if we follow Schutz, develops an objectivity of its own. Phenomenological description tells us that the world of common sense is built on the foundation of *typicality* and, accordingly, does not require a knowledge that reduces an act to a specific or named human actor. To understand his behavior, "it is sufficient to find typical motives of typical actors which explain the act as a *typical* one arising out of a *typical* situation. There is a certain conformity in the acts

---

[36] G. K. Chesterton, "The Mad Hatter and the Sane Householder," *Vanity Fair* (January, 1921), p. 54. Cited in Walter Lippmann, *Public Opinion* (New York: Harcourt Brace, 1922).

of priests, soldiers, servants, farmers, everywhere and at every time."³⁷ Perhaps we should also note that the process of identification is no more than the assignment of an instance to a class or type. We do this when we say *that* act is political, *that* organization is decentralized, *that* man is a bureaucrat. Our very language attests to an almost perpetual repetition of behaviors in a multitude of domains.

In fact, there appears to be so much regularity before us as to enable one critic of the scientific movement to ask, ". . . what kind of political world came into being which rendered the application of scientific methods fruitful and its criteria of truth plausible?" This question implies that the order presupposed by a science is a recent or modern phenomenon. Thus Wolin suggests that prior to the sixteenth century, "the political orders of Europe were characteristically decentralized. Uniform legal systems were a rarity and centralized bureaucracies still in the formative stage. Order itself was not a presupposition of daily life but a precarious achievement. Habits of civility were dictated by local loyalties, and the whole complex of national duties, rights, and codes of deference were only slowly being developed. In brief, political life lacked those qualities of uniformity, regularity, routine, and settled expectations that we now take for granted."³⁸

This last conclusive statement is ambiguous. If it means that life styles then were different from now—well, of course. If it means that pre-sixteenth century Europe lacked patterns of behavior (typicality), the statement must be false. Apparently, it is the latter meaning that Wolin intends, for he adds, "To the extent that scientific theory presupposes order and regularity in

---

37 Alfred Schutz, "The Social World and the Theory of Action," in A. Brodersen (ed.), *Collected Papers* (The Hague: Martinus Nijhoff, 1964), p. 13.

38 Sheldon S. Wolin, "Political Theory: Trends and Goals," in David L. Sills (ed.), *International Encyclopedia of the Social Sciences*, Vol. 12 (New York: Macmillan and Free Press, 1968), p. 325.

phenomena, political societies prior to the establishment of the modern, centralized, bureaucratized state could not furnish the necessary basis for scientific theorizing."[39]

Notice immediately that Wolin's description is couched as a generalization—an empirical generalization which treats of the "political orders" of Europe. It tells us that these were "decentralized," "localized"; that characteristic behaviors were not of the "type" that we find associated with the modern centralized state. Assuming standard meanings for these terms, the evidence we have indicates that the description is correct. Even further, hidden in its prose is a law of political development so dear to modern political science: that systems develop along a decentralization-centralization continuum. Nor is it necessary to add that the fixing of points on this scale is the marking out of "formative stages." Hence, the absence of those properties associated with "nation-alized" or "centralized politics" does not mean that no regularities were present (there were obviously "orders"—or "institutions"); rather, that they were different, and of such character as to be found on the lower side of the scale. If they cluster together, we are liable to name them—as when we say *medieval* Europe or *the Renaissance*. Thereafter, when we identify a condition as medieval, we have located it on this scale. In short, there is no reason why we can't "theorize" about political life in pre-sixteenth century Europe—any less than we can with modern or developed societies. Wolin himself did so. If we turned directly to that stage of our history, allowing for cultural differences, we would probably find the same parameters in effect there as, say, in much of the Third World today. It is also probable that processes of socialization, dynamics of class, status, and power, and the like would also be seen as similar. And it is a safe prediction that in this circumstance we would find that prevailing epistemological premises required that scientific criteria of truth be treated as

[39] Ibid.

heresy.[40] As they are in some parts of the discipline today! But this in no way constitutes evidence that for such societies "the necessary basis for scientific theorizing" does not exist. To assert this is to propose that behavior in pre-sixteenth century Europe was a random affair. Which, clearly, is the implication of the standard free-will formulation.

There is one aspect of this argument that merits serious attention. It is exemplified in the following passage: Where "Predictions of the return of Halley's comet do not influence its orbit ... the rumored insolvency of Millingville's bank did affect the outcome. The prophecy of collapse led to its own fulfillment."[41] This quotation calls attention to what philosophers of science refer to as "the problem of reflexive prediction." Placed in the literature of sociology by Robert Merton, on the foundations of W. I. Thomas' *reality theorem,* this phenomenon is more popularly known as "the self-fulfilling (or self-denying) prophecy."[42] Its implications are quite clear and lead to a crucial question: if the phenomenon of reflexivity in social science predictions confounds the possibility of discovering the kind of law that describes the physical world, does this not mandate a separate and distinct mode of inquiry in the social domain?

We should extend this a bit. A reflexive prediction is one in which the prediction is itself a factor which may materially alter the projected or anticipated outcome. As Merton puts it, "... since ... predictions can be taken into account by the very people to whom they refer, the social scientist everlastingly faces the possibility that his prediction will enter into the situation as a *new and dynamic* factor, changing the very conditions under which the prediction initially held true. This characteristic of

---

40 See Martin Landau, "Decision Theory and Development Administration," in E. W. Weidner (ed.), *Development Administration in Asia* (Durham, N.C.: Duke University Press, 1970).

41 Robert Merton, *Social Theory and Social Structure* (Glencoe: The Free Press, 1957), p. 423.

42 See also Lippmann, *Public Opinion,* op. cit.

Science and Political Science

predictions is peculiar to human affairs."[43] Innumerable illustrations of this can be brought to mind: economists predict a fall in the stock market; traders act on this hypothesis in such a manner as to insure confirmation. Or the reverse: on a forecast of oversupply, producers curtail their production so as to invalidate the initial hypothesis. In politics, one notable example is the "bandwagon effect."

At the very least, this exercise of volition makes it extremely difficult to test hypotheses. If only this was involved, we would simply face a formidable, not an insurmountable hurdle. But the more pressing problem is this: if public knowledge of a social science prediction can affect its probability value (positively or negatively), then men are volitional agents who can, as Alan Gewirth has suggested, change social science law. And if men can do this, there must be a profound difference between a natural and social science, a difference of such quality that it is folly to employ natural science modes of analysis for social problems. The laws of the latter, susceptible to changes by the very actors who are presumed to be covered, must, obviously, render such modes quite inadequate.

This position is not the usual anti-social scientific posture. Rather, it points to a prime difficulty that must be overcome by those who assert a unity of the sciences, social and physical. Somehow, they have to show that human volition does not constitute the obstacle it appears to be.

In this regard, Adolf Grunbaum, whose critique prompted Merton to amend his original position, has drawn upon cybernetic systems to demonstrate that reflexivity is by no means unique to social science.[44] Doubtful of this, Roger Buck, in an exhaustive analysis of reflexive prediction, has nevertheless concluded that they do not offer any special or *in-principle* barriers to a social

---

[43] Merton, op. cit., p. 129. Emphasis in the original.
[44] Adolf Grunbaum, "Historical Determinism, Social Activism, and Predictions in the Social Sciences," *British Journal for the Philosophy of Science*, Vol. 7 (1956).

science. In the first instance, the fact of reflexivity is itself an empirical matter and, further, it is quite possible that the effect of "advance information" on a causally relevant public can be incorporated as a variable.[45] A correct prediction, thus, depends on a knowledge of what Herbert Simon has called "the reaction function." All of this would be somewhat removed except that Simon, in dealing with bandwagon effects, has not only demonstrated that correct predictions can be made, but has also contributed to the solution of the practical difficulties involved.[46] (Nor should this occasion surprise. The social logic of reflexive prediction is a common phenomenon: in the real world situation a considerable amount of second guessing the effects of advance information [that supplied by a prediction] often meets with considerable success.) Upon analysis, then, this aspect of the volitional argument turns out to be much less methodological and far more empirical. It is not an *in-principle* objection; rather, it serves to indicate something of the magnitude of the tasks that confront a social science.

On Mannheim's Paradox

If, then, free will in both its standard and sophisticated forms of presentation does not stand as an insurmountable barrier, what does? Here we confront an interesting irony. Where, historically, the central thrust of the anti-scientific movement was built upon the doctrine of self-determination, the "now" formula is that man is so fully a product of social forces, so completely culture bound, so determined socially as to thoroughly subvert the principle of "objectivity." Accordingly, "the detachment of the individual

---

[45] Roger Buck, "Reflexive Predictions," *Philosophy of Science*, Vol. 30 (1963). See also *Comment* and *Rejoinder* by Grunbaum and Buck. But see, too, Alan Gerwirth, "Can Men Change Laws of Social Science?" *Philosophy of Science*, Vol. 21 (1954).

[46] Herbert Simon, "Bandwagon and Underdog Effects of Election Predictions," *Public Opinion Quarterly*, Vol. 18 (1954).

Science and Political Science

from the group," from "the matrix of which [he] thinks and experiences" is a fiction. All knowledge is "dependent upon the subjective standpoint and the social situation of the knower," and "it is impossible to conceive of absolute truth existing independently of the values and position of the subject and unrelated to the social context." The thought of all parties in all epochs, Mannheim insists, is of an ideological character.[47]

There is, Euben has asserted, a failure to confront this paradox, and among "new political scientists," one hears this frequently.[48] But what is today referred to as "Mannheim's paradox" entangles Mannheim and those who have adopted his argument.

The phrase itself we owe to Geertz; its popularity in political science is probably due to La Palombara.[49] And it is used to deny even the possibility of objectivity in the social sciences. For the social scientist is locked into a matrix from which he cannot escape. All formulations offered as statements of fact are at best "partial truths." The *partiality* is always there—such is the nature of the paradox. A statement, for example, on the "decline of ideology," is itself ideological, as are hypotheses about equilibrium or pluralism, and findings with respect to political behavior. These mask an ideology, conceal bias, hide valuations, and are always, *of necessity,* reflections of the interests of some social group, class or the Establishment itself. Even conscious awareness of these liabilities does not help—"for the truth which a mind thus socially conditioned is able to grasp is likewise

---

47 Karl Mannheim, *Ideology and Utopia* (New York: Harcourt, Brace & World, Harvest Edition, 1965), pp. 28, 77, 79.

48 J. Peter Euben, "Political Science and Political Science," in P. Green and S. Levinson (eds.), *Power and Community* (New York: Vintage, 1969), p. 27. See also McCoy and Playford, op. cit. and Surkin and Wolfe, op. cit.

49 Clifford Geertz, "Ideology as a Cultural System," in David Apter (ed.), *Ideology and Discontent* (New York: The Free Press, 1964); Joseph La Palombara, "Decline of Ideology: A Dissent and an Interpretation," *American Political Science Review*, Vol. 60 (1966).

socially conditioned."[50] This is the paradox from which the social scientist cannot extricate himself.

La Palombara urges that we attend to its implications, and so we should, for they are frightful to contemplate. But let us look first at the actual paradox—i.e., that bind that Mannheim placed himself in. And if I hesitate to add words to the discussion of this problem, it is only because the invalidity of Mannheim's position is self-evident, and because it has been pointed to so many times. Examine, for example, the following:

1. Robert Merton:

Mannheim's conception of the general total ideology . . . leads at once, it would seem, to radical relativism with its familiar vicious circle in which the very propositions asserting such relativism are *ipso facto* invalid.[51]

2. Virgil Hinshaw:

I do not wish to whip a dead horse but, after surveying much of the recent literature, I find that, though occasionally enfeebled, this horse is not quite dead. If we agree with Mannheim that the entire structure of one's thought is ideological, then even science, especially social science and history, becomes necessarily bound to historical social position and is consequently invalid. Such relativism, however disguised, *is self-referentially inconsistent*.

[50] Morgenthau, op. cit., pp. 445–446, where he writes: "The mind of the political scientist is molded by the society he observes. His outlook, his intellectual interests, and his mode of thinking are determined by the civilization, the national community, and all the particular religious, political, and economic and social groups of which he is a member. The 'personal equation' of the political scientist both limits and directs his scholarly pursuits. The truth which a mind thus socially conditioned is able to grasp is likewise socially conditioned. The perspective of the observer determines what can be known and how it is to be understood. In consequence, the truth of political science is of necessity a partial truth."

[51] Merton, op. cit., p. 503. This essay also appears in the 1949 edition. Emphasis in the original.

Science and Political Science

How can one find out about the social determination of knowledge if even the validity of the attempt is historically conditioned?[52]

3. Gustav Bergmann:

As some of the classical philosophers . . . with quixotic heroism denied the existence of the physical universe, so Mannheim . . . denies in principle the possibility of an objective social science. Or, to say the same thing by means of the familiar terms as I use them and he, naturally, doesn't, he insists that every rationale is an ideology. This formulation has the merit of revealing, in a pattern only too familiar to the historian of philosophy, the intrinsic difficulty of a position like Mannheim's. *If this proposition that every rationale is an ideology is itself objectively true, how can he know it?* If it is not, why should we pay any attention to it? And what is the value of a social science thus construed?

Bergmann also treats Mannheim's answer to the last question—the theory of the free intelligentsia which asserts that the intelligentsia construct composite ideologies capable of finding acceptance and achieving progress:

A subjectivist cannot in this manner define progress and, in particular, approximation toward an objective truth whose very existence he in principle denies.[53]

4. Ernest Nagel:

What is the cognitive status of the thesis that a social perspective enters essentially into the content as well as the validation of every assertion about human affairs? Is this thesis meaningful and

---

[52] Virgil Hinshaw, "The Objectivity of History," *Philosophy of Science*, Vol. 25 (1958), p. 53. Emphasis added. And see also Hinshaw, "The Epistemological Relevance of Mannheim's Sociology of Knowledge," *Journal of Philosophy*, Vol. 40 (1943) and "Epistemological Relativism and the Sociology of Knowledge," *Philosophy of Science*, Vol. 15 (1948).

[53] Gustav Bergmann, "Ideology," *Ethics*, Vol. 61 (1951), p. 132 Emphasis added.

valid only for those who maintain it and who thus subscribe to certain values because of their distinctive social commitments? If so, no one with a different social perspective can properly understand it; its acceptance as valid is strictly limited to those who can do so, and social scientists who subscribe to a different set of social values ought therefore to dismiss it as empty talk. *Or is the thesis singularly exempt from the class of assertions to which it applies, so that its meaning and truth are not inherently related to the social perspectives of those who assert it? If so, it is not evident why the thesis is so exempt; but, in any case, the thesis is then a conclusion of inquiry into human affairs that is presumably 'objectively valid' in the usual sense of this phrase—and if there is one such conclusion, it is not clear why there cannot be others as well.*[54]

5. A. R. Louch, on the self-defeating character of Mannheim's formulation:

For it has the form, we can never be sure of x because we are sure of y, but y turns out to be an instance of x.[55]

6. Benjamin Walter:

S–1: All empirical propositions about social life are (a) perspectively conditioned, and (b) therefore lack objectivity. But it is also the case that
S–2: S–1 is an empirical proposition about social life. . . .
Thus do the epistemological claims of the sociology of knowledge collapse in one inescapable and baffling contradiction.[56]

Do we need more to suggest that it is not presumptuous to claim to have solved the paradox? In point of logic, Mannheim's

---

[54] Ernest Nagel, *The Structure of Science* (New York: Harcourt, Brace & World, 1961), p. 500. Emphasis added.

[55] A. R. Louch, *Explanation and Human Action* (Berkeley and Los Angeles: University of California Press, 1969), p. 205.

[56] Benjamin Walter, "The Sociology of Knowledge and the Problem of Objectivity," in L. Gross (ed.), *Sociological Theory: Inquiries and Paradigms* (New York: Harper and Row, 1967), p. 349.

Science and Political Science

position, as Karl Popper would put it, maintains its own falsity.[57] To indicate this is immediately to show that the thesis which asserts the necessary impossibility of an "objective validity" in the social sciences is itself invalid. The paradox confronts Mannheim, not social science.

Understand, however, that we are addressing the implications of the sociology of knowledge for the problem of objectivity—not that of the relation between social position and thought. On this problem the powerful work of Mannheim is not easily to be dismissed and his hypothesis that the categories in which experiences are subsumed, collected, and ordered vary in accordance with social context occupies considerable attention in the social sciences. In fact, it constitutes the basis of much research into political behavior. Nor is there doubt that thought, even scientific thought, is influenced by extra-theoretical factors, that these can have more than peripheral effect in the selection of problems and the genesis of ideas. From the standpoint of a Zeitgeist (a favorite of sociologists of knowledge) we are all plagiarists, which is to say that no one clearly understands the sources of his own ideas.[58] But to draw from this a set of epistemological conclusions about objectivity is, as we have seen, a most doubtful deduction. There is no logical connection between the two. We can, therefore, close this phase of our discussion by observing, as Mannheim himself did, that the two aspects of his theory (the empirical and the epistemological) "are not *necessarily* connected and one can accept the empirical . . . without drawing the epistemological conclusions."[59]

Suppose that we draw them away. What would happen? Is it possible that theoretical proposals, research reports and find-

[57] Karl R. Popper, *The Open Society and Its Enemies* (London: Routledge & Sons, 1945) Vol. II, p. 217. And see his statement on the paradox of the liar, p. 335, footnote 7.

[58] E. G. Boring, "The Dual Role of the Zeitgeist in Scientific Creativity," in P. Frank (ed.), *The Validation of Scientific Theories* (New York: Collier, 1954).

[59] Mannheim, op. cit., pp. 266–269.

ings would be received as "characterized by conservatism, fearful of popular democracy, opposed to any massive extension of democratic participation?" Is it possible that their authors would be stigmatized as manufacturers of processed voters, Neronians, trivialists—even as they specialize in the art (or is it science?) of emasculation? Or that one would find the following statement: ". . . his method of studying only these issues is an ideological cover for this political stratum since he agrees with their definition of the relevant political issues."[60]

Karl Popper is right. The notion that all thought is ideological is liable to destroy the rational basis of any discussion. For we are obliged under this rubric to search for hidden motive as we seek to pierce disguise, uncover the covert, and expose the "higher cunning" of the social scientist. A theory, as the prophet Theodore Dwight Woolsey ruled a century ago, is now to be tested by the morality of the theorist. And the standard is the approved relevance system of the appointed social grouping. What a happy circumstance this is. Evidence, necessarily tainted, is no longer of concern, and one need not use his brains to explain an untoward event or a surprising circumstance because any proposition can be assigned to the class of correct statements by merely demonstrating its symmetry with the interests of any annointed group. In fact, error does not matter save as it relates to strategies of conflict pursued by warring parties in their ideological struggles.

It follows, then, that one should not confuse any issue with fact. And it follows, too, that when confronted with a hypothesis (say, *the stability of a complex society varies with overlapping group membership*), we should ask the following questions:

1. What is it that prompts David Truman to advance a claim in terms of stability? Why doesn't he emphasize change? Why doesn't he point up the human significance and normative implications of his claim?

60 McCoy and Playford, op. cit., p. 95.

Science and Political Science

2. What are Truman's ideological presuppositions? Where does he stand on the Columbia crisis, the Vietnam war, non-decisions, pornography, private property, and the fact-value dichotomy?
3. What kind of a person is he: what is his basic attitudinal set? What's his score on the "F" scale?[61]
4. With whom does Truman consort? Who are the members of his primary communication nets? What are his primary reference groups?
5. Now: ask these questions of Arthur Bentley, V. O. Key, James M. Burns, Theodore Newcomb, Conrad Arensberg, C. H. Pritchett, the President and Trustees of Williams College, Miss Ethel Richmond, the staff of the Williams Library and Mrs. Truman.[62]

It is possible, however, to risk reputation and approach Truman's hypothesis by demanding justification. We could ask:

1. Do we have a hypothesis here: or does it constitute a disguised tautology?
2. Are the properties of the concept *stability* stated with sufficient clarity so as to enable the unambiguous choice of an instance? Do the concepts *complex, group* and *membership* meet this criterion?
3. What is the character of the evidence which is adduced?

---

[61] We agree in advance that the determination of the sociological position of Mr. Truman would require a much more detailed instrument. In fact, it might be necessary to take Mr. Truman's entire life history—possibly even on a couch. But because the validity of this hypothesis depends upon Truman's social position and his overt and covert motivation, the time and expense involved would appear to be warranted. It is, after all, important to find out why he didn't postulate a hypothesis dealing with change.

[62] These people are mentioned in the preface of *The Governmental Process,* in which the original proposition appears, as having given especially important advice, criticism, and assistance in the preparation of the book.

Does it constitute a sufficient warrant for the acceptance of the proposition?
4. What counter-evidence is there? Is the hypothesis so constructed as to protect itself against negative findings? Can we mount a study to confound its claims?

These, of course, are simple tests, but if we wanted to apply even more stringent criteria, we could insist that the hypothesis not be accepted as correct, or warranted, or confirmed until it is evaluated in terms of the whole family of theories that treat with the problem at issue.

It would be comforting if it could now be said that the first "test-set" is facetious. But these are queries that now abound, and their implications are too frightful to contemplate. All we need do is contrast both test sets to realize that the former enshrines ignorance, exalts the *ad hominem,* and establishes the validity of an empirical claim *senatus consultum.* Once we allow this, we are in a circumstance in which dogma prevails. And it is then that a "scholar" can appear before his colleagues and declare with utmost confidence: "My theory is confirmed. So has our senate decreed."[63] Dogma, we should remember, admits of no error and, therefore, requires no evidence.

---

[63] Z. A. Medvedev, *The Rise and Fall of T. D. Lysenko* (New York: Columbia University Press, 1969).

CHAPTER 2
Objectivity, Neutrality, and Kuhn's Paradigm

IN political science, those who argue for the principle of the relativity of knowledge frequently point to recent developments in the philosophy of science as support for their claims. Citing the works of Norwood Hanson, Stephen Toulmin, Michael Scriven, Paul Feyerabend, among others, they have taken note of prevailing challenges to orthodox positions (for example, to the classical two tiered D-N model of explanation) and have dismissed objectivity as a tattered remnant of an outmoded positivism. (I beg off those positions that have fortified themselves with a measure of phenomenology, a dose of ordinary language analysis, a pinch of structural linguistics in a stock of existentialism: it is a heady brew which results in indisposition, not intoxication.) But the main thrust of their argument derives from Thomas S. Kuhn's *The Structure of Scientific Revolutions*.[1] Because of its profound influence, this work requires careful consideration; before we turn to this it will be helpful to extend our discussion of objectivity.

The mention of objectivity in political science is certain to call forth the idea of scientific neutrality, which, invariably, is expressed in terms of the value-free observer. Discussion, then, centers on one issue: "Whether or not the social investigator can place his values in abeyance."[2] We should understand, however, that there is a profound difference between this formulation and

[1] Thomas S. Kuhn, *The Structure of Scientific Revolutions* (Chicago: University of Chicago Press; Phoenix Edition, 1964).
[2] Fred M. Frohock, *The Nature of Political Inquiry* (Homewood, Ill.: Dorsey Press, 1967), p. 165.

Political Theory and Political Science

the concept of scientific objectivity: that *neutrality* and *objectivity* are not synonymous. For it is precisely the enormous difficulties involved in attaining neutrality, in bracketing values, that have demanded the system of regulatory control that constitutes objectivity in science.

Science does not require that observers exhibit the pristine purity of total detachment. No one, save perhaps a tyro, suggests that a scientist be so chaste, or that "scientific habits of mind" are incompatible with "passionate advocacy, strong faith, intuitive conjecture, and imaginative speculation."[3] All of us, scientists included, are subject to countless influences so well hidden as to be uncoverable either by socio- or psychoanalysis. To transform a scientist into that fully aseptic and thoroughly neutral observer of legend is a virtual impossibility. There is no doubt that "there is more to seeing than meets the eyeball"; that what we see is "theory-laden" or "field-determined." We can admit out of hand that there is no such process as "immaculate perception." Arguments, therefore, which seek to sustain objectivity by predicating neutrality are doomed to fail. They are also irrelevant. Even if such neutral observers could be manufactured, Popper tells us, "they could not possibly attain to what we call scientific objectivity."[4]

For the crux of this concept rests on the fact that men, even scientific men, are not angels. Indeed, the entire system of science is based on a variation of Murphy's Law—the prime assumption that any scientist, no matter how careful he may be, is a risky actor; that he is prone to error; that he is not perfectable; that there are no algorithms which he can apply so perfectly as to expunge any and all biasing effects. Accordingly, all his proposals must be subject to error-correcting procedures. The goals of the

[3] Israel Scheffler, *Science and Subjectivity* (New York: Bobbs-Merrill, 1967), p. 2. I am greatly indebted to this powerful and cogent book.

[4] Karl R. Popper, *The Open Society and Its Enemies* (London: Routledge & Sons, 1945), Vol. II, p. 206. And see his *The Logic of Scientific Discovery* (New York: Science Editions, 1961), pp. 44–48.

Objectivity, Neutrality, and Kuhn's Paradigm

enterprise demand a network of highly redundant[5] and visible public checks to protect against the inclusion of erroneous items in the corpus of knowledge. Such networks are *institutionalized control procedures* which continually subject "all scientific statements to the test of independent and impartial criteria": not men, but criteria, for science recognizes "no authority of persons in the realm of cognition."[6] This is the decision rule that is called objectivity.

But what are these criteria? The answer to this question cannot be written as a recipe. Veridical knowledge (truth, if you will), though presupposed by the concept of error, is a problem that has confronted philosophers for a long time. Their literature reflects continuous analysis of such concepts as verification, falsification, justification, warranted assertability, and confirmation. However these may differ, insofar as the class of contingent (empirical) statements is concerned, whether one is a verificationist or a falsificationist does not alter the fact that the prime test here is the test of experience.[7] There is a necessity to this position which derives from the nature of a hypothesis: constituting an assertion about or an anticipation of experience, a hypothesis is a claim which, by definition, is not known to be true or warranted or confirmed or corroborated. As such, the only evidence that is relevant in determining its factual adequacy is

---

5 For an analysis of redundancy as a theory of error suppression see Martin Landau, "Redundancy, Rationality, and the Problem of Duplication and Overlap," *Public Administration Review*, Vol. 29 (1969).

6 Scheffler, op. cit., p. 1.

7 "I shall certainly admit a system as empirical or scientific only if it is capable of being *tested* by experience. These considerations suggest not that the *verifiability* but the *falsifiability* of a system is to be taken as a criterion of demarcation. In other words, I shall not require of a scientific system that it shall be capable of being singled out once and for all, in a positive sense; but I shall require that its logical form shall be such that it can be singled out, by means of empirical tests, in a negative sense: *it must be possible for an empirical scientific system to be refuted by experience.*" Popper, *The Logic of Scientific Discovery*, op. cit., pp. 40–41. Emphasis in the original.

the experience anticipated by the hypothesis itself. It is for this reason that a hypothesis which cloaks itself in privilege or protects itself from observation is on its face faulty, for it is then impossible to reach a decision as to the adequacy of its assertions (the accuracy of its anticipations). The factual status of a hypothesis can only be determined by examining, directly or by consequence, the phenomena it points to. Nor can such examination be waived, proscribed, falsified, tampered with, compromised, fabricated, or evaded. As the necessary standard by which empirical claims are to be decided, *evidence* (that which is evident upon examination) must be open to inspection by anyone at any time. Hence it is that the rule of objectivity is a public rule which instructs that experience is to provide the criteria, to play the role of independent controller and impartial arbiter of all such claims. It is in this context that we should understand, as Scheffler has put it, that the moral thrust of positivism turned, despite its excesses, on the demand that all empirical assertions impose a primary obligation—the submission of those assertions to the arbitration of experience. The unity of science doctrine "granted no holidays from such responsibilities" even to the social sciences.[8] An attitude of moral indifference, as Max Weber would say, has no connection with scientific objectivity. But an attitude that affirms the "responsibility of assertion" would lead us to a concept of *scientific honesty* "which consists of specifying, in advance, an experiment such that if the result contradicts the theory, the theory has to be given up."[9]

That there is a profound difference between objectivity and neutrality may, perhaps, be readily agreed upon. But it can properly be said that the circularity of the observational process, indicated by the use of such terms as "theory-laden," still remains

---

8 Scheffler, op. cit., p. 5.
9 Imre Lakatos, "Falsification and the Methodology of Scientific Research Programmes," in Imre Lakatos and Alan Musgrave (eds.), *Criticism and the Growth of Knowledge* (Cambridge: Cambridge University Press, 1970), pp. 96, 123.

Objectivity, Neutrality, and Kuhn's Paradigm

as a problem. There is a considerable evidence for the suggestion that the act of observation is itself inherently faulty—incapable of providing the necessary check because we see what we are conditioned to see. If this is the case, the relation between expectation and observation tends to be reflexive, and observation may thus be a self-fulfilling prophecy. Stated in more familiar terms, the argument runs along the following lines: if there is a prior control of our observations, if they are theory-laden, if our linguistic categories determine what we see, then how can we hold experience to be the basis of a system of external checks by means of which we render our proposals accountable? Even further, Scheffler has called attention to the "paradox of categorization" that confronts us: if categories of thought (conceptualizations) determine observation, observation cannot then provide an independent control of thought; and if such categories do not determine what is seen, then what is seen cannot provide an independent check because it is uncategorized—formless and nondescript.[10] We seem here to be in a double bind from which there is no exit. In such a circumstance, it should be clear, we would be unable to assess, evaluate, support, or refute any claim. We should have to take all assertions as equally valid, and we should have to do away with the concept of error. The whole structure of science, to say the least, collapses by this stroke.

But why restrict this to science alone? Why not carry the paradox to the construct system, the linguistic habits, the "informed" perception of any man in any structured social situation? Does not the bind operate here as well—and by the same dynamic? Yet, if it did, how could there be any change? And how could our linguistic habit contain such categories as truth, error, problem, novelty, anomaly, surprise—not to speak of discovery? If we see only what we are taught to see, then why do discrepancies between anticipation and event amaze, astonish, or disturb us, or why—to use a popular locution—do we need any feedback? And how does it happen that we so anticipate error that we now

10 Scheffler, op. cit., p. 13.

employ the term "likelihood" or "probability" even for our most time-tested hypotheses? Or is there any doubt that each of us continually *tests against* experience—that we probe, experiment, investigate, try out, feel our way—all the time *learning* that our conceptualizations are not intractable? Notice, too, that upon the contrary, when *in fact* we observe people with conceptualizations that are forever fixed, we will say of them that they are blind, have tunnel vision, or that they are biased and prejudiced and that their categories are really stereotypes. Most of us, however, do seem to rely on external empirical checks, for we do *discard, amend, revise,* and *correct* our categories. Not always, not easily, but quite often. And it sometimes happens that we even invent new ones—"feedback," for example.

It is possible, of course, that we are "cultural dopes"—that we are too dumb to understand that we are caught in a paradox or to realize that we are imprisoned by our linguistic categories. But we do learn, and the television works, and there are now lasers, space ships, and artificial hormones. So, it appears, there must be some escape from the bind. Or perhaps the equation between our conceptual categories and our observational processes does not hold; that the latter do play their regulative role so that we are able to reject an assertion, solve a problem, and design an artifact.

To say, then, that conceptualization affects observation is not necessarily to say that it controls or determines observation. *But it is to call attention to the fallibility of observers and their potential for error.* As regards the paradox, Scheffler has demonstrated that upon careful analysis the contradiction disappears.

"Conceptualization" is a broad and rather ambiguous term that breaks down into two distinct sets: categories on the one hand and expectations on the other. In the former case, we can substitute such terms as concepts, classes, predicates; in the latter, we have propositions, statements, and hypotheses.[11] The

---

11 Ibid., Chapter 2, especially pp. 36–40. See also Chapter 7 of this book.

Objectivity, Neutrality, and Kuhn's Paradigm

difference here has to do with the distinction between the intension of a term and its extension, between its connotation and denotation.[12]

The intension of a term refers to the property (or set of properties) that an entity must have in order for the term to be correctly applied to it, to cover it. The extension is the term's range of application—the population of entities which may be so classified. The extension of a class, it should be clear, is always informed by its intensional properties. But these do no more than provide criteria of membership. A class property may have an intended range of application, it may presuppose a universe of objects, but by itself it cannot tell us that such objects exist. In fact, there may be no objects to be covered—as in the case of the "centaur," the "unicorn" or the "three-eyed man." If a category commits us to anything, it is to the identification or recognition of instances.

The assignment of an object to a class is another matter. Here we entertain an expectation, a hypothesis. If one says that object A is a legislature and this (class) term has been provided with clear criteria of membership, then one expects to find that A exhibits these properties. If it does not, and we can only find this by observation, it cannot be assigned to this class. Assignment, thus, constitutes a hypothesis.

Accordingly, it is the difference between "category" and "assignment" that permits observation to play a regulatory role. The hypothesis is clearly category-laden. It is thoroughly informed by categorization. And yet it remains subject to an independent check.

To make this argument more immediate, and to provide an illustration of the way in which experience alters even the most durable of our categories, the concept of "separation of powers" may be taken as a case in point.

This category-system consists of three distinct classes of behavior: legislative, executive, and judicial. To say that they

[12] See Chapters 4 and 6 of this book.

Political Theory and Political Science

are distinct is to say that they are mutually exclusive—a condition that not only accords with the logic of classification but provides us with the concept of "separation." For most of us, the triad is so familiar as to appear quite "natural"; it remains unquestioned and non-problematical. Each of its terms seems to be "given"—and this "givenness" derives from the fact that our government was patterned in accordance with this system and in such manner as to provide for each class a directly observable referent (Congress, Presidency, and Supreme Court). The combination of a pair of factors—that the category system dates back centuries and a government designed to exemplify it—allows us to assign the category names to the divisions of government without *a second glance*. There is the danger, then, that the categories of the system will be employed as reifications (in which case no distinction will obtain between a category and that which is assigned to it). When this happens, we are indeed prisoners of the system. For all classifications, no matter how natural they appear, are invented. They are constructs which permit us to take a *first glance,* to engage in a search, to make observations. If we permit them to congeal, if we reify them, if we fail to make the necessary distinction between class and object, between category and assignment, then we rob ourselves of the opportunity to take a second glance (research). One needs to emphasize that category-informed observation takes the form of a search and that the concept of a re-search constitutes an error-correcting device. When we forget this, we tend to become immured in the system.

Having said this, let us adopt a posture of innocence and turn to the category *legislative*. We take its defining properties to be (a) the initiation of rules (laws), and (b) the promulgation (enactment) of rules. These properties generally accord with common usage and will serve to identify a legislative body. The intension of the term is clear (we shall so assume), but the extension of the category denoted by its intension shall remain prob-

Objectivity, Neutrality, and Kuhn's Paradigm

lematical. Now, by itself, what does this concept tell me? Well, it tells me one thing: whenever I write the word legislative, I can substitute for it phrases (a) and (b). More importantly, it provides me with a measure (standard)[13] by means of which I can make assignments to the class. But it tells me nothing about the things "out there" that I am interested in. For all I know, a legislative body may turn out to have the existential status of a unicorn, and my concept may soon be consigned to the realm of mythology. That is, to construct the term *legislative* is not to say anything that is true or false; it is not to make an empirical claim of any sort—whether as to the existence of such bodies or their distribution. What I can do is identify those which can properly be assigned to this class.

I do this by means of observation. And if I learn (observe) that a body can be so classified, I *know* something about it. Placing the Congress in this class, for example, is tantamount to the assertion that it (a) initiates, and (b) promulgates rules. Notice that this hypothesis is fully informed by the category *legislative*—which is why I searched as I did. But it often happens that seemingly similar phenomena are assigned to the same class only to *find* that an *error* has been made. Once and with too hasty a glance (or was it because I fell prey to the naturalness of reification?) I took the New York City Council to be a legislative body. After all, the City Charter referred to it in these terms. Accordingly, I predicted its behavior—invariably incorrectly. It soon dawned on me that to admit the Council to the class *legislative* was a gross error; I was amazed (astonished, startled, taken aback) to find that a law "initiated and promulgated" by the Council was vetoed by the Board of Estimate on the grounds that the Department of Traffic had already issued a regulation which

---

[13] As noted earlier, we define measurement as the comparison of an unknown entity with a known fixed standard. If we want to treat this concept in terms of numbers, we define measurement as the comparison of an unknown quantity with a known fixed unit quantity.

the Council's action contravened! One would be hard pressed to take this body as an exemplification of a legislature.[14]

Or, by an opposite turn, we tend to allow the customary connotations of conventional terms (which generally possess a subjective intension) to obscure similarity because of surface differences. So, I did not place the Presidency in the class *legislative,* only to find that it does initiate and promulgate rules. And when I extended my observation here, these activities assumed such prominent proportions that I began to refer to this office as the "chief legislator." The moment I did this, I introduced an adjective which qualified the original category. And I was soon forced, on the appearance of "borderline" cases, to create an additional qualification—"quasi-legislative." And upon further examination of the Court, it also turned out to be *legislative*—sufficiently so as to permit the use of the term "judicial-legislation." Then, I discovered that my initial hypothesis was quite questionable: the Congress seems to satisfy criteria (b) but a re-search continues to suggest that (a) does not figure very prominently in its behavior. On the contrary, it appears that (a) better describes the Presidency. And when, finally, I turned to the bureaucracy, an agency readily assigned to a new category, *administrative,* my bewilderment only increased on the discovery that it possesses both (a) and (b).

Evidently, the original classification scheme is not appropriate to its task. My observations, though category-laden, do not allow for any clear-cut assignments. The units under investigation do not behave "characteristically." They seem to offer a resolute resistance to the category-system. And in the effort to retain some utility, I have had to introduce some peculiar qualifications. Adjectives are normally employed to limit and thereby provide more specific characteristics (criteria of membership), but in this case they have rendered the categories more opaque and less

[14] It is frequently said in New York City that the only "legislative" power possessed by the City Council is its ability to change the names of streets.

Objectivity, Neutrality, and Kuhn's Paradigm

exact. *Separation of powers* does not describe the government adequately—i.e., the assignment of units of government to its various categories produces only surprise.

At this point, I am left with several options. It may be possible to make the criteria of each class unambiguous and exact by the addition of more properties. But here I run the risk of "death by qualification." As I continue to enlarge the set of criteria, the utility of the category diminishes: when the intension of a term is increased (by the addition of properties), its extension (range of application) is thereby decreased. I could, for example, approach exact specification by employing the descriptive elements of Article I of the Constitution, to define (make definite) the category *legislative*. I would then have a class of one member; there would be no other legislative bodies. And if I did this for the various branches of government, with due allowance for statutory and judicial revision, the system would become its own best description. This is what some have called "legal formalism." Or, it may be that the phenomenon under scrutiny defies the category-system because it is not disjunctive (dichotomous). If so, we will have to create some clearly defined dimensions that will permit the construction of rating-scales. Or, perhaps, a thorough reconceptualization (a new category-system) is in order: the old system is beyond repair; it simply must be abandoned. Which is what has happened: the theoretical reconstructions of Deutsch, Easton, and Simon, for example, are based on this conclusion. One usually begins to reconceptualize (theorize) on the continual violation of expectation.

So it is that the category-system itself can be held accountable —for it is both alterable and replaceable on the basis of observational results. No matter how closely one may adhere to the system (and the more closely the better), the assignment of an item to a category constitutes a hypothesis. And there is no a priori way of reducing the uncertainty that attends this claim —i.e., there is nothing that so predetermines the hypothesis as to place it beyond the probability of error. Nor is there anything that predetermines the distribution of items which fall into the category; and there is nothing to prevent the raising of alternative and contrary hypotheses. The same category-system can be used to generate sets of competing and conflicting hypotheses (as in Max Weber's system) which, though category-laden, can only be resolved by resort to experience. Observation, then, may indeed be category-laden and still serve as an independent check on hypotheses that are also category-laden. It is certainly the case that there can be no description without prior categories, but these do not so control our descriptions as to place them beyond accountability. It is accountability, not neutrality, that marks the principle of objectivity.

Before returning to a discussion of Kuhn, one more note needs to be added. Much of the controversy that besets the philosophy of science is often employed by political scientists to warrant one position or another with respect to such problems as explanation. What is obscured, rather frequently, is the fact that a good deal of this ferment has to do with the effort to find more effective systems of error control. The assumption that seems to prevail is that the construction of a foolproof or fail-safe system is beyond our reach—that no matter how much we approach a "perfect knowledge," we cannot achieve it. Nevertheless, the effort must be made. For this reason, the concept of independent external check, or experience as arbiter, or "testability" has been expanded so as to comprehend a system of mutual rational control by critical discussion.

In fact, Popper has defined science as the "systematic criticism of error."[15] The implications of this are pointed: in the absence of such criticism, there is only change; when it constitutes an institutionalized procedure, there is progress. And this extends even to the principle of objectivity. More immediately, what we are to understand is that every theoretical choice, like every

---

15 Karl R. Popper, *Conjectures and Refutations* (London: Routledge & Kegan Paul, 1963), pp. 216–217.

Objectivity, Neutrality, and Kuhn's Paradigm

hypothesis, is a risky guess. This means that there can be no authoritative personages—that we address theories, not people. "A scientist may offer his theory with the full conviction that it is unassailable. But this does not necessarily impress his fellow scientists; rather, it challenges them. For they know that the scientific attitude means criticizing everything, and they are little deterred even by authorities."[16] Perhaps the latter phrase is best read by substituting "should be" for "are," but the statement is not so much descriptive of practice as it evidences the demand for more stringent, less lenient, tests. In this regard, Feyerabend insists that even the most well-confirmed theory must be continually challenged for fear that it will degenerate into dogma. Hence he demands a "theoretical pluralism [as] an essential feature of all knowledge that claims to be objective." Alternative theories are to be so framed that even problems considered to have been solved can be subject to reexamination. These provide the *necessary criticism*—a criticism that may even be sharper than the comparison of a theory with a domain of experience. For however much a theory reflects experience, its factual adequacy should come only after a confrontation with strong alternatives.[17] Feyerabend, whose treatment of theoretical pluralism and whose pragmatic theory of observation often gives rise to the allegation of relativity,[18] states his purpose: "The model which underlies my own discussion has as its aim the maximum test-

---

16 Popper, *Open Society* . . ., op. cit., p. 206.

17 Paul K. Feyerabend, "How to Be a Good Empiricist," in Bernard Baumrin (ed.), *Philosophy of Science—The Delaware Seminar*, Vol. 2 (New York: John Wiley & Sons, 1963).

18 Scheffler, op. cit., pp. 50–52. Scheffler's discussion turns on Feyerabend's questioning of "meaning invariance." If one is interested in pursuing this, see J. J. C. Smart, "Conflicting Views About Explanation"; Wilfred Sellars, "Scientific Realism or Irenic Instrumentalism"; Hilary Putnam, "How Not to Talk About Meaning"; and Paul K. Feyerabend, "Reply to Criticism," all in Robert E. Cohen and Marx Wartofsky, (eds.) *Boston Studies in the Philosophy of Science*, Vol. II (New York: Humanities Press, 1965).

ability of our knowledge."[19] Objectivity stands as a cardinal rule which requires of scientific practice a strict and continuous regulation on the foundation of observational results and systematic criticism.

Political Science and the Paradigm

The last sentence suggests the rather widely held view that the history of science is one of carefully sanctioned cumulative knowledge. But this concept of development, sometimes referred to as a linear progression of constant accretion, is exactly that feature of our usual understanding which Kuhn finds in error. In his estimate of the situation, the classical model of progressive accretion is patently false. On the contrary, science has, *in fact,* proceeded in terms of revolutions—those "non-cumulative developmental episodes in which an older paradigm is replaced in whole or in part by an incompatible new one."[20] Moreover, Kuhn ties to this thesis a rejection of the categorical distinction between discovery and justification and assigns subjective considerations a pre-eminent place in scientific development. These penetrate scientific criteria so thoroughly and so deeply as to render the principle of independent control sheer utopianism. In his reading of history, the "rational" evaluation of conceptual alternatives must yield to "gestalt switches" and "conversion experiences." For the moment, let us fix upon Kuhn's developmental scheme, the central concepts of which are *normal science, paradigm,* and *revolution*. The description is as follows:

Sciences pass through stages that may be considered *normal.* "Normal science" is the condition that exists when a particular community of scholars accepts a "common paradigm." Paradigms are "universally recognized scientific achievements that

---

19 Feyerabend, op. cit., p. 223. What we have here is a demand for a multiplex system or the application of the principle of redundancy as an error suppression device. See Landau, op. cit.
20 Kuhn, op. cit., p. 91.

Objectivity, Neutrality, and Kuhn's Paradigm

for a time provide model problems and solutions to a community of practitioners." Acceptance of the paradigm provides the necessary consensus for a common field of inquiry. It generates a distinctive and coherent research tradition which constitutes the foundation of normal science. In this stage, work is cumulative but limited to those problems which the paradigm calls for; and neither creativity nor innovation are promoted as intrinsic values. Creativity in normal science is creative "puzzle-solving" within the terms and conditions of the paradigm. Innovation means finding ingenious solutions to puzzles. What is sought is not surprise, not the unexpected, not new theories and models, but findings that will lend greater clarity and precision to the paradigm and thereby extend its range of application. Problems which are outside the paradigm, which are not anticipated by paradigmatic theory, are apt to be dismissed "as metaphysical, as the concern of another discipline, or sometimes as too problematic to be worth the time."

But when anomalies appear and persist, or there are consistent failures to solve paradigmatic puzzles, a crisis may be produced. Crisis begets a loss of "faith" in the paradigm and the way is open to alternatives. Where before there was sharp resistance to change, to extra-paradigmatic factors, there now arises a willingness to try anything. Competing schools arise, extraordinary research occurs, and there is marked recourse to philosophical debates. The science is now in ferment and a revolution occurs when the older paradigm is replaced by an "incompatible successor." There then ensues a new era of normal science.

Steady accumulation or incrementalism describes only the period of normalcy. The history of science proper shows its development to be in terms of "non-cumulative episodes," each of which is literally revolutionary in character.[21]

This is the scenario that has overwhelmed political science. Its appeal has been so immediate, so powerful, so universally com-

[21] Ibid., pp. x, xi, 11, 24, 37, 42, 52, 68, 77, 90–92. (All further page references to this work are given in parenthesis in the text.)

pelling that it seems as if a massive conversion experience has taken place. In the face of the discord and upheaval that characterizes the discipline today, all sides of the science controversy derive sustenance and solace from the Book of Kuhn. It is not stretching the metaphor to suggest that it has appeared as a "godsend."

Two recent presidential addresses in search of a political science draw immediate inspiration from Kuhn. Following his outline faithfully, David Truman and Gabriel Almond tell us that we have had a paradigm in political science, but it has broken down in the face of anomaly. The tension that now besets us is quite natural, for we are in the throes of a competition that augurs well for the emergence of a new normal science, a new paradigm, and a new consensus. In fact, one need not despair: the structure of the new paradigm is clearly visible.[22] Then, there is David Easton's presidential statement which pleads that "behavioralism," the last of a chain of paradigms which have bound the discipline, be replaced in order to serve relevance.[23] And, most recently, we find Karl Deutsch's discussion of theory complete with obeisance to Kuhn.[24] The present president-elect, Heinz Eulau, in the same tradition, has highlighted the anomalies of the "normal science" of representation and invites a new and open competition on the ground that the existing paradigm "will not get us out of our theoretical quandary."[25] Our presidents, surely, bear the sign of Kuhn—but it is not restricted to them. In their examination of comparative politics, Holt and Turner make easy

22 David Truman, "Disillusion and Regeneration: The Quest for a Discipline," *American Political Science Review*, Vol. 59 (1965), and Gabriel Almond, "Political Theory and Political Science," *American Political Science Review*, Vol. 60 (1966).

23 David Easton, "The New Revolution in Political Science," *American Political Science Review*, Vol. 63 (1969).

24 Karl Deutsch, "On Political Theory and Political Action," *American Political Science Review*, Vol. 65 (1971).

25 Heinz Eulau, "Changing Views of Representation" in Ithiel de Sola Pool (ed.), *Contemporary Political Science* (New York: McGraw-Hill, 1967).

Objectivity, Neutrality, and Kuhn's Paradigm

use of Kuhn, organize the field in terms of competing paradigms, and go so far as to explicate the properties of the concept of *paradigm*—something that even Kuhn himself has not done.[26] And, in an innocent moment, I once attempted to defend the principle of continuity in research through the use of the paradigmatic formula.[27]

I shall return to this later, but what of the anti-Establishment, the anti-science advocates, those oriented to a *political* political science? Once again the power of Kuhn is evident. The editors of the "Caucus Papers" demand that the prevailing "pluralist paradigm" be shattered and, consistent with this locution, invoke Kuhn's "poignant description of 'normal science.' "[28] Sanford Levinson, making much of the textbooks of normal science which "socialize the scientific novice into his discipline" so as to insure work in an "approved manner," builds his case for the overthrow of the prevailing paradigm in accordance with a fundamental dictum of Kuhn: in the shift from one paradigm to another, there is no decision rule by means of which the validity of one or the other can be established.[29] Writing in the same "anti-textbook," one finds Euben rather fearful that the hopes of Truman and Almond may be realized. For, as Kuhn instructs, a normal science reduces both the field of experience and imagination, diminishes sources of inspiration, and routinizes and circumscribes mind and

---

[26] Robert T. Holt and John M. Richardson, "Competing Paradigms in Comparative Politics" in Robert T. Holt and John E. Turner (eds.), *The Methodology of Comparative Research* (New York: Free Press, 1970).

[27] See "Sociology and the Study of Formal Organization" in D. Waldo and M. Landau, *The Study of Organizational Behavior, Special Series No. 8* (Washington: American Society for Public Administration, 1966).

[28] Marvin Surkin and Alan Wolfe, (eds.), *An End to Political Science: The Caucus Papers* (New York: Basic Books, 1970), pp. 6-7.

[29] Sanford Levinson, "On Teaching Political Science" in P. Green and S. Levinson (eds.), *Power and the Community* (New York: Vintage, 1969).

action. So Euben tells us that "The real world of behavioralism is a paradigm which like all paradigms is . . . supported . . . by those authorities who are given or assume responsibility for maintaining the (politically) scientific community, and who are thus able to define in broad terms what constitutes appropriate and inappropriate behavior for 'professionals' and to punish 'deviancy.'" A normal science is then "an orthodoxy supported by authorities who enforce distinctions" between those who are and are not in the scientific community.[30]

All of this, it must be borne in mind, rests upon one fundamental assumption: in choosing between competing paradigms there is no objective basis for determining which is valid. In political science, this aspect of Kuhn's argument has been relied on by Wolin to challenge the "cumulative" progress of science, to warn of the repressive features of normal science, and to caution that the selection of a paradigm has more to do with power than with truth.[31]

Kuhn's achievement is as perplexing as it is monumental. What can there be in his theory that permits such divergent, even mutually exclusive, positions to rest so heavily upon it? To answer this question is to provide an analysis of a model of scientific development that has provoked considerable controversy among philosophers of science. Before political scientists, on either side, employ the Kuhnian formula as a court of last resort, it would be well for them to make contact with the problems that have been raised.

The Question of Descriptive Accuracy

The first of these turns on the question of accuracy. Does the abrupt discontinuity between normal science and revolution

[30] J. Peter Euben, "Political Science and Political Science," in Green and Levinson, op. cit., pp. 20–21, 31.
[31] Sheldon S. Wolin, "Paradigms and Political Theories" in Preston King and B. C. Parekh (eds.), *Politics and Experience* (Cambridge: Cambridge University Press, 1968).

Objectivity, Neutrality, and Kuhn's Paradigm

adequately describe the history of scientific development? Is this history one that turns on the temporal separation of periods of normalcy and those of crisis and revolution? Or are the latter simultaneous and interacting? Questions of this sort cannot be answered by political scientists; we simply do not have the knowledge necessary to assess Kuhn's claims—and that is all they are at the present time. But if doubts have been expressed by Toulmin, Popper, Feyerabend, Lakatos, and Shapere—none of whom can be assigned to the classical school (logical empiricism) —then it certainly behooves us to take cognizance of them. At the very least, this procedure may save us from some rather damaging errors.

If we run down this list of philosophers of science, it becomes quite apparent that the concepts of *normal science, revolution,* and *paradigm* are not received with the enthusiasm that they have generated amongst the untutored. In Toulmin's view, "There was always an element of rhetorical exaggeration in [Kuhn's] statement of the matter." Exaggeration or not, Toulmin holds that Kuhn is wrong: the "absolute" (incompatible) character of revolutionary change, which itself provides the criteria of recognition for such an occurrence, is not only debatable but in error. Conceptual incongruities are rather frequent developments in science and new generations of scientists, often possessed of ideas of their own, are just as often at cross-purposes with their predecessors. Toulmin agrees that science does not develop by accretion alone. But if it is the case that there are frequent incongruities, then the idea of a grand and total revolution which stands as a dramatic (and incomprehensible) interruption of normal science is incorrect. He also observes that Kuhn is able to provide only one illustration of an authentic "revolution" during the last three hundred years. In fact, Toulmin suggests that Kuhn has already accepted the criticism that profound conceptual changes are going on all the time. While Kuhn has denied this, the list of revolutions he provides in rebuttal does seem to aug-

Political Theory and Political Science

ment the notion of a "revolution in perpetuity."[32] In this event, the most distinctive element of Kuhn's hypothesis is refuted.

As far as Karl Popper is concerned, Kuhn's account is false.

> Although I find Kuhn's discovery of what he calls "normal science" most important, I do not agree that the history of science supports his doctrine (essential for his theory of rational communication) that "normally" we have *one* dominant theory—a "paradigm"—in each scientific domain, and that the history of a science consists in a sequence of dominant theories, with intervening revolutionary periods of "extraordinary" science; periods which he describes as if communication between scientists had broken down, owing to the absence of a dominant theory.
>
> This picture of the history of science clashes with the facts as I see them.[33]

While Popper finds normal science "important," Feyerabend suspects that it "is not even a historical fact." Feyerabend's general critique is both interesting and powerful, but it would take us afield to try to present it. One of its features may be emphasized, however. According to Kuhn, normal science is monolithic: it is tenacious, resistant to change, hostile to the proliferation of new theories, virtually a closed system. The process that he describes has a specific sequence which instructs that proliferation emerges only upon crisis; crisis is "the appropriate prelude to the emergence of new theories" (p. 85). Thereafter, competition sets in for the new paradigm, and when one is triumphant we are back to normalcy. What Feyerabend does, by an examination of late nineteenth century physics, is to show that "normal periods, if they ever existed, cannot have lasted very long and

---

[32] Stephen Toulmin, "Conceptual Revolutions in Science" in Cohen and Wartofsky, op. cit., Vol. III, especially pp. 337–341. See also Toulmin, "Does the Distinction Between Normal and Revolutionary Science Hold Water?" in Lakatos and Musgrave, op. cit., pp. 43–47, and Kuhn's reply, "Reflections on my Critics," ibid., pp. 249–259.

[33] Karl R. Popper, "Normal Science and Its Dangers" in Lakatos and Musgrave, op. cit., p. 55. Emphasis in the original.

Objectivity, Neutrality, and Kuhn's Paradigm

cannot have extended over large fields either." At that time, three distinct paradigms existed (we need only mention them)—classical mechanics, the phenomenological theory of heat, and Maxwell's electrodynamics. These were not "quasi-independent" theories competing for paradigmatic ascendancy in the face of crisis. Rather, it was precisely their interaction which set up the tensions between Maxwell's theory and Newtonian mechanics that finally led to the special theory of relativity. Or, to provide another example, the discovery of the quantum involved the bringing together of "different, incompatible, and occasionally even incommensurable disciplines." Feyerabend's point is that this "proliferating minority" produced such progress even as the great majority of workers continued to work on "paradigmatic puzzles" in the face of the "great revolutions" which were then occurring. While this has profound implications for Kuhn's assignment of the properties of success and progress to periods of normalcy, it also strikes a devastating blow at Kuhn's rhythmical pattern. That is, the temporal separation of periods of proliferation and periods of monolithic normalcy that Kuhn describes is simply not accurate.[34] Both are always present: they do not belong to successive periods. Indeed, when they are synthesized, as Lakatos has indicated, a more powerful picture of scientific development emerges.[35]

Ambiguity

There is, in addition, the matter of identifying a paradigm. It is a rather ambiguous concept; neither its meaning-in-intension nor its meaning-in-extension is very clear, which means that we do not have a well-defined concept or any ready referents. One critic of Kuhn, and a friendly and sympathetic one at that, has found not less than twenty-one different senses in which Kuhn uses *paradigm*. These she reduces to three (metaphysical, sociological,

---

[34] Paul Feyerabend, "Consolation for the Specialist" in Lakatos and Musgrave, op. cit. See pages 207–208.
[35] Lakatos, op. cit.

and construct or artifact paradigms), but her reductions are themselves not too helpful.[36] With such a multiplicity of meanings, one may properly raise question as to what is *not* a paradigm. It is, as Shapere has observed, "too easy to identify a paradigm"—which is, perhaps, why it is such an "in" word to political scientists. But "it is also not easy to determine, in particular cases treated by Kuhn, what the paradigm is supposed to have been in that case."[37] Paradigm is so elastic a term, it can be stretched so far, as to render its use quite questionable. It covers, following Masterman: scientific achievements, myths, philosophy, constellation of questions, classic work, textbook, tradition, analogy, metaphysical speculation, model, pattern, tools, type of instrumentation, gestalt figure, set of political institutions, standard, organizing principle, epistemological viewpoint, new way of seeing[38]—to which we can add theory, frame of reference, conceptual scheme, and the like. The notion that paradigms control the researches of a normal science may be guaranteed, not by investigation, but by the breadth of the term itself,[39] which is, upon reflection, immense.

Carried over to political science, its reach, as we have indicated, is almost as large. The elasticity of the term permits diverse students to employ it as they see fit. And in no case can one say that any of them are using it incorrectly. Where Truman finds "realism" to have been the paradigm of political science from 1880 to 1930, this period did have a tradition, it had its textbooks and did possess a constellation of questions. If Wolfe and Surkin find "pluralism" to be a paradigm, it, too, has its textbooks, its set of questions, its standards, and its models. If Wolin wishes to say that the paradigm of normal political science is the ideolog-

---

[36] Margaret Masterman, "The Nature of a Paradigm" in Lakatos and Musgrave, op. cit., pp. 61–65.

[37] Dudley Shapere, "The Structure of Scientific Revolutions," *The Philosophical Review,* Vol. 73 (1964), pp. 385–386.

[38] Masterman, op. cit.

[39] Shapere, op. cit.

Objectivity, Neutrality, and Kuhn's Paradigm

ical paradigm of the political community, this also is a reasonable usage.[40] In fact, methodism itself can be taken as a paradigm and Holt and Richardson do so in their chapter on competing paradigms in comparative politics. They don't use the term "methodism," but they do include "atheoretical approaches," marking factor analysis as the most sophisticated form of contemporary Baconianism. The other competitors are structural-functionalism (Almond), systems analysis (Deutsch, Easton), and psychological approaches (Pye, Riker).[41] If the confusion attending the use of paradigm in political science is not sufficient reason for its abandonment, this chapter may provide what is required.

Conversion and the Selection of a Paradigm

We now understand, on the foundation of Kuhn, that paradigms compete. When a normal science begins to break down in the face of mounting anomaly, there appears a proliferation of theories, each of which becomes a prime candidate for reconstituting a consensus. But Kuhn tells us that the selection of the new paradigm is not a function of evidence, of the principle of external independent control. On the contrary, it involves a gestalt switch, a conversion, which occurs on other than objective grounds. Hence it is that Wolin can ask: "Is there an objective way for deciding between the competing claims of game theory, bargaining theory, equilibrium models, systems analysis, communication theory, functional theory or structural-functional theory?" His answer is in the negative: and he adds that "what matters is not which is the truer paradigm, but which is to be enforced."[42]

Prevailing paradigms, say behavioralism or pluralism, are,

---

[40] Sheldon S. Wolin, "Politics as a Vocation," *American Political Science Review,* Vol. 63 (1969), p. 1064.

[41] Holt and Richardson, op. cit.

[42] Wolin, "Paradigms . . .," op. cit., pp. 134-135. And see his "Politics . . ." op. cit., p. 1063.

therefore, not a function of their truth value or of any demonstrated scientific power. Their choice, to begin with, is not based on any evident superiority, and their staying power is dependent only on the ability of the normal scientific community to command and distribute desired resources. It is by means of such sanctions that the paradigm can be enforced. Enforcement, of course, and enforcers are necessary precisely because there are no objective criteria which control selection. In this context, it is quite appropriate for the authors of the "Caucus Papers" and of the anti-textbooks to insist that the issue is not evidence, but governance. Paradigmatic struggles, they hold, cannot be decided on scientific or scholarly grounds; their outcome is never dependent on scientific superiority. The struggle is political. The issue is power.

Now I have often heard it said that Wolin misreads Kuhn. That the emphases he places on paradigmatic resistance to change, on paradigmatic control, on the suppression of novelty, on the socialization—better still, indoctrination—of students, on the isolation of deviants, and upon "enforcement" are misplaced. But all of this is Kuhn's description, not Wolin's. And if it is further alleged that Wolin's resort to Polanyi's "tacit knowledge" reduces to the level of personal fideism, it is to be remembered that Kuhn introduces Polanyi (p. 44). I suspect, however, that the reason why Wolin is presumed to be guilty of misinterpretation is because one can find Kuhn stating, "This is not to suggest that new paradigms triumph ultimately through some mystical aesthetic" (p. 157). Yet the fact is that a frequent inconsistency of expression[43] in no way obscures Kuhn's basic hypothesis: acceptance of a paradigm is a subjective matter best described as a conversion experience.

Here, in evidence, is Kuhn:

---

[43] The only political scientist I know of who has commented on the inconsistencies of Kuhn's position is Nelson W. Polsby: "The Sociology of Scientific Change: A Glance at Kuhn's Contribution," unpublished manuscript (1968).

Objectivity, Neutrality, and Kuhn's Paradigm

1. Like the choice between competing political institutions, that between competing paradigms proves to be a choice between incompatible modes of life. Because it has this character, the choice is not and cannot be determined merely by the evaluative procedures characteristic of normal science. (93) (108)
2. The issue of paradigm choice can never be unequivocally settled by logic and experiment alone. (93)
3. Anomalies and crises are not terminated by deliberation and interpretation but by a relatively sudden and unstructured event like the gestalt switch. No ordinary sense of the term "interpretation" fits these flashes of intuition through which a new paradigm is born. (121–2)
4. The proponents of competing paradigms, which are incommensurable, practice their trades in different worlds. (149)
5. Just because it is a transition between incommensurables, the transition between competing paradigms cannot be made a step at a time, forced by logic and mutual experience. (149)
6. I would argue that in these matters neither proof nor error is at issue. The transfer of allegiance from paradigm to paradigm is a conversion experience that cannot be forced. (150)
7. The man who embraces a new paradigm at an early stage must often do so in defiance of the evidence provided by problem-solving. A decision of that kind can only be made on faith. (157)

Notice the language: paradigmatic shifts are not determined by rational rules; they do not depend on logic and experiment, nor on deliberation and interpretation. They are sudden, matters of faith, conversions. These are some of the reasons why Kuhn's peers find his work to be so much at fault. Crisis gives rise to unstructured gestalt switches. So, Lakatos writes, it begets "a contagious panic. Then a new 'paradigm' emerges, incommensurable with its predecessor.... The change is a bandwagon effect. Thus *in Kuhn's view scientific revolution is irrational, a matter for mob psychology*." And if it is not this, then it "is a mystical conversion which is not and cannot be governed by rules of reason...."[44] For Marx Wartofsky, what started out as a corrective alternative to positivism ends up as the "abandonment of the rational objectivity of science and substitutes a voluntarist obscurantism."[45] The situation is not too much different for Scheffler: "In place of a community of rational men following objective procedures in the pursuit of truth, we have a set of isolated nomads, within each of which belief forms without systematic constraints."[46] While Toulmin tells us that many theoretical physicists lived through the shift from Newton's to Einstein's physics and they could and did explain the "reasons" why they changed to relativity. "So, prima facie at least, the switch... represented something more than a 'conversion.' "[47] And Popper instructs that what Kuhn presents is the logic of *historical relativism*—a thesis which he regards as wholly mistaken and which he refers to as the "Myth of the Framework." I have already spent considerable time in the attempt to refute this thesis (and its linguistic counterpart), but it is just as well to allow Popper to tell us that it is simply a dogma—"a dangerous dogma" at that. If we are prisoners of our theories, expectations, history, and language, this is so in only a "Pickwickian" (simple-minded) sense: "If we try, we can break out of our framework at any time." If this means moving into a new one, it can be better and roomier, and we can at any moment break out of it again. "The Myth of the Framework is, in our time, the central bulwark of irrationalism."[48] And, by way of summation, Shapere writes as follows:

relativism, while it may seem to be suggested by a half-century of deeper study of discarded theories, is a *logical* outgrowth of con-

---

[44] Lakatos, op. cit., pp. 93, 178. Emphasis in the original. It is interesting in this respect to compare Kuhn's description of scientific change with Anthony F. C. Wallace's "Revitalization Movements," *American Anthropologist,* Vol. 58 (1956).
[45] Cohen and Wartofsky, op. cit., Vol. III, pp. 149–150.
[46] Scheffler, op. cit., p. 19.
[47] Toulmin, "Conceptual Revolutions . . ." op. cit., pp. 340–341.
[48] Popper, "Normal Science and Its Dangers," op. cit., p. 56.

Objectivity, Neutrality, and Kuhn's Paradigm

ceptual confusions, in Kuhn's case owing primarily to the use of a blanket term. For his view is made to appear convincing only by inflating the definition of "paradigm" until that term becomes so vague and ambiguous that it cannot easily be withheld, so general that it cannot easily be applied, so mysterious that it cannot help explain, and so misleading that it is a positive hindrance to the understanding of some central aspects of science; and then, finally, these excesses must be counterbalanced by qualifications that simply contradict them.[49]

Even the sympathetic Margaret Masterman must disagree with Kuhn's "conception of verification (or the absence of it)." And, she adds, "on this . . . the philosophical empiricist world has indeed a case against him."[50]

The Normative and the Empirical

There is one more aspect of Kuhn's analysis that is of special interest to social scientists. It is not unusual for social scientists to take their models from the natural sciences—often with undesirable consequences. But in Kuhn's work, a reversal is in evidence: the mode of his inquiry is political, and in addition to the base concept of revolution, such critical psychological concepts as the "gestalt switch" loom large. These are fortified with much sociological metaphor and we have, all told, a volume written in an idiom that is quite familiar to social scientists. This, perhaps, is the reason that they have generally hailed the book as a "realistic" description of actual scientific practice.

In rather sharp contrast, however, one can find philosophical critics concerned that Kuhn's book may be descriptive of the sociology of science but not its methodology.

On this score, there is much confusion in political science—especially when it is said that methodological studies should provide accurate and realistic accounts of our actual scientific practices. We can observe an irony here, for it is often those political

---

49 Shapere, op. cit., p. 393. Emphasis in the original.
50 Masterman, op. cit., p. 61.

Political Theory and Political Science

scientists disturbed by "realistic" descriptions of political behavior who want this procedure to be applied to "scientific" behavior. In fact, the irony is further extensible: while they insist that the study of politics must be taken as a normative inquiry, they are adamant in the demand that methodological inquiry be empirically grounded. This is patently evident in the work of the "new political science."

Yet it is quite clear that methodology is a normative practice. It is usually taken in terms of "rational reconstruction," having to do with optimal forms of scientific procedure and not with the actual processes of thought. Philosophers of science are not psychologists and they are concerned with what may be considered "idealized" scientific maxims—with standards that must be followed in order to practice science properly. If, for example, one should ask Popper why we need to axiomatize, he will answer that it is not a goal but a means to an end. Taken as means, deductive systems are indispensable because it is necessary to develop our theories in this form. "This is made quite unavoidable by the logical strength, by the great informative content, which we have to demand of our theories if they are to be better and better testable."[51] Or, as J. W. N. Watkins puts it, "Methodology ... is concerned with science at its best, with science as it should be conducted, rather than with hack science."[52]

Feyerabend expresses what is involved here very pointedly. He insists that the normative interpretation of methodology must be followed even though actual scientific practice corresponds to its rules only more or less closely. If such norms are not upheld, the result will be an increased leniency with respect to questions of test. As against a "maximum testability of our knowledge," the grounds for the acceptance of a claim may become those of conformity. To illustrate this he uses a medical hypothesis that "is

---

[51] Popper, *Conjectures,* op. cit., p. 221. Popper's position does not accord with the usual Newtonian view that the goal of science is an axiomatic deductive system. Ibid. Section V.

[52] Lakatos and Musgrave, op. cit., p. 27.

Objectivity, Neutrality, and Kuhn's Paradigm

accepted, and retained, despite the fact that independent tests are not available, and its further use is defended by reference to the fact that it is in accord with the 'logic of medicine.' " He then points out that the phrase "logic of medicine" is a maneuver which propagates the acceptance of unsatisfactory hypotheses on the ground that this is what everybody is doing. "It is conformism covered up with high-sounding language."[53]

In the social sciences, as we have indicated earlier, an example of this kind of conformism is provided by the Meehl-Lykken analysis of the use of "statistical significance" in much of our researches.[54] Indeed, it flies in the face of "what everybody is doing" to suggest that significance levels are not very important, that they are never a *sufficient* reason for corroborating a theory or establishing a finding, and that they "promote increased leniency with respect to questions of test." If we took the description of actual research technique as our standard, we would be enshrining "hack science." And we would never ask why a *relativist* like Kuhn resorts to the *objective* facts of history to *prove* his thesis.

Nor would we, as Feyerabend does, raise a query as to whether Kuhn has written a purely descriptive ("void of any evaluation element") account of science or a methodological prescription. Accordingly, there are many commentators who see Kuhn as preferring "normal science" while he deprecates "revolutionary science."[55] Normal science is "mature" science, while revolution-

---

[53] Paul K. Feyerabend, "Explanation, Reduction and Empiricism" in Herbert Feigl and Grover Maxwell (eds.), *Scientific Explanation, Space and Time,* Minnesota Studies in the Philosophy of Science, Vol. 3 (Minneapolis: University of Minnesota Press, 1962), pp. 60–61.

[54] Paul Meehl, "Theory-Testing in Psychology and Physics: A Methodological Paradox," *Philosophy of Science,* Vol. 34 (1967). And see David T. Lykken, "Statistical Significance in Psychological Research," *Psychological Bulletin,* Vol. 70 (1968). See also D. E. Morrison and R. E. Henkel (eds.), *The Significance Test Controversy* (Chicago: Aldine, 1970).

[55] This theme runs throughout the various commentaries in Lakatos and Musgrave, op. cit.

ary science is crisis science, marked by schism, confusion, and conflict. And progress, we will recall, is the movement from paradigm to paradigm, with intervening periods of breakdown. Well, whether or not Kuhn extols normal science as the preferred condition, it is quite clear that one segment of political science is without doubt on this score. If we take Truman, Almond, Eulau, Holt and Richardson, it is rather evident that they are looking toward the day when a normal political science will emerge. They long for a disciplinary consensus, for the paradigm that eliminates dissensus as it produces science, and a "mature" science at that. But they may be asking for more than they anticipate.

To see this requires us only to state some of the properties that Kuhn assigns to normal science: it consists of mopping-up operations, is intolerant of new theory, drastically restricts vision, investigates areas that are miniscule (p. 24). These restrictions are not only "essential to the development of science" (p. 24), but there must also be conformity as to choice of problems and the rejection of extra-paradigmatic problems as metaphysical (p. 37) —in short, normal science constitutes a rigid and close-knit community (p. 49). Its education is narrow—on a par with theology (p. 165), and it is not inappropriate to regard the typical member of the normal scientific community as Orwellian (p. 166). If what is described here is not monolithic (p. 49), then it surely is monopolistic. There is, clearly, ample reason for Watkins to describe Kuhn's picture of normal science as an "essentially closed" society. It is as if Kuhn has erected the principle of the closed shop as the paradigm of normal science.

But this metaphor may be inappropriate because it is too weak. One could, as Watkins does, employ the image of the church—in which case "conversion" is certainly appropriate. And so are heresy, sin, and excommunication. Or, if we add to our discussion Kuhn's essay on "The Function of Dogma in Scientific Research,"[56] we make contact with a science that is also authoritar-

[56] In A. C. Crombie (ed.), *Scientific Change* (London: Heinemann, 1963).

ian. Normal science, so pictured, is not anything a reasonable scholar should look forward to.

There is, then, ample reason to damp the optimism of those seekers after a normal science. Moreover, if they think that a consensus built upon one paradigm, which then permits a turn to puzzles, will beget a science, they are, says Kuhn, "badly misconstruing my point."[57]

What now of the use of Kuhn by practitioners of the "new political science"—by Wolfe, Surkin, Levinson, Euben, and Wolin? Where Truman, Almond, and company turn on "normal science," this group zeroes in on "crisis science." And their arguments are quite consonant with Kuhn's formulations. Recall that in the crisis period, alternative, incommensurable theories compete with each other, and there is no objective way of determining the relative merits of each candidate. Hence, the conversion process. But here again we might switch our imagery, for we are dealing with a revolutionary situation. And "revolutions," Kuhn tells us, "close with a total victory for one of the two opposing camps" (p. 165).

One can, therefore, understand the intensity of the attack that is launched against that which is presumed to be a normal political science. And one can further appreciate the insistent refrain that what exists exists only as a consequence of power. For if, as Lakatos points out, "in science there is no other way of judging a theory but by assessing the number, faith, and vocal energy of its supporters, then this must be even more so in the social sciences: truth lies in power."[58] Despite Kuhn's caveat on this subject, might does seem to make right; and the "revolutionaries" have dug in for a monumental battle that will end with total victory. The task is to destroy "the hegemony of political science over its students" by "denouncing the current paradigm and

---

57 Kuhn, "Reflections on My Critics" in Lakatos and Musgrave, op. cit., p. 245. And see Feyerabend, "Consolation for the Specialist," op. cit., p. 198.

58 Lakatos, op. cit., p. 93.

Political Theory and Political Science

moving toward the creation, along with other radical caucuses, of . . . a social science that is *political*."[59] It was no doubt quite unintentional, but Kuhn's work has contributed in some measure to the current irrationality that holds the test of a theory to be its politics. If we are now in the throes of "extraordinary science," then a good part of the new politics movement stands as evidence for Watkin's assertion that extraordinary science is not science at all.[60]

There is now the rather influential position of Wolin to consider. In his view, the prevailing research program in political science, behavioralism or methodism, exhibits all the restrictive features of a normal paradigmatic science and has thereby impoverished the educational process, trivialized theory, and threatened the scientific imagination. It appears, though it is not always clear, that he wishes to expand the reach of our theories by eliminating the strictures of the prevailing paradigm, that he believes its monopoly status must be broken, that ipso facto it must be challenged; otherwise, it will remain incapable of comprehending the range of experience that stands as its task. It will cut itself off from its own vital sources as it becomes the handmaiden of the status quo.

I hesitate now to use the term, but it does not require too much thought to see that science is fundamentally a "revolutionary" enterprise. By taking as problematical those features of the common-sense world that remain unquestioned; by "re-presenting" forms of behavior that have been enshrined; by creating theories that challenge the "givenness" of commonly accepted explanations; and by the discovery of facts (findings) which undermine the received and revered truths of the day, theoretical science is clearly subversive of any status quo if it remains faithful to its values. Perhaps this is why Adam and Eve were kicked out of the garden—why science has always elicited a hostile response.

59 Surkin and Wolfe, op. cit., p. 7. Emphasis in the original.
60 Lakatos and Musgrave, op. cit., p. 29.

Objectivity, Neutrality, and Kuhn's Paradigm

But whether or not Wolin's criticisms are designed to advance scientific development, a monolithic or monopolistic paradigm must be eliminated because it promotes dogma, not science. The question arises, however, as to whether contemporary political science is so dogmatic. Clearly, there is much disagreement—but over what? Paradigm is so ambiguous, so elastic a concept as to permit any claim—and on any side. All the same, let us assume that Wolin's charges are not without point, and that we need to resist the "normal science" of Kuhn.

Let us note immediately that this cannot be done by adopting the thesis of "truth by consensus"—a doctrine advanced by both Kuhn and Polanyi. For this leads right back to the sins of normalcy. Nor will the resort to a "tacit political knowledge" help very much—for this bestows upon a claim precisely the kind of privileged status that excepts it from the principle of accountability and thereby places it beyond criticism, beyond test, and beyond science.

On the contrary, what is required to break monopoly is, by definition, competition. And the principle of "maximum empirical testability," with testability understood as the rule of independent external check, guarantees this by demanding that all theories, no matter how unorthodox, be considered. Not to consider them is to risk the loss of facts which can refute other theories.

While this principle encourages a theoretical competition, it also suggests that theories should not be discarded too easily. One of the interesting things that Kuhn has documented is the "tenacity" with which theories are held to even in the face of conflicting evidence.[61] That a theory should be defended vigorously is desirable so that it can not be eliminated before its resources have been fully explored.[62] But if it is defended in the face of clear and unequivocal refutation, it has become a dogma.

61 Lakatos, op. cit., pp. 175–176, and 211.
62 Lakatos and Musgrave, op. cit., p. 28.

Here, then, we have a strategy that is congenial to a theoretical pluralism, tolerant of tenacity, informed by the principle of accountability, and highly resistant to closed paradigmatic dogmas. If progress, scientific progress, is to be taken as the systematic elimination of error (and, consequently, the systematic accumulation of truth), it must be understood that this strategy cannot be followed when theories are empty of empirical content, constructed so that failure is impossible, or are that type of mixture best described as "Chinese metaphysics."[63]

It remains for me to acknowledge that I have omitted, almost completely, Kuhn's defense of his own position. I have not done this out of malice, nor because I consider his response to be without weight—although I remain unconvinced. Rather, my point stands as originally stated: when so much doubt attends Kuhn's proposals, when these have been subjected to such searching, often telling, criticism by his peers, this alone is sufficient cause for political scientists to hesitate before grounding their positions on his theory. But I cannot resist quoting Kuhn on two critical items:

> It is emphatically *not* my view that "adoption of a new scientific theory is an intuitive or mystical affair, a matter for psychological description rather than logical or methodological codification." On the contrary, the chapter of my *Scientific Revolutions* from which the preceding quotation was abstracted explicitly denies "that new paradigms triumph ultimately through some mystical aesthetic," and the pages which precede that denial contain a preliminary codification of good reasons for theory choice. These are, furthermore, reasons of exactly the kind standard (sic.) in philosophy of science: accuracy, scope, simplicity, fruitfulness and the like. It is vitally important that scientists be taught to value these characteristics and that they be provided with examples that illustrate them in practice.[64]

63 See Chapter 8 of this book.
64 Kuhn, "Reflections . . . ," op. cit., p. 261. Emphasis in the original.

Objectivity, Neutrality, and Kuhn's Paradigm

And second:

no part of the argument here or in my book implies that scientists may choose any theory they like so long as they agree in their choice and thereafter enforce it.[65]

---

65 Ibid., p. 263.

CHAPTER 3
On the Use of Metaphor in Political Analysis

> Thinking is radically metaphoric. Linkage by analogy is its constituent law or principle, its causal nexus, since meaning only arises through the causal contexts by which a sign stands for (takes the place of) an instance of a sort. To think of anything is to take it *as* of a sort (as a such and such) and that "as" brings in (openly or in disguise) the analogy, the parallel, the metaphoric grapple or ground or grasp or draw by which alone the mind takes hold. It takes no hold if there is nothing for it to haul from, for its thinking is the haul, the attraction of likes.
>
> I. A. RICHARDS

Such phrases as "living constitution" and "balanced governments" are daily encounters in political discussion. We speak and we write in metaphors, and we could scarcely get along without them. But the consequence may be more than felicity of phrase, for though figurative language can provide powerful analytic tools, it can also be the source of distortion and misrepresentation. Analysis is a function of the language we employ, and frequently "our thoughts do not select the words we use; instead, words determine the thoughts we have."[1] When this happens, language may impose on entities properties they do not in fact possess, or relationships

---

[1] Weller Embler, "Metaphor and Social Belief," in S. I. Hayakawa (ed.), *Language, Meaning and Maturity* (New York: Harper, 1954), p. 125.

Reprinted, with modifications, by permission from Martin Landau, "On the Use of Metaphor in Political Analysis," *Social Research*, Vol. 28, No. 3 (Autumn 1961).

On the Use of Metaphor in Political Analysis

that do not in fact exist; language, which is intended to clarify and illuminate, may then have just the opposite effect. In any case, the consequences of metaphoric expression, both substantively and methodologically, should not be minimized.

My purpose here is to examine the methodological implications of metaphoric usage in political analysis, with primary emphasis on the organizing power that has been demonstrated in American political thinking, by the concepts of mechanism and evolutionism. Each has served to impose a distinctive pattern of analysis on the field. Mechanism underwrote a rigidly structured formalism that made possible an almost wholly deductive study of politics. Evolutionism stimulated the "pragmatic revolt" that overthrew formalism and transformed political science into an empirical discipline. The contemporary revival of a theoretical politics derives much from prevailing models of "system," few of which are mechanical (closed), most of which are biological (open).[2]

I

A typical textbook provides many examples of the metaphors to which political scientists have grown accustomed.[3] Constitutions and governments, the student reads (pp. 33, 83), "are *growing* and *evolving* organisms" (italics in original), which must be "adapted to changing conditions." If government is to be "functional" for a society in change, it must itself change, following the laws of evolution as it "adapts" to new conditions. In

[2] See R. L. Schanck, *The Permanent Revolution in Science* (New York: Philosophical Library, 1954); P. Meadows, "Models, System, and Science," *American Sociological Review*, Vol. 22 (1957); L. von. Bertalanffy, *Problems of Life* (London: Oxford, 1952); D. Easton, "An Approach to the Analysis of Political Systems," in *World Politics*, Vol. 9 (1957); M. A. Kaplan, *Systems and Process in International Politics* (New York: John Wiley, 1957).

[3] J. M. Burns and J. W. Peltason, *Government by the People* (New York: John Wiley, 1957). Page numbers from this volume are in parenthesis in the text.

Political Theory and Political Science

this process all sorts of "disorders" arise to threaten "integration," and these may result in "stasis" (p. 564). One is presented with a "diagnosis of the main ills," with "proposals for cure," with clinical prescriptions designed to maintain or restore "health." We have here the image of an *organism,* and it is fully consistent with this image to employ a set of biological concepts to order analysis and discussion. But in the same volume, and sometimes in the same chapter if not on the same page, our student will find a language particularly appropriate to the image of a *machine*. He is told of the "operations of governmental machinery," of the "friction" between President and Congress, of the means whereby an effective "balance" might be engineered. He finds references to the "political pendulum," to "political leverage," to "inertia" in bureaucracy, to obsolescence ("out-of-date party machinery"), and to "efficiency" in the "running of the machine." In this context, it is not too difficult to set the President at the center of government with the control box before him and "his fingers on countless levers that shape the making of public and private policies" (p. 432).

If our student is perceptive he will wonder about the effects of such metaphors, about the identities that are thereby established. But if this escapes him he will no doubt observe that two "dominant metaphors" are indiscriminately mixed, and this, as his English instructor must have taught him, can serve only to obscure imagery and confuse meaning—indeed, to involve one in essentially contradictory statements. Thus if "American federalism has not been a static affair" and "has been molded by our dynamic society" (p. 84), then federalism cannot be a "mechanical arrangement" (p. 140). If it is "self-evident" that such social alterations as urbanization and industrialization have a "powerful impact on the government" (p. 105), if "forms" and "patterns" so intermesh (p. 889) that "alterations in procedures ... have an impact upon ... structure" (p. 902), and if "the pattern of federalism is being altered" (p. 121) in such a way that "the original system has been adapted to meet the problems of a

On the Use of Metaphor in Political Analysis

nation going through vast . . . changes" (p. 32), then it cannot follow that "the structure of our federalism is little changed" although "its actual operation has been drastically altered" (p. 101). It is only when we confuse evolutionary and mechanical models that we can hold to this conclusion and yet maintain that there are "few aspects" of the economy not national in scope (pp. 102–07) and that "the national government today . . . has sufficient constitutional power to dispose of virtually any problem of national extent" (pp. 137–38).

II

Bronowski has written that "the action of putting things which are not identical into a group or class is so familiar that we forget how sweeping it is. The action depends on recognizing a set of things to be alike when they are not identical. . . . Habit makes us think the likeness obvious", but "this ability to order things into likes and unlikes is . . . a human ability; we trace and to some extent inject the likeness, which is by no means planted there by nature for all to see."[4] Nevertheless, to seek likeness between things that are apparently unlike—to search for analogies—is a fundamental means of scientific inquiry. Its great value is to enable us to see a single "logical form" in things that appear to be quite different—as when Newton perceived the likeness "between the fall of an apple and the swing of the moon in its orbit," a likeness expressed by the concept of gravitational attraction. In science "we take from the world around us a few models of structure and process and when we research into nature, we try to fit her with these models."[5] By rendering different things as in certain respects equivalent, a class or category, a generalization, is established. Through such a process the empirical complexity

---

4 J. Bronowski, *The Common Sense of Science* (Cambridge, Mass.: Harvard University Press, 1953), pp. 21–22.
5 J. Bronowski, "Science as Foresight," in J. R. Newman (ed.), *What is Science?* (New York: Simon and Schuster, 1955), p. 428.

of an environment is reduced. So ordered and simplified, it need no longer be responded to in terms of the unique.

When, therefore, we come across something new we liken it to something familiar to us. We treat the new entity "as if" it were like the known entity, which, because known, has a name and is a part of our language. A language is a classification system. Each of its basic terms, its nouns and verbs, is a category defined in terms of a set of characteristics. To liken the new to the old (the known) is to suggest that the new possesses some of the characteristics of the known, that the two are somehow analogous.[6] And this is the way inquiry must proceed, for "how can we apprehend new relations except by viewing them under old categories? . . . In trying to visualize the unknown, the imagination must clothe it with attributes analogous to the known."[7]

For this reason metaphorical expression may be considered the "omnipresent principle of language." By using the more familiar as a representational base for the less familiar, we acquire a hypothesis to be tested. As Cohen puts it, metaphors express vague and confused but primal perceptions of identity, which through analysis and research may be transformed into a clear statement of the common properties possessed by two different objects.

There is another way in which metaphor serves as a useful organizing device. We frequently engage in a "conscious identification of avowedly diverse objects," both of which are quite familiar to us. This action, by transferring the actual referent to a new context, stimulates a reorganization of thought that may

---

6 See W. H. Werkmeister, *The Basis and Structure of Knowledge* (New York: Harper, 1948), pp. 34–39. Charles Morris, in *Sign Language and Behavior* (New York: Prentice-Hall, 1946), pp. 136–37, defines a metaphorical "sign" as one that "is used to denote an object which it does not literally denote in virtue of its signification but which has some of the properties which its genuine denotata have."

7 Morris A. Cohen, *A Preface to Logic* (New York: Holt, 1944), pp. 83–84, also Chapter 5. See J. S. Bruner, J. J. Goodnow, and G. A. Austin, *A Study of Thinking* (New York: John Wiley, 1956); E. Cassirer, *Language and Myth* (New York: Harper, 1946), Chapter 6.

On the Use of Metaphor in Political Analysis

be quite productive. It prompts us to revise our former conceptions of the object, and it gives rise to new hypotheses that may yield a significant increment. To call a government a machine (when we know that it is not literally a machine) directs us to the task of determining in what sense government is like (or unlike) a machine.

Thus metaphorical transfer—the substitution of analogy for actuality—may serve to "reveal new attributes or disclose old ones in a new light," thereby adding to the corpus of our knowledge. But while serving as a basic instrument of scientific analysis it must be attended by an awareness of the tentative character of the proposed analogy (in this chapter I do not consider its emotional function, but only its use as an analytic tool). If, through research, the analogy is verified, well and good; we have learned something. If the transfer is revealed to be false—if no analogous properties can be demonstrated—we have also learned something. Difficulty arises, however, when we allow a metaphor to congeal, to harden into a rigid set—when we take it literally. What we then do is to allow a presumed analogy to become an identity, an assertion of fact that may be, and usually is, entirely erroneous. To take a metaphor literally is to create a myth, and the more conventional myths become, the more difficult they are to dislodge.

In political science, as in social science generally, this danger is further aggravated by the fact that those metaphors in longest use have not been the product of explicit formulation or conscious transference. They have been, for the most part, rather implicit, and more often than not they have been taken as quite literal expressions precisely because of their familiarity and conventionality. And where the transfer is not explicitly formulated (as it is in the scientific use of a model), we work without a clear conception of the steps that led from the original to the metaphorical meaning, we fail to realize the hypothetical character of our statements, and we remain unaware that our thoughts and our observations are being shaped and directed by a particular

Political Theory and Political Science

image. If the analytic power of metaphors is to be properly exploited, metaphorical representation must be a matter of deliberate conceptualization. Only then can we proceed with that "full recognition of its limitations" which makes for "hygiene" in metaphorical usage.[8]

III

Historians often suggest that an era is best known by the metaphors it keeps. It should not surprise us that for the last four centuries these have been drawn primarily from the domain of the natural sciences. Because of the spectacular successes of modern science, those models of structure and process that science itself accepts as most warranted have been readily transferred to the domain of social inquiry, to become what Nagel calls the "set of necessary principles for ordering, acquiring, and interpreting all knowledge."[9] Or, in Oppenheimer's phrase, the findings of physical science have been prone to such extensive generalization as to profoundly affect the "common understanding" of a time. One central unifying image seems to distinguish the way men think. In the eighteenth century it was the machine that provided this image, and it was the Newtonian system that was taken as the model on which all rational inquiry was to be based.[10] So strong were these influences that numerous scholars of the Enlightenment have regarded the form of the American Constitution as a direct product of mechanism, and have held that as a result of the profound effect of the Constitution on political analysis,

---

[8] A. Rapoport, *Operational Philosophy* (New York: Harper, 1953); see Chapter 17.

[9] E. Nagel, *Sovereign Reason* (Glencoe, Ill.: Free Press, 1954), p. 122.

[10] J. R. Oppenheimer, *Science and the Common Understanding* (New York: Simon and Schuster, 1954), pp. 4-6, 15-16, and Chapter 4. See also Nagel, op. cit.; E. Cassirer, *The Philosophy of the Enlightenment* (Boston: Beacon Press, 1951); Crane Brinton, *The Shaping of the Modern Mind* (New York: New American Library, 1953); Bronowski, op. cit.

On the Use of Metaphor in Political Analysis

mechanism has been the dominant influence on American political science.

There are many uses to which the term *mechanism* is put, but since we are dealing with metaphorical transfer it is necessary to indicate only its literal meaning. In physics a system is called mechanical, as with Newton, "if and only if its basic entities are particles that move in orbit." That is, it must be a closed system consisting of discrete bodies, each possessing a specific set of properties (such as mass and position) that act over space and time in accordance with fixed law. The motion of a body is unequivocally determined by the action of external forces, and these forces arise from the action of other bodies in the system. Changes in position are always and solely a function of the masses of the system members and the distances between them. In such a system there is only lawful behavior: from a definite configuration of particles there will always follow the same results; there are no alternatives, and there is nothing any part of the system can do about it. It is possible, therefore, to build a completely predictable structure. Because the state of the system at any one time determines its state at another, one may predict the future if one knows the present. Hence, the method of analysis is to reduce any process to its irreducible elements or parts, and to treat process as the resultant of these separate parts acting externally on one another.[11]

This model, the most powerful in the history of scientific enterprise until very recently, was formulated by Newton "sudden and entire." From a puzzle of loose observations, from the empirical generalizations of his predecessors, this great physicist produced a system of such utter simplicity, of such "sweep and finality,"

---

[11] Nagel, op. cit., p. 23. See also E. Nagel, "The Causal Character of Modern Physical Theory," in H. Feigl and M. Brodbeck (eds.), *Readings in the Philosophy of Science* (New York: Appleton-Century-Crofts, 1953), pp. 420–427. For an extensive analysis of the properties of a mechanical system, see G. Bergmann, *Philosophy of Science* (Madison, Wis.: University of Wisconsin Press, 1957), Chapter 2.

Political Theory and Political Science

that nature seemed indeed to have given him "her profoundest secret." To the eighteenth century the Newtonian system constituted a cosmological formula so powerful that "Newton became not so much the name of a man as of an infallible world outlook."[12]

Accordingly, society came to be thought of in terms of mechanics. Social processes were seen as determined processes, directed into given paths by the action of impersonal external forces. The motion (behavior) of bodies (human beings) was preset and controlled according to the laws of nature. Natural man, whose properties included natural rights, was directed by natural forces to form societies. A society was no more than the sum of its constituents, a state no more than the sum of its discrete parts, its elemental bodies. Social and political processes resulted from the action of the separate parts on one another. And the perfect working of a state, as of any machine, depended only on the perfection of adjustment of the pushes and pulls of its constituent elements.

When, however, scientific models are transferred from their areas of literal meaning, they frequently give rise to a set of moral principles which precondition the goals to be obtained. What is in science an empirical hypothesis becomes in society a system of norms; what is in the original domain a descriptive proposition becomes in the social context a prescriptive instruction. It is this transfer that explains the "moral Newtonianism" of the Enlightenment, which was later to give rise to utilitarianism.[13] The hypothesis became the norm, and the image the goal. To achieve the harmony and balance of the physical universe it was necessary only to discover nature's way. And nature, in Thomas Paine's phrase, was "the law by which the universe was governed." Once this law, the natural order of human affairs, was

---

[12] J. W. N. Sullivan, *Isaac Newton* (New York: Macmillan, 1938), p. 259.

[13] See Elie Halévy, *The Growth of Philosophical Radicalism* (Boston: Beacon Press, 1955), Chapter 1.

On the Use of Metaphor in Political Analysis

discovered and applied, society would achieve the symmetry of the great machine.

In turning to the influence of mechanics upon the American Founding Fathers, we need not be concerned with the origins of their ideas about a mixed constitution or a balanced government. There is no doubt that these ideas predate the Newtonian era.[14] What is to the point is the sense of certainty that was attached to the concept of balance, and the fact that this assurance reflected the triumph of mechanism. With but few exceptions the constitution-makers thought that the government they were constructing was in accord with nature's design: in establishing the separation and balancing of power they were following nature's way. This was the ideal that was struck in Philadelphia—a government of law, not of men; one that by its natural properties minimized the risks of human passion. The true principle of government, said Hamilton, is this: "Make the system *complete* in its structure; give a *perfect proportion* and *balance* to its *parts*, and the power you give it will never affect your security."[15] We may not find footnotes to Newton's *Principia,* but the master model emerges so clearly that one may ask, with Lippmann, "Is there in all the world a more plain-spoken attempt to contrive an automatic governor—a machine which would preserve its bal-

[14] J. A. Robinson, "Newtonianism and the Constitution," in *Midwest Journal of Political Science,* Vol. 1 (1957), makes much of this fact in rejecting the influence of Newtonian mechanics on American constitutional philosophy. But his observations are quite irrelevant to his conclusions. He sampled the writings of the Founders (using as guide the indexes of various editions of their papers) and failed to find any "significant acknowledgement of intellectual debts to Newton"; on the contrary, they "referred more frequently to seventeenth century and classical figures than to the Newtonians." Robinson thus transformed the problem from that of the influence of mechanics on the Founders to whether or not they "acknowledged" Newton—thereby failing to understand the nature of a dominant metaphor. Metaphors may be so implicit that a lack of acknowledgment means only a lack of awareness that a transfer is in process.

[15] Quoted in Richard B. Morris, *Alexander Hamilton and the Founding of the Nation* (New York: Dial Press, 1957), p. 238. Emphasis added.

ance without the need of taking human nature into account?"

And it could scarcely have been otherwise. The Founders were no more able to throw off the fundamental typifications and conceptualizations of their day than we of ours. That they had differences in interest, attitude, and opinion is without doubt. But they possessed a certain habit of mind, a way of perceiving problems, which inevitably affected their projected solutions. Thus Lippmann[16] could remark that had the Founders "written the Constitution in the fire of their youth, they might have made it more democratic—I doubt whether they would have made it less mechanical." However hardheaded they were, however practical in adapting their prior constitutional experience, they still bathed willy-nilly in eighteenth-century thought: "Arguments for balance were all about them, in pamphlet and treatise, in legal commentary, in reports of parliamentary debates, in encyclopedias, in classical works, in books on education, on morality, on philosophy, as well as in John Adams's book—the whole of it a learned defense of balance—which they were all reading in the spring of 1787, and in Madison's doctrinaire pronouncements on the convention floor."[17] This "stream of thought" is what is commonly referred to as the American Enlightenment and, like its European counterpart, it was set firmly on the mechanistic hypothesis. Adams's *Defence* is most interesting in this context, for, in his words, it "was written to lay before the public a specimen of that kind of reading and reasoning which produced the American constitutions." On its title page one finds this line from Pope: "All Nature's difference keeps all Nature's peace." And this was the defense of the United States.

Its people exhibited "the first example of governments erected

---

16 Walter Lippmann, *A Preface to Politics* (New York: Macmillan, 1913), pp. 14–15.

17 Stanley Pargellis, "The Theory of Balanced Government," in Conyers Read (ed.), *The Constitution Reconsidered* (New York: Columbia University Press, 1938), pp. 38–39. Adams's work is *A Defence of the Constitutions of Government of the United States of America*, 3 vols. (London, 1787–88).

On the Use of Metaphor in Political Analysis

on the simple principles of nature." Compelled by their circumstances to erect new governments, they held this to be a problem of the same order as "arts and sciences, only more important." Faced with a rational problem, they turned to rational inquiry. They examined history, consulted theorists, studied past governments, compared the theories to the governments—all "to inquire how far both the theories and the models were founded in nature." And nature's principle (so happily verified by Newton) was action and reaction, thrust and counterthrust, check and balance. There are, said Adams, in his *Defence,* three branches in any government, and "they have an unalterable foundation in nature"; "to constitute a single body with all power, without any counterpoise, balance, or equilibrium," is to violate the laws of nature, but "to hold power in balance is a self-evident truth," which stands as the basis of "decency, honesty, and order in society."[18]

Is this not what the *Federalist Papers* attempted to demonstrate? Set squarely on the foundations of mechanism, they had to be written "in the most precise Newtonian language."[19] The image was the "perfectly proportioned complete structure"—Jonathan Swift's scale—always to be held in poise by equal weights on each side of the beam. In the celebrated No. 10, it will be recalled, Madison based stability and order on a balance of rival interests, on the neutralization of counterforces. Faction was to be checked by faction, class by class, one part of government by another—all to achieve the equilibrium of nature. A "natural" government was such that "its several constituent parts may, by their mutual relations, be the means of keeping each other in their proper places." A "natural" government, after all, was a transcript of nature, and nature was but a machine.

[18] G. A. Peek, Jr. (ed.), *The Political Writings of John Adams* (New York: Liberal Arts Press, 1954); see pp. 115–118, 142, 188–192.

[19] See R. Hofstadter, *The American Political Tradition* (New York: Alfred A. Knopf, 1938), Chapter 1. H. S. Commager, *The American Mind* (New Haven: Yale University Press, 1950), pp. 312–313, speaks of a "vocabulary . . . eloquent of mechanistic concepts."

Political Theory and Political Science

Look at this world, Hume wrote; "You will find it to be nothing but one great machine, subdivided into an infinite number of lesser machines . . . adjusted to each other with an accuracy which ravishes into admiration all men who have ever contemplated them." Look at these United States, Jefferson might have paraphrased, that great federation of lesser units—states, towns, and wards—all "adjusted to each other with an accuracy. . . ." "In time," he ventured, "all these as well as their central government, like the planets revolving around their common sun, acting and acted upon according to their respective weights and distances, will produce that beautiful equilibrium on which our Constitution is founded, and which I believe it will exhibit to the world in a degree of perfection, unexampled but in the planetary system itself. The enlightened statesman, therefore, will endeavor to preserve the weight and influence of every part, as too much given to any member of it would destroy the general equilibrium."[20] So, too, Hamilton cautioned that the "public burthens" must be so distributed that they do not fall too heavily on parts of the community, lest disorder ensue; "a shock given to any part of the political machine vibrates through the whole."[21]

It is possible to extend this parade at great length, but it would only weary. In one form or another, in greater or lesser degree, the Founders' thought rested on the image of the world machine. Even man was a machine, not only for La Mettrie but for Benjamin Rush, to whom life itself was the purely mechanical effect of material causes. It is beyond the scope of this essay to consider the psychology of the time, but its essential environmentalism, or elemental behaviorism, was a function of mechanism. Eighteenth-century psychology began with Hobbes' sensationalism—all that

---

[20] Quoted in H. W. Schneider, *A History of American Philosophy* (New York: Columbia University Press, 1946), pp. 46–47. See C. E. Merriam, *American Political Theories* (New York: Macmillan, 1903), pp. 159–160, and J. L. Blau's discussion of Jefferson and Paine in his *Men and Movements in American Philosophy* (New York: Prentice-Hall, 1952).

[21] R. B. Morris, op. cit., pp. 84–85; and see *Federalist Papers*, No. 17.

On the Use of Metaphor in Political Analysis

exists is body, all that occurs is motion, and the fundamental element of life is body (matter) in motion. It extended to Locke, for whom an external nature wrote its images on a *tabula rasa* (an interesting metaphor), and for whom the laws of retention and association became the equivalent of the force of gravitational attraction. And it reached into the American Enlightenment to underwrite, beyond Rush's psychology, the doctrines of individualism, equality, and perfectibility. Man was a discrete body, rationally contrived, governed by the play of natural forces. It was to order the interaction of these discrete particles in accordance with the laws of nature that Adams would check passion with passion, G. Morris set vice against vice, and Madison ambition against ambition. Small wonder that, as Pargellis tells us,[22] "few voices were raised in the convention, as too few in the eighteenth century, to offset the clear-cut, beautiful, unreal symbolism of government as an equipoise of equal powers." The set of this time, the prevailing habit of mind, made it axiomatic that government constituted a problem in mechanics, and its solution a matter of balance. The Constitution of the United States may well be taken as "a deliberate monument" to the image of the machine.

IV

The dominance of the mechanical metaphor in eighteenth-century political thought may be regarded as inevitable, given the historical circumstances. But it is the appropriateness of the metaphor and its consequences for political science that is our central problem. In considering these questions it is instructive to refer to Woodrow Wilson and J. Robert Oppenheimer, who have on occasion been quoted in opposition to each other. Wilson regarded the Constitution as built on a theory "which Newton might readily have recognized as suggestive of the mechanism of the heavens," but Oppenheimer, it has been suggested,[23] is hard

---

22 Pargellis, op. cit., p. 49.
23 Robinson, op. cit.

Political Theory and Political Science

put to find any appreciable influence of Newtonian mechanics on eighteenth-century political thought. When we place their positions in context, however, they make the point of this chapter.

At the time Wilson began to write, the influence of developments in the biological sciences was such that a new metaphor had begun to take hold. Darwin had appeared. And the rise of a new dominant metaphor has important methodological consequences. The transfer of meaning from one context to another serves to introduce new modes of thought, new systems of analysis, which profoundly affect the "received axioms" of the past. A change in image is a change in method.

To those who have studied Wilson he appears as a "realist," one of the first American political scientists to break with nineteenth-century tradition. Chafing under the "literary theory," the "paper pictures" of the Constitution, the young Wilson pressed as much for a reform of political science as of government. As early as *Cabinet Government* (1879) and certainly by his doctoral dissertation *Congressional Government* (1885), he appeared as an advocate of Walter Bagehot's "fresh and original method," which, "if applied to the exposition of our federal constitution, would result in ... a revelation"; even the most acute constitutional students, he held, had been dominated by the images of the *Federalists Papers,* and these images, "with a strange, persistent longevity of power, shape the constitutional criticism of the present day." As a result, one who looks at the living reality of government would wonder at the contrast to the paper description: he would see in life much that was not in the books, and in the rough practice of government he would not find the many refinements of the literary theory. If one wished to write practically and critically of government, he must "escape from theories and attach himself to facts ... striving to catch its present phases and to photograph the delicate organism ... exactly as it is today."[24]

24 Woodrow Wilson, *Congressional Government,* Meridian edition, with introduction by Walter Lippmann (New York: World Publishing Co.,

On the Use of Metaphor in Political Analysis

Here then is the shift in metaphor. The organism is to replace the machine. There is no mention of Darwin, but the evolutionary model that structures Wilson's analysis is evident throughout the work. Where once the language of physics was applied to government, it is now the language of biology that is relevant. The Constitution has become "a living and fecund system," and the terms Wilson used to describe it are growth, development, change, adaptation, and alteration. This was the approach that would provide an escape from a political science that "thinks, argues, and dogmatizes only about the *constitution;* about the nature of the state, . . . of sovereignty." Two decades later, still concerned with transforming political science into a descriptive, empirical discipline, Wilson issued his ringing protest: "government is not a machine, it is a living thing. It falls not under the theory of the universe, but under the theory of organic life. It is accountable to Darwin, not to Newton. It is modified by its environment, necessitated by its tasks, shaped to its functions by the sheer pressure of life."[25] A few years thereafter, on the eve of World War I, Walter Lippmann wrote a preface to a new political science cut in this image. The times, he stated, require a different order of thinking: we cannot expect to meet our problems with a few inherited ideas, uncriticized assumptions, a foggy vocabulary, and a machine philosophy. "Feckless—that is what our politics is. It is literally eccentric: it has been centered mechanically instead of vitally. *We have, it seems, been seduced by a fictitious analogy.*"[26]

To both Wilson and Lippmann, then, the historic assumption of an analogy between a political system and a mechanical system

---

1956), pp. 11, 30. See also Wilson's "The Study of Administration," *Political Science Quarterly,* Vol. 56 (1941), reprinted from Vol. 2 (1887); and D. Easton, *The Political System* (New York: Alfred A. Knopf, 1953), Chapter 6.

25 Woodrow Wilson, *Constitutional Government in the United States* (New York: Columbia University Press, 1908), p. 56.

26 Lippmann, op. cit., p. 23. Emphasis added.

was false. There was, in fact, no correspondence between the properties of a machine and those of a government; the "symbolism" was unreal. The proper analogy was to evolution; the appropriate image was the biological organism. And it was, indeed, the Darwinian metaphor that served as the foundation of the practical, "realistic" political science which was to emerge.

Now Oppenheimer enters this discussion because of the following statement: "What there is of direct borrowing from Newtonian physics for . . . politics is mostly crude and sterile. What there is in eighteenth-century political and economic theory that derives from Newtonian methodology is hard for even an earnest reader to find. The absence of experiment and the inapplicability of Newtonian methods of mathematical analysis make that inevitable."[27]

This statement is particularly significant because his book has to do in large measure with metaphorical transfer, and with the use of the physical sciences as a model both for other sciences and for the "common understanding." While Oppenheimer considers physical science a source of fruitful analogies, he reminds us of the dangers involved in uncritical transfer—especially when scientific findings are so generalized as to affect "the way men think about things which are not themselves part of science." The limiting terms and conditions, "the special circumstances of the discovery of scientific truth," act "as a protecting sheath against their unlimited and universal acceptance," but this holds only when these circumstances are understood. When they are not, we are faced with "misapplications of findings," which can result only in misrepresentation and confusion.

Let us fix on this quotation. If it is read carefully, Oppenheimer is seen not to be in conflict with Wilson; on the contrary. He does not say that the Newtonian model was not applied: he says that it was misapplied, that the application was crude and sterile,

---

27 Oppenheimer, op. cit., pp. 15–16.

On the Use of Metaphor in Political Analysis

that the transfer was quite uncritical. And this misapplication was precisely what underlay the criticisms of Wilson and those who came after him. What passed as Newtonian methodology in eighteenth-century, and most of nineteenth-century American political theory did indeed bear very little visible relation to Newton's system. Perhaps the reason was, as Oppenheimer says, the inapplicability of Newtonian mathematical analysis. But examination suggests that a deeper reason for the misapplication of the mechanistic metaphor in the eighteenth century, and for its "strange, persistent longevity of power" over nineteenth-century political and social inquiry, was the distortion of the role of mathematics. What made it inevitable that Newton's name would be taken in vain was that the scholarship of this era was not born of Newton's "rules of reasoning."

The world that Newton dealt with, from which he had banished all notions of a priori certainty, was a world of sensible phenomena, and was limited to the "phenomena of motions." While some aspects of nature, in his view, possessed mathematical characteristics, he was not at all certain that we could "derive the rest of the phenomena of nature by the same kind of reasoning from mathematical principles." As Burtt paraphrased him, "the world is what it is; so far as exact mathematical laws can be discovered in it, well and good; so far as not, we must seek to expand our mathematics or resign ourselves to some other less certain method" (Newton's invention of the calculus was such an expansion, although his *Principia* used the language of geometry). Unlike Descartes, Newton distinguished mathematical and empirical truth, insisting that the process of mathematical deduction must culminate in the process of experimental verification. Thus all propositions, all hypotheses, were to be empirical in character. Metaphysical assertions, unverifiable hypotheses, a priori speculation in general, were to be cast out of science: if such hypotheses are to be "the test of truth and reality of things," stated Newton, "I see not how certainty can be obtained in any science." The

Political Theory and Political Science

union of mathematics (logic) and experimentation (experience), set firmly on the rule of observation, was the essence of Newton's methodology.[28]

But this was not the methodology that characterized the Age of Reason. Its measure of knowledge, though taken under the authority of Newton, derived less from him than from the great rationalists who preceded him. It is ironic that the "universal geometry" of Descartes expresses more of the character of "reason" than does the mathematical-experimental method of Newton. Geometry, as Nagel tells us, was taken as the method of nature, indeed as the prototype of reason. The only familiar system of deductive mathematics, it was assumed to mark off the inherent boundaries of human reason. The lack of alternative systems was construed as evidence of their impossibility; thus geometry and mechanics were riveted in the final structure of reason and nature. "The true system of the world," D'Alembert could therefore write, "has been recognized, developed, and perfected."[29] Hence the overwhelming emphasis on "self-evident principles," on "axioms of right" and "primary truths." Things became knowable in advance of experience, requiring no more verification than intuitive self-evidence (compare Hamilton's "rules" in *Federalist Papers,* No. 31). In the common currency of the time, sovereign reason moved on a priori knowledge. From "first principles," through a network of deductions, results were arrived at, and if logical they were deemed incontrovertible.

This summary provides, without too much danger of error, a statement of the general methodology of academic thinkers of the eighteenth and nineteenth centuries in the sphere of American social inquiry. The curriculum researches of Anna Haddow sustain the observation that the nineteenth century inherited and pre-

---

28 E. A. Burtt, *The Metaphysical Foundations of Modern Science* (New York: Doubleday, Anchor edition, 1954); for an extensive discussion of Newton's methodology see Chapter 7. See also A. R. Hall, *The Scientific Revolution* (New York: Beacon Press, 1954).

29 Cited in Cassirer, op. cit., p. 3.

On the Use of Metaphor in Political Analysis

served a political thinking that was a priori in method, mechanistic in form, and moral in character.[30] During this time the study of politics was the study of moral philosophy. Ethics was the overwhelming concern of instruction, and the logical elaboration of primary truths was the subject of countless disputations. Empirical research was frequently minimized as "beneath the dignity . . . beside the purpose of philosophical institutions." Philosophy, after all, was "inquiry by reason," and if it had laid aside revelation, neither was it linked to experience. The first empirical study of Congress was not made until Wilson published his dissertation (1885), and the first empirical study of parties came only with Lord Bryce's *American Commonwealth* (1888). Until Bryce, the "conspiracy of silence" on the political party was virtually unbroken.[31] Francis Lieber, our first "political scientist," could write two volumes *On Civil Liberty and Self-Government* (1853) and devote a page and a half to the role of the party; in 1890 John W. Burgess, the founder of the Columbia School of Political Science, could ignore parties even as he tried to describe presidential elections.[32]

And so it went with respect to almost every sphere of governmental activity. It seems strange now, but the activities or operations of government did not become the subject matter of political science until the last decade of the century. Before that the preoccupation of political research, such as it was, was law: the law of the Constitution. What was not provided for in law, or in acceptable philosophies of law, was either of no concern or downright dangerous. Thus, to Lieber, the movement for an eight-hour work day was a "dangerous tampering with im-

---

30 Anna Haddow, *Political Science in American Colleges and Universities* (New York: Appleton-Century, 1939). And see T. I. Cook, "The Methods of Political Science," in *Contemporary Political Science*, UNESCO Publication No. 426 (Paris, 1950).

31 See E. E. Schattschneider, *Party Government* (New York: Rinehart & Co., 1942), pp. 4–5; also Easton, op. cit., Chapters 3, 6.

32 For an excellent analysis of Lieber and Burgess, see B. Brown, *American Conservatives* (New York: Columbia University Press, 1950).

mutable law." Even administrative law was suspect until the pragmatic Frank Goodnow made it respectable—but this did not occur until the new metaphor had taken hold. Indeed, it took a veritable social revolution to dislodge the eternal and immutable law that had been so fortified by mechanism, and to prove that there existed other systems of analysis. To those to whom self-evident principles were the starting points of a geometric deductivism, the life of the law was not experience; it was logic.

There was another aspect of this period which made the "certain systems" of the eighteenth century even more rigid. Those scholars who dominated the emerging discipline of political science were heavily influenced by German idealism: the line ran from Kant to Hegel. With Lieber and Burgess, and the returning *Herren Doktoren,* political science drew its first principles from a "higher kind of truth" and built grand deductive systems that were carefully protected from the eroding force of experience. They spoke science, but they were speculative scholars who relied on intuition and frequently resorted to an active Providence to validate their propositions. Even their concept of change, a type of organicism that had emerged as a reaction to the dissolving individualism of the closed and static world of the "Newtonian," was confined within its own predestined system, bounded on all sides by the high walls of morality.[33] They may have opened this world to break through the "social contract," but they closed it right back again with a moral absolutism.

Nor is their kind of organicism to be confused with the evolutionary political science that was soon to take root under the promptings of pragmatism. To be sure, they treated the state as a biological organism, but the state was to be distinguished from government—and with respect to government their treat-

---

[33] See M. G. White, *Social Thought in America: The Revolt Against Formalism* (New York: Viking Press, 1950), Chapter 2; R. Hofstadter, *Social Darwinism in American Thought* (Boston: Beacon Press, 1955); also Haddow, op. cit., and Cook, op. cit.

ment remained typically mechanical. Beard, in recalling his schooling under Burgess, reminds us of a time when the Constitution was the thing, when a judge was presented as a master mechanic, when the "weighing, measuring and logistical method of 'learning' constitutional law was a way of life," and when the analysis of a case was "an adventure in deductions drawn from a major premise grounded in the ineluctable nature of things."[34]

The Darwinian metaphor overthrew all of this. The story is a long one, but its substance is that the epistemological implications of evolution exerted a mighty influence on those who laid the foundations of pragmatism. Discarding old-world forms of rationalism and empiricism, the group of scholars who came together in their Metaphysical Club (Charles Peirce, William James, Oliver W. Holmes, and Chauncey Wright, among others) searched for a new "rule of method" to clarify ideas and to test claims of truth. And out of the welter of their thought came a new empirical temper.[35]

And this was the hallmark of the political science of Wilson and Frank Goodnow, of Henry Jones Ford and J. Allen Smith— it was pragmatic, evolutionary, and empirical. Politics became a descriptive science, abandoning the isolation of first causes for a functional analysis of how things worked. The old language yielded to the new as fixed and final notions gave way to a vocabulary whose essential terms were function, process, development, and change. System building and theorizing were minimized, and the "thin abstraction" fell before the "thick particular fact." The fact became the thing; to get it sure, "to polish it until it sparkled"—this was the goal of the new pragmatist and of the generation that followed. Observation was to come first, the fact stood inviolate, and the secondary, even dangerous character of theory was stressed, a stress that led to a fragmentary political

---

[34] Charles A. and Mary R. Beard, *The American Spirit* (New York: Macmillan, 1942), pp. 347–354.

[35] See P. Wiener, *Evolution and the Founders of Pragmatism* (Cambridge, Mass.: Harvard University Press, 1949).

science that we are only now beginning to question. These were the results of the new metaphor.[36]

V

The implications of metaphors are such, then, as to call for the clearest understanding of their uses and limitations. It is neither possible nor necessary that exacting care be taken with every metaphorical expression; many of them have been made so synonymous with what is to be represented that we are unaware of their metaphorical character; many of them are not important. But where a metaphor is dominant, it is a very powerful instrument. It structures inquiry, establishes relevance, and provides an interpretive system. Hence it must be used with full awareness, and must be made fully explicit. The use of a dominant metaphor always involves us in a basic form of comparative analysis. We compare B to A in order to pursue a more or less systematic analysis of B. A is our representational base, our model. If very little is known about A, the likelihood of any significant yield is minimal; if we do not understand A's characteristics, the comparison is pointless. It is only when we understand the structural form, the concepts involved, and the properties and features of the model that we can make an educated guess as to the validity of the analogy.[37]

Thus to reject mechanism for evolutionism does not mean that the latter is necessarily more appropriate. A mechanical model, properly employed, may yield considerable increment. Improperly employed, we know, it quickly "hardens into a rigid prison of system" and will serve only to retard the development of the field. It may be that social institutions are more analogous to biological organisms than they are to machines, but this is only a

---

[36] See Chapter 5 of this book for a full discussion of this movement.
[37] See May Brodbeck, "Models, Meaning and Theories," in L. Gross (ed.), *Symposium on Sociological Theory* (Evanston, Ill.: Row, Peterson and Co., 1959); also A. Rapoport, "Uses and Limitations of Mathematical Models in Social Science," ibid.

On the Use of Metaphor in Political Analysis

guess that must be tested out. Whether social institutions in fact possess properties and features that are similar to those of biological organisms becomes, under this metaphor, the empirical problem. To attack this problem requires that the concepts involved be clarified.

There are any number of concepts that have been transferred from biology to the sphere of social science. But just what does it mean to apply these terms to social institutions? To what in political life do these concepts refer? What is being placed in correspondence with what? What does the concept *evolution* itself mean in political science? (It is interesting that Wilson and Lippmann tried to clarify what it was in mechanism that they rejected; their attack rested on the fact that mechanism assumes a closed system while that of social life is open.) The proper employment of the Darwinian metaphor, no matter on what level of generality, requires that these questions be dealt with before we can proceed to a determination of whether the properties of the organism and the government are in fact analogous. Failure to make such clarification provides us with a proposal (hypothesis) that is so vague, so ambiguous, as to be of little usefulness in the organization of our efforts.

The long history of metaphorical transfer in political science may well be pondered by those who fret over the increasing use of models today—be the models mathematical, biological, electronic, or other. It may justifiably be said that some of this is more a product of fashion than a scientific tool relevantly employed.[38] But fashion is by no means the whole story. Just as mechanism once ordered the domain of politics, and evolutionism proposed to reorder it, new models are now employed to provide some system in a field that remains, after some seventy-five years of hyperfactualism, without any substantial theory. Some of these, as applied to politics, may be quite inadequate, and the methodology they engender quite inappropriate, but in the minds of

[38] See H. Goldhamer, "Fashion in Social Science," *World Politics*, Vol. 6 (1954).

sophisticated workers their "as if" quality remains clear, their proposals are recognized as hypothetical, their limitations are understood. It is therefore possible to evaluate them with ease and economy. This is to be contrasted with the use of concealed metaphors, which invariably begins with an "as if" proposition and ends with an "it is" statement without in any way demonstrating correspondence and similarity.

Political science has always resorted to metaphors, to the device of proceeding from the known to the unknown. Those who criticize the use of models need to understand that they too must use them. Accordingly, much of the conflict over the use of models is spurious. The choice is not between models and no models, but between a critical consciousness of their use and an uncritical acceptance. An open and "hygienic" use of models may or may not aid us in developing empirically sound political theory, but it would enable us to run far less risk than we take with the hidden, implicit, and rigidified metaphors so frequently in the textbooks of political science.

CHAPTER 4
On the Use of Functional Analysis in American Political Science

It is problematical as to whether any violence is done to the present state of affairs in American political science when it is asserted that its domain of inquiry is excessively random.[1] Indeed, it is this fact—a high information level and a low theoretic yield—that has prompted the rather extensive efforts at theory construction that are so readily apparent today. For the most part, however, theory in political science has come by way of transfers from a wide variety of sciences[2]—all in the hope of systematizing the field. Structural-functionalism, immediately drawn from sociology (but with a long history in anthropology and biology), constitutes one such rather popular transfer.

My task in this chapter is to convey "an idea of just what functionalism means in American political science." In doing so, I will avoid any extended comment on functionalism in sociology, although the temptation to do so is strong on two counts: not only is it the source of the transfer but as a theoretical enterprise it is far more developed. Nor will I inquire into the status of

---

1 See David Easton, *The Political System* (New York: Alfred Knopf, 1953); Richard C. Snyder, "A Decision-Making Approach to the Study of Political Phenomena" in Roland Young (ed.), *Approaches to the Study of Politics* (Evanston: Northwestern University Press, 1958); David B. Truman, "Disillusion and Regeneration: The Quest for a Discipline," *American Political Science Review*, Vol. 59 (1965).

2 See Chapter 8.

Reprinted, with modifications, by permission from Martin Landau, "On the Use of Functional Analysis in Political Science," *Social Research*, Vol. 35, No. 1 (Spring 1968).

Political Theory and Political Science

teleological formulations with all their attendant problems. This critique, and the analysis of sociological functionalism, has been executed by philosophers of science with far more logical skill than is at my disposal.[3] Accordingly, this chapter is limited to political science proper.

As for the assignment itself, I will employ a concept of *meaning* that has functional connotations—namely, the uses to which this type of analysis has been put. Such judgments as I make, I hasten to add, are to be taken as tentative. For in political science, functionalism constitutes a theory that is—like all theories in their initial states of application—both incomplete and ambiguous. To offer any final judgment as to its value is to predict its future. And this no one can do with any certainty. Theoretic proposals of this order are only possibilities: it takes hard logical work and much empirical research to transform them into probabilities. In political science, the setting of odds is quite premature.

To begin with, it is necessary to treat the problem of ambiguity—if only to identify what it is that we are talking about. And since I am operating on the assumption that functionalism is a distinctive mode of inquiry, I have sought to reduce its ambiguity by means of the energy-transfer model that it expresses. In the remainder of the chapter, I have dealt with what I consider to be the important applications of functionalism in political science: first, as a classification system by means of which a wide variety of countries can be ordered and analyzed and, second, as a technique by means of which anomalous political developments can be dealt with. The first expression of this latter formulation came

---

3 See Ernest Nagel, *The Structure of Science* (New York: Harcourt, Brace & World, 1961); Carl G. Hempel, "The Logic of Functional Analysis" in L. Gross (ed.), *Symposium on Sociological Theory* (Evanston, Ill.: Row, Peterson and Co., 1959); Max Black, "Some Questions About Parsons' Theories" in Max Black (ed.), *The Social Theories of Talcott Parsons* (Englewood Cliffs, N.J.: Prentice-Hall, 1961); Robert Brown, *Explanation in Social Science* (Chicago: Aldine, 1963). In the interest of brevity, I make no references to the "functionalism" of physical and social anthropology.

Functional Analysis in American Political Science

at the turn of the century under the influence of pragmatism and evolution but was unfortunately lost because our pragmatic forebears were not given to statements of formal rules. I shall hold discussion of this for Chapter 5.

I

Philosophers of science, in evaluating such sociological functionalists as Talcott Parsons, Marion J. Levy, Jr., and Robert K. Merton (who are, collectively, the primary source of functionalism in political science), have often observed that there is no agreement as to the distinctive properties of functional analysis. And in a recent volume, Richard S. Rudner points to this condition in no uncertain terms. Functionalism, he states,

> has been the topic of a discussion so voluminous and widespread in texts and treatises, that no one who has engaged in even a peripheral study of the social sciences can fail to have been confronted with references to it. *Yet to be thus confronted is, unfortunately, usually to become convinced that the major task of saying clearly what constitutes functionalism still remains.*[4]

If the concept of "functionalism" is not clear, or if there is no agreement as to its defining properties, we face a rather difficult problem: we have no definite standards by which identification of instances of functional analysis can be made. In strictly formal terms, the correct denotation of a class term (say, functionalism) is arrived at on the basis of its designative or intensional properties. That is, the set of characteristics that defines a concept is the set of characteristics that phenomena must exhibit in order to be denoted (counted). This, in fact, is how an instance of a class is correctly determined. That such determination cannot be made with any significant degree of confidence unless and until the class term is assigned a definite meaning bears emphasis. Here, it

---

4 Richard S. Rudner, *Philosophy of Social Science* (Englewood Cliffs, N.J.: Prentice-Hall, 1966), pp. 84–85. Emphasis added.

appears, the grounds for such determination are so vague that anything and everything can be classified as functional. Conversely, everything and anything can be excluded.

One illustration of this can be found in Eugene Meehan's analysis.[5] There we discover that Easton's *The Political System* is a "landmark" work in functional analysis "though [its] functionalism is latent rather than manifest"; that Gabriel Almond's work "is functional in name only"; and that Morton Kaplan's *System and Process in International Relations* is a "typical" functionalism, to be grouped with William Mitchell's *The American Polity* and David Apter's *Gold Coast in Transition*. In this analysis it is rather startling to encounter Kaplan as a functionalist —and a typical one at that—especially when Meehan states that his model is mechanistic! Nor is it made clear on what basis Easton's work is treated "as an interesting variant of functionalism." In the case of Almond, who has introduced all of his work over the last decade as a "functional" approach, and who has generally been accepted as a functionalist, Meehan's idiom may simply indicate his dissatisfaction with Almond's work; then too he may be excluding him from the set. Although quite elusive, there must be some principle of classification operative here other than the fact that any theory is, by its systemic nature, deemed to be functional.

A further indication of the difficulties that arise is to be seen in the commentary of Flanigan and Fogelman.[6] Called upon to evaluate functional analysis, they find it necessary to order their efforts by offering a classification scheme that suggests that func-

---

[5] Eugene J. Meehan, *Contemporary Political Thought* (Homewood, Ill.: The Dorsey Press, 1967), pp. 112, 180–181, 168. Parenthetically, Mitchell does not see much Parsonian influence on Kaplan's work. See William C. Mitchell, *Sociological Analysis and Politics* (Englewood Cliffs, N.J.: Prentice-Hall, 1967).

[6] William Flanigan and Edwin Fogelman, "Functionalism in Political Science" in Don Martindale (ed.), *Functionalism in the Social Sciences* (Philadelphia: The American Academy of Political and Social Science, 1965).

Functional Analysis in American Political Science

tionalism has taken three forms in political science: eclectic, empirical, and structural-functionalism.

In the eclectic brand, the researcher asks, "What function does X perform?" But he does not derive this question from any formal theoretical apparatus nor is he working to test any theory. Whatever theory is involved is implicit and the researcher, accordingly, is free to ask a variety of additional questions.

Empirical functionalism is differentiated as a more explicit formulation. Analysis is more consistent, and the orientation is structured, thereby presenting a degree of discipline that is absent in eclectic functionalism. This type of analysis looks upon a general functional theory as premature and, our authors note, "was given its greatest impetus and its most convincing justification"[7] in Merton's analysis of the political machine.[8] And, following Merton, one of its primary features is the need to distinguish manifest (intended and recognized by participants in the system) from latent (unintended and unrecognized) functions.

The third category, structural-functionalism itself, represents an effort at general theory. Its leading advocates, Parsons and Levy, propose a full-scale social theory. Parsons' work constitutes something analogous to a unified field theory in social science while Levy's is limited to the structure (logic of relationships) of society and proceeds primarily in terms of what he calls "requisite analysis." Both proposals, it is to be noted, are framed within a systems perspective with such attendant hypotheses as self-regulation and functional interdependence.[9]

---

7 Ibid., p. 113.

8 Robert K. Merton, *Social Theory and Social Structure* (Glencoe, Ill.: Free Press, 1957), Chapter 1.

9 Flanigan and Fogelman see the following as characteristic features: an emphasis on the whole system as the unit of analysis, postulation of particular functions as requisite to the maintenance of the system and concern to demonstrate the diverse structures within the system. See op. cit., pp. 115–116. For a bibliography of Parsons' work see Mitchell, op. cit. or Black, op. cit. Marion Levy's theoretical statement is *The Structure of Society* (Princeton: Princeton University Press, 1950). And

Political Theory and Political Science

In the instance of eclectic functionalism, one may now ask, why should we even bother with such a classification if, as Flanigan and Fogelman say, the "functionalist aspect [is not] considered in any way primary or exceptionally significant."[10] The answer they give is that eclectics not only are found in all branches of political science but can be identified by their *tendency* to frame questions in terms of functions. And this tendency is marked; so well marked that its measure is 100 per cent. For our commentators hold that "it is not too much to say that we are all functionalists now." In this context, Kingsley Davis is quite right in insisting that functional analysis is indistinguishable from analysis in general.[11]

Actually, there is a point here that should not be glossed over. "Function" has been a concept in the English language for hundreds of years. And it is one that has had, as Edward Rose puts it,[12] a natural sociological meaning, whose essence is "the kind of action proper to." In the earliest dated usage, 1533, it was action proper to a person belonging to a particular class, "especially the holder of any office." Shortly thereafter it became the "special kind of activity proper to anything," and by 1590, "the mode of action by which (anything) fulfills its purpose." Thus there has been a teleological cast to this term for close to four hundred years. After all this time, given its staying power, "function" stands as a very powerful conventional concept. It was there in the lexicon for anyone—whether Durkheim, Radcliffe-Brown or even Leibnitz—to use.

Conventional concepts, however, are rarely defined so as to permit a precise statement of their properties. That they are ambiguous, that they carry surplus meaning, is an old story. The

---

see Robert T. Holt, "A Proposed Structural-Functional Framework for Political Science," in Martindale, op. cit.

10 Ibid., p. 112.

11 Kingsley Davis, "The Myth of Functional Analysis," *American Sociological Review*, Vol. 24 (1959).

12 Edward Rose, "The English Record of a Natural Sociology," *American Sociological Review*, Vol. 25 (1960).

Functional Analysis in American Political Science

easy employment of task, role, mission, purpose, part, and place as synonyms of function makes this eminently clear. When, therefore, inquiry is inaugurated around or in terms of this concept, its referents cannot be identified in any scientific sense. The paradox that is evident in this situation stems from the fact that denotations are habitually known but the properties by which we know them are not. That is, through custom and usage what "function" points to is easily recognizable, the things it denotes are relatively clear—but the ground upon which identification is made remains implicit.

This is the feature that characterizes eclectic functionalism and because of this feature we can dismiss it from our considerations. It represents an initial stage of inquiry which does not possess, in and of itself, any distinguishable formal properties nor any distinguishable subject matter other than those bequeathed by custom and tradition. If political scientists, or anyone else for that matter, inform their researches by the conventional concept "function," their work is bound to be loose and ambiguous, undisciplined and eclectic. It is as a matter of convention, not theoretical science, that this form of analysis so abounds. That it does in great measure is perhaps a mark of our "development"—a term that, not so incidentally, is defined by the same dictionaries as "making manifest that which is latent."

It is the latter pair, empirical and structural-functionalism, that are of interest to us. And even as they are presented, they constitute not so much two types as two strategies. In Merton's view, we should adopt the well-known rule of the middle range, but this is a praexiological proposal, not a theoretical one. Parsons and Levy, on the other hand, are willing to entertain the greater risks (and the greater pay-offs) of a more comprehensive scheme. But all three have long since abandoned the pretheoretic concept (of ordinary usage) and have moved toward an autonomous designation of "structural-functionalism." If it is necessary to distinguish Parsons, Levy, and Merton, it is best to do so in terms of a descending order of generality.

Political Theory and Political Science

The clarity thus far achieved does not meet the requirements of logicians or philosophers of science and leaves unresolved many problems, both of a theoretical and empirical character. Nor is this situation eased by the propensities of American political scientists to innovate. Finding little value in continuity, they tend to grasp a central theme and, even before the hold is secure, mount variation upon variation sometimes to the point of nonrecognition, sometimes to the point of inconsistency. Nevertheless, there appears to be a common core of meaning to functionalism in political science, sufficient to provide some working rules of inquiry. To demonstrate this requires some preliminary statements about "systems."

II

Structural-Functionalism: An Energy-Transfer System

Any ordered set of relations may be taken as a system, but in political science (as in social science generally) this term is usually employed as an abbreviation of "general systems theory." In a somewhat oversimplified fashion, this theory is an amalgam of two distinct formulations: the biological model of energy transfer and the communications model of information transfer. Although neither formulation has yet been reduced to the other, they do possess a striking similarity, which begins with the concept of an open set of variables. Taken together, and in an integrated manner, they form the information-energy model which interprets general systems theory.

These closely related theoretic schemes are often treated as distinctive proposals even though they overlap considerably. General systems theory finds, for example, a major expression in David Easton's work[13]—and it is, no doubt, the element of overlap that

---

13 See David Easton, *A Systems Analysis of Political Life* (New York: John Wiley & Sons, 1965).

Functional Analysis in American Political Science

enables Meehan to classify this work as "functionalist." Information transfer is given a specific treatment in Karl Deutsch's work.[14] Functionalism, however, is to be understood primarily in terms of the biological model of energy transfer. A clue to this is to be found in the almost inevitable resort to biological metaphor by functionalists. Accordingly, a statement of the primary characteristics of this model[15] provides the context for an understanding of functional analysis. These are:

1. Every living system is "open." That is, it maintains itself in a continuous exchange of matter and energy with its environment. That which enters the system from the environment becomes a part of its internal processes. Changes in the environment have far-reaching effects upon the system. Conversely, that which is discharged into the environment can grossly affect it.[16] A system, then, is always changing, constantly taking in and putting out, breaking down and building up its own substance.

    This process enables the statement: *"Living forms are not in being: they are happening."*[17]

2. Every living system is "self-regulating." Though in a state of constant exchange, it acts to keep both its internal condition and external environment stable. It is capable of main-

---

14 See Karl Deutsch, *The Nerves of Government* (New York: Free Press of Glencoe, 1963).

15 The following discussion is based primarily upon L. von Bertalanffy, *Problems of Life* (New York: Harper Torchbook, 1960) and Felix Mainx, "Foundations of Biology," in *International Encyclopedia of Unified Science* (Chicago: University of Chicago Press, 1955), Vol. 1, Part 2.

16 The study of living systems in their total environment is known as ecology. It appears that discharges into the environment have so grossly affected ecological balance as to create a survival problem of considerable magnitude for all mankind. One may hope that the disturbances have not reached the point as to be beyond homeostatic controls—i.e. the capacity of the system to right the imbalance.

17 Von Bertalanffy, op. cit., p. 124.

Political Theory and Political Science

taining this stability (sometimes called "steady state") against extensive disturbance and variation both within and without by a process of self-regulation. Regulatory processes[18] are *manifold, complex,* and *redundant* and serve to protect against threats to the system. Only if the disturbance exceeds certain limits will these self-regulating or adaptive processes fail and the system be irreversibly destroyed.

Despite ceaseless change, there is a constancy to the system. *What is constant, however, is not its material substance but its forms and process.*

3. Every living system constitutes a set of processes that are functionally interdependent. Systems cannot be broken down into isolated elementary components. They cannot be taken apart and put together again like machines. The behavior of an individual unit that is isolated differs from its behavior in the context of the whole: *it loses its systemic properties.* Within the system, each unit depends not only upon its own internal condition but on the condition of the whole. All units and processes, whatever their level of complexity, work in mutual interdependence so as to guarantee the maintenance of a steady state. It is this complex of mutual involvement and functional interdependence that enables a system to regulate disturbance and adapt to changed conditions.

   The meaning of any part or process, thus, *is the function it performs for the system as a whole.*

4. In living systems, *structure and function* are distinguished by their rates of change. Structure is understood not as the sum of separate parts acting upon each other but as a close relational process of long duration. Function is a rapid process of short duration and is distinguished from structure by the rate of change involved. While both are dynamic in character, structure appears stationary or fixed, relative to func-

[18] Self-regulatory processes are often referred to as homeostatic. The term homeostasis refers to constancy of condition or steady state.

tion.[19] What we take as structures are not only connected to each other and to the system by functions but may themselves serve as functions, depending upon the vantage point of the observer.

5. The organization form of a system tends toward hierarchy. Its various forms and processes are arranged in terms of levels (hence the notion of subsystem) with the higher levels comprehending the lower. This rank-order arrangement is further marked by the principle of specialization, or division of labor. As a system develops, not only does it increase in size, but its parts assume definite structures and functions. These *differentiated structures and specialized functions,* further, become subject to a central control. The system exhibits the property of *centralization*. The concept of *development* refers to this process of differentiation, and the more developed the system, the greater the degree of specialization. With increased specialization, certain structures take control over others and operate to *integrate* the various behaviors within the system.

In summary, then, an energy-transfer system possesses the properties of boundary exchange, mutual interdependence, self-regulation, adaptation to disturbance, and approaches to a steady state. Its direction of movement is from the simple to the complex. As it develops, its organizational form becomes hierarchical, structurally differentiated, functionally specific, and centrally controlled. The more developed the system, the more these features become descriptive of the system. And in its structure and function, it displays a purposeful construction that is adapted to the environment in which it normally exists.

From this general model, we extract two formulations: first, that the meaning of any part or process is the function it performs

---

[19] Descriptions of structure, therefore, are frequently presented in static terms, but such descriptions always presuppose a stoppage of time and are, in reality, a momentary glimpse of what is happening.

for the system as a whole; and second, the principle of differentiation and specialization. Both are to be understood only within the context of an energy-transfer model. Both are cardinal elements in functional analysis. We will discuss them in reverse order.

III

Structural-Functionalism: Theory of the Political System

Those who are familiar with the work of Parsons and Levy will immediately recognize that this general model lies at the base of their theorizing. In a technical sense, both have raised the grand hypothesis that societies (systems of social action) share the properties of an energy-exchange system. Their work, up to now, has largely consisted of clarifying the basic concepts and relationships involved, and the linkages that exist amongst them. And while they do not deal with those problems that we usually refer to as "operational," they are not Chinese metaphysicians,[20] nor do they mix their metaphors.[21] They are, as Max Black might say, genuine theorists in the work they do.[22]

In political science there are two similar attempts to formulate a generalized theory. By intent, their range of application is limited to politics or the political (sub) system. There is, of course, the architectonic world of Easton, but since this is grounded upon an information-transfer model, it is not necesary to consider it here. In regard to structural-functionalism proper, there is William Mitchell's work in American politics[23] and that of Fred Riggs in the comparative area. Both draw directly from Parsons, but Mitchell derives primarily from the four "functional imperatives" that Parsons has postulated as requisite to any social sys-

20 See Chapter 8 of this book.
21 See Chapter 3 of this book.
22 Black, op. cit., p. 274.
23 William C. Mitchell, *The American Polity* (New York: Free Press of Glencoe, 1962).

Functional Analysis in American Political Science

tem: (G) goal attainment, (A) adaptation, (I) integration, and (L) latency or pattern maintenance and tension management. Despite Mitchell's earlier optimism that Parsonian formulations seem "to offer the best possibilities for eventually developing a general theory of American politics and of political systems,"[24] he has chosen not to continue this rather important initial attempt and is now inclined toward economic models on the strength of their more formidable deductive powers.[25] This represents an abrupt shift—not simply because it is a move from a macro- to a microposition, as the cliché goes, but because it rests on the principle of "methodological individualism" and thereby denies the assumption of "emergent" levels so necessary for functional analysis. Requisite analysis, however, is sufficiently interesting to political science to allow the suggestion that Mitchell's first effort to order the American polity in functional terms will not stand in isolation.

Riggs, on the other hand, has applied functionalism to the analysis of politics and administration in developing countries for a solid decade. His contributions exhibit a consistent and sustained effort, and many have been unusually brilliant. Unfortunately, Riggs's analysis is marred by the use of an esoteric vocabulary that weakens efforts to standardize the use of working concepts and often results in the employment of the same concept under several aliases. Moreover, he has written rather prolifically[26]—his output is also Parsonian—and has yet to take the time to codify and systematize this vast product; his willingness to accept and try new ideas only compounds the problem. As a

---

24 Ibid., p. vii.
25 William C. Mitchell, "The Shape of Political Theory to Come," in S. M. Lipset (ed.), *Politics and the Social Sciences* (New York: Oxford University Press, 1969).
26 His works are too numerous to cite here. But see *Administration in Developing Countries* (Boston: Houghton-Mifflin Co., 1964); and *Thailand: The Modernization of a Bureaucratic Polity* (Honolulu: East-West Center Press, 1966). And see Chapter 6 of this book on Names and Concepts.

consequence, his general effort appears sprawling, untidy, and uneconomical, and has not generated the research it warrants.

It is with respect to the thorny problem of traditional, transitional, and modern or developed systems that Riggs demonstrates the utility of a structural-functional orientation. His fundamental point of departure is the principle of structural differentiation and functional specialization which he has coupled to the Parsonian pattern variables.[27] The disjunctions provide the polar points of a scale that permits the identification of crucial differences in such gross types as traditional, transitional and modern systems. We set aside the special language of the "theory of prismatic society," as Riggs calls it, to note that it stands as an important attempt to provide an orderly framework for both diachronic and synchronic analysis. This framework is what a theory aims at and what structural-functionalism was originally intended for. As such, it is truly comparative—not because it covers numerous countries but because it takes these countries as instances of types that may be plotted (described) along a fixed scale. From the structural-functional viewpoint, development constitutes the process of differentiation and specialization. The Parsonian pattern variables assume this and, further, mark a range of variation within which societies can be ordered. Riggs's formulations, in directing us specifically to a scale of differentiation, tend to move us "from the classificatory, qualitative level of concept formulation to the quantitative one."[28]

Riggs, however, does not remain alone. For the field of comparative politics has, for the last decade or so, evidenced a sur-

[27] For Parsons, "A pattern variable is a dichotomy, one side of which must be chosen by an actor before the meaning of a situation is determinate for him." The variables are: affectivity or affective neutrality, ascription or achievement, diffusion or specificity, particularism or universalism, collectivity or self-orientation. See Talcott A. Parsons and Edward A. Shils (eds.), *Toward a General Theory of Social Action* (New York: Harper Torchbook, 1962), Part 2, Chapter 1.

[28] Hempel's phrase. See Carl G. Hempel, "Typological Methods in the Social Sciences" in M. Natanson, *Philosophy of the Social Sciences* (New York: Random House, 1963).

prising degree of order—if we make due allowance for the state of political science in general. This is directly the result of the influence of structural-functionalism, and it has not been obscured despite the apparently invariant tendency of political scientists to be novel. Here again the informing theme is the principle of differentiation. As Lucien Pye puts it:

> This is particularly true in the analysis of institutions and structures. Thus, this aspect of development involves first of all the differentiation and specialization of structures. . . . With differentiation there is also, of course, increased functional specificity of the various political roles within the system. And, finally, differentiation also involves the integration of complex structures and processes. That is, differentiation is not fragmentation and the isolation of different parts of the political system but specialization based on an ultimate sense of integration.[29]

A few additional illustrations may suffice to show the importance of the postulate of differentiation to this domain of inquiry. La Palombara speaks of a "gamut" (scale) that runs from the most primitive functionally diffuse to the most modern, the latter defined by a "very high degree of specialization and differentiation of both structure and function."[30] Accordingly, the "degree of structural differentiation" becomes a measure of change. La Palombara offers this as only one measure of four, but in reality it is the primary scale. We can observe this by noting that his second dimension, "magnitude," is defined as the ratio of political activity to all other activity. Magnitude, then, can appear only upon the occasion of differentiation, i.e., only when political structures have been differentiated. And if the logic holds, it may be used as a measure of differentiation. The situation is similar

[29] Lucien W. Pye, "The Concept of Political Development," *The Annals of the American Academy of Political and Social Sciences,* Vol. 358 (1965), p. 12.

[30] Joseph La Palombara, "Bureaucracy and Political Development" in La Palombara (ed.), *Bureaucracy and Political Development* (Princeton: Princeton University Press, 1963), p. 34.

with respect to a second pair of dimensions that he employs—achievement orientation and degree of secularization.[31]

If we now turn to Gabriel Almond, the original chairman of the Social Science Research Committee on Comparative Politics (which has generally supported and pursued this line of analysis), the same formulation dominates.[32] Structural differentiation and functional specificity constitute the *fundamentum divisionis* in Almond's classification system, and the same scale is operative here as with Riggs. But where Riggs has drawn his polar points very sharply on the basis of the pattern variables, Almond often urges that their use leads to an "unfortunate theoretical polarization," that as "pure types" they are empty classes, that as "limits" they are exaggerated, and that the obvious appearance of *structural multifunctionality* in highly differentiated societies requires that political science work with "mixed types."

These criticisms make it appear that Almond is advocating something different in the way of an organizing or classifying principle, but, as I have shown elsewhere,[33] the mixed type is a point on the same scale. Insofar as the notion of structural multifunctionality is concerned, the systemic character of structural-functionalism predicts this phenomenon. This is missed only when the distinction between, say, specialized and nonspecialized structures is reified, for the regulatory processes of an energy-transfer system, especially in a developed stage, are manifold, complex, and *redundant*.[34] Structural multifunctionality is pre-

[31] Ibid. See pp. 39–48. I have also dealt with such predications in "Decision Theory and Development Administration" in E. W. Weidner (ed.), *Development Administration* (Durham, N.C.: Duke University Press, 1970).

[32] Gabriel Almond, "A Functional Approach to Comparative Politics" in Gabriel A. Almond and James S. Coleman, *The Politics of Developing Areas* (Princeton: Princeton University Press, 1960). See also Gabriel A. Almond and G. Bingham Powell, *Comparative Politics* (Boston: Little Brown & Co., 1966).

[33] See "Decision Theory and Development Administration," op. cit.

[34] See Martin Landau, "Redundancy, Rationality, and the Problem of Duplication and Overlap," *Public Administration Review*, Vol. 29 (1969).

cisely the redundancy that permits self-regulation and adaptation. Often we refer to this in terms of "latent function." But this usage, of course, does not exhaust the concept of multifunctionality.

What may now be suggested is that structural-functionalism has constituted the most acceptable framework for the study of politics and administration in developed, developing and underdeveloped countries—as we ordinarily use these terms. More specifically, it is the *organizational properties of an energy-transfer system* that have been taken as the primary basis for classifying and ordering such countries. This application, expressed as structural-functional relationships, has generated a considerable amount of theorizing and has moved us toward the construction of ordered metrics. Whatever the difficulties involved, whether of a conceptual or operational character, functional analysis in this domain has brought us closer to "ordering concepts of the purely comparative kind."

IV

Functionalism: The Middle Range and Discontinuity

We turn to our second formulation: that the meaning of any part or process is the function it performs for the system as a whole or for any part of its parts.

The basis for this rule is the systemic property of "functional interdependence." What this means is that no part or process of the system possesses properties independent of any other part. They are, so to speak, defined in terms of each other, and their defining properties are systemic in character. The moment a unit or process is disengaged from the system, it loses its systemic properties and becomes something else. If, therefore, one wishes to analyze such a part, it must be done as it operates within the system. And since all parts and processes have objective consequences for each other and for the system, the consequences they do have are the functions they perform. Given the additional properties of an energy-transfer system, functions may be interpreted

Political Theory and Political Science

in terms of the contribution they make to the maintenance of a specified state or condition. This, it should be obvious, is the essential feature of functional analysis.

The question that invariably arises has to do with the deployment of this rule. Applied to societies, i.e., taking a whole society as the object of inquiry, the difficulties involved are as numerous as they are notorious. In fact, such major theorists as Parsons and Levy are prone to issue cautions even as they continue their work, fully cognizant that their proposals remain in a "highly tentative untested stage of development." So far as philosophers of science are concerned, they urge that structural-functionalism is best conceived as a program for research rather than as a body of theory. In Hempel's phrasing, functionalism "might more profitably be construed as expressing a directive for research, namely to search for specific self-regulatory aspects of . . . systems and to examine the ways in which various traits of a system might contribute to its particular mode of self-regulation."[35]

This, generally, is the rule that Merton adheres to. It is the strategy that is laid out in his justly famous paper on "Manifest and Latent Functions,"[36] which preceded Hempel by a decade. Expressing the central orientation of functionalism as "the practice of interpreting data by establishing their consequences for [the] larger structures in which they are implicated,"[37] Merton limits his analysis to specific social structures, emphasizing "latent functional analysis" as a means of clarifying "seemingly irrational social patterns." He presents three case studies, one of which—the analysis of the boss and the political machine—remains a classic for political scientists.[38] As we have already noted, Flanigan and Fogelman have pointed to its inspirational effect, and Meehan insists that it should be "required reading" for just about

---

35 Op. cit., p. 301. See also Nagel, op. cit., pp. 520–535.
36 Merton, op. cit.
37 Ibid., p. 47.
38 The other two are the Hawthorne Studies and the pattern of conspicuous consumption.

Functional Analysis in American Political Science

every political scientist because no better functional treatment of the boss can be found anywhere.[39]

There is, however, a special irony here, and to note it is in no way to disparage Merton's work. It arises from the fact that Flanigan and Fogelman assert (contrary to Merton and Levy, incidentally) that functionalism is brand-new to political science: "At no time has [it] been a prevalent mode of analysis in political science."[40] But in the course of his exposition, Merton, always sensitive to the need for theoretical continuity, refers to one instance of a gross discontinuity in the development of sociology. He quotes Shils with approbation: "A problem is stressed by one who is an acknowledged founder of the discipline, the problem is left unstudied, then, some years later, it is taken up with enthusiasm as if no one had ever thought of it before."[41] In the next chapter we will demonstrate a similar discontinuity in the case of political science. Strangely enough, our primary vehicle will be the political machine.

---

[39] Op. cit., p. 188.
[40] Op. cit., p. 111.
[41] Merton, op. cit., p. 67. Reference here is to the study of the primary group.

CHAPTER 5

The Myth of Hyperfactualism in the Study of American Politics

To introduce his work on functionalism, Robert Merton[1] employs that intriguing phrase of Whitehead's: "A science which hesitates to forget its founders is lost." If Whitehead meant to caution against allowing past generations to "impose their stencils upon an unknown future,"[2] who, in a scientific domain, can possibly quarrel with this injunction? But Whitehead also remarked (as Merton noted) that everything of importance has been said before by someone who did not discover it. Whether so or not, it is germane to my purpose to change some wording and suggest that everything of importance has been said before by someone who did not *name* it. In substituting the act of naming for that of discovery, I mean to emphasize the crucial importance of close inquiry into the logic and procedure of analysis. For a science which forgets its founders too soon may lose in considerable measure. What it loses it must again find, often at great waste of time and energy.

The title of this chapter was selected with this in mind. It has to do also with the altogether too hasty use of such terms as hyperfactualism and traditionalism. These have become synonyms in contemporary political science and they are used to refer to a

[1] Robert Merton, *Social Theory and Social Structure* (Glencoe: Free Press, 1957), p. 3.
[2] This is Walter Lippmann's phrase. *Public Opinion* (New York: Macmillan, 1960), p. 137.

Reprinted, with modifications, by permission from Martin Landau, "The Myth of Hyperfactualism in the Study of American Politics," from the *Political Science Quarterly*, 83 (September 1968), 378–99.

Hyperfactualism in the Study of American Politics

mode of inquiry which employs real types, whose research is informed by meliorism, and whose rules of procedure lead only to fact-gathering and social prescription. They designate, in short, a normative orientation frequently described as a premature policy science that suffers from a "theoretical malnutrition and surfeit of facts." Moreover, this tradition is traced back to the founders of the modern discipline.[3] They were the ones who set us on this track.

A theory, however, is more than its trappings; and a concept is more than its name. That is, I am concerned that the easy use of hyperfactualism obscures a powerful continuity in political science and misrepresents the line of analysis pursued by the founders. An understanding of their mode of inquiry makes it eminently clear—quite to the contrary of Flanigan and Fogelman[4]—that functional analysis is a continuation of their approach. Functionalism, reintroduced by way of sociology in recent years and absorbed by the notion of system, has forced its devotees to relearn formulations known to our fathers who, most unfortunately, forgot to name them.

I

When Lord Bryce, Henry Jones Ford, and Frank Goodnow are joined with Woodrow Wilson, we have the nucleus of that original group of early "realists" who set the future of the discipline on the rule of observation.

The magnitude of this development may be measured by the fact that "no American institution [of higher learning] honored the function [of empirical research] until Johns Hopkins opened in 1876."[5] Where before the discipline had been marked by a

---

[3] David Easton, *The Political System* (New York: Alfred A. Knopf, 1953), Chapter 3.

[4] See Chapter 4 of this book.

[5] W. H. Cowley, "Critical Decisions in American Higher Education," in *Current Issues in Higher Education* (National Education Association,

Political Theory and Political Science

high warfare of principle, legendary debates over sovereignty, the veneration of legal discourse, and the construction of grand systems, now it was the problematic character of the institutions of government that was to claim its attention. We are the first to doubt, the young Wilson wrote, the first to think of new models, the first to propose new forms.[6] No longer was it to be assumed "that the founding fathers had handed from Sinai all we needed to know about government."[7]

Viewed from contemporary perspectives, it may seem plausible to suggest that the architects of the new realism were not as pioneering as their words indicate. Indeed, so far as Easton's analysis is concerned, the early realists "stood with one foot securely lodged in traditional legal description."[8] The full formulation of Easton's appraisal is this: when looked at from their own time perspective, the realists took a tremendous stride beyond legal phenomena; when examined in the perspective of the whole progress of empirical political science, they took only a short, "although vital," step. Short, in the sense that the efforts of the realists were still largely confined to the formal structure of government or such near-governmental structures as party; vital, in that they rejected legal description as a true picture of government and sought to discover the actual locus of power in government and the ways in which it was distributed. This, as Easton notes, led to the consideration of a new class of phenomena and thereby extended the definition of the "political situation" so as to comprehend, beyond law, the actual patterns of political relations in government. Yet, he holds, the "genus of data" was the same in that it was confined to the formal features of govern-

---

1963), Chapter 1. See also Anna Haddow, *Political Science in American Colleges and Universities* (New York: Appleton-Century, 1939).

6 Woodrow Wilson, *Congressional Government* (New York: World Publishing Co., 1956), p. 27. The first edition was published in 1885.

7 This is Henry Seidel Canby's phrase, quoted in Haddow, op. cit., p. 178.

8 Ibid., p. 167; see also pp. 161–170.

Hyperfactualism in the Study of American Politics

ment. Accordingly, he considers them to be "captives of the juristic framework of thought" to the extent that they failed to pass beyond the legal structure to the broader political matrix which conditioned it. There is, however, a point to be missed by such appraisals and it has precisely to do with "the framework of thought."

The crux of the change that occurred is not to be seen in the concept of "scope of coverage" despite the fact that this concern has so often been a feature of disciplinary criticism. In political science, the negative connotation and persuasive use[9] of the term "narrow" is suggestive of the notion that the larger the number of variables or classes of phenomena to be considered, the richer is the discipline—an assumption which may be quite at variance with the production of knowledge. Scope, moreover, is initially hypothesized by whatever definitions of politics are employed.[10] In Easton's case, his appraisals are grounded on a definition of politics that is so extensive as to comprehend all social activity influencing the "authoritative allocation of values." Given so comprehensive a field of interest, the early realists must perforce appear narrow. But what this means is that the class of phenomena they chose as relevant to their purpose constitutes a subset of Easton's general reference class.[11] That is, they chose to delimit

---

[9] See C. L. Stevenson, "Persuasive Definitions," *Mind*, Vol. 47 (1938). See also Chapter 6 of this book.

[10] All definitions of politics that are not ostensive are the products of "abstractive differentiation." They are concepts. In theoretical sciences, the scope of a concept is a hypothetical matter. That is, its range of coverage is determined by empirical research. "Scope," thus, cannot be legislated nor is it. It is always demonstrated. And it sometimes happens that a particular formulation originally thought of as "narrow" is shown to possess a range of application that is truly extraordinary. See Chapter 2 of this book for a discussion of category and assignment.

[11] Against the standard of general systems theory or the general theory of social action, Easton's formulations also appear "narrow." The important factor in appraisals of this sort, however, is not "bandwidth," but what—with respect to a given problem—offers the more powerful explanation.

Political Theory and Political Science

a more restricted segment of experience as their object of inquiry. They chose to fix upon that class of behavior that manifested itself as concrete governmental activity. This was their field of focus and their treatment of it bore as much resemblance to the juristic tradition as Wilson did to Theodore Dwight Woolsey. For in the course of development of the discipline, their decisions must be understood as reflecting the profound epistemological shift that had occurred.

II

We must at this point recall that a dominant metaphor entails important methodological consequences. The transfer of meaning from one context to another serves to introduce new modes of thought, new systems of analysis, which undoubtedly affect and oftentimes subvert the procedural rules that have guided a given generation. A change in image is a change in method.[12]

At the time that Wilson began to write, the implications of the theory of evolution were of such proportions that no field of intellectual endeavor remained beyond its influence. Like mechanics earlier, it was so widely extrapolated as to alter the "common understanding" of the day. The rich afterglow of the Enlightenment had faded and its images lay shattered. Where once the universe had constituted a closed system, now it was to be seen as an open and endless process of change. The human mind, "more time-conscious than it had ever been under the reign of Euclidean and Newtonian science,"[13] no longer carried its formulas as impeccable doctrine. The Zeitgeist had been transformed and all that was became problematical. Even physics was not immune, as when Charles Sanders Peirce asked, "who will deliberately say that our knowledge of these laws [gravitation, elasticity, electricity, and chemistry] is sufficient to make us

---

12 See Chapter 3 of this book.
13 Philip Wiener, *Evolution and the Founders of Pragmatism* (Cambridge, Mass.: Harvard University Press, 1949), p. 10.

reasonably confident that they are absolutely eternal and immutable, and that they escape the great law of evolution?"[14] Nothing in science, in art, and in philosophy, it seemed, escaped this great metaphor—whether in England, on the continent, or in the United States. For American political science, its most important effect is to be seen in the development of pragmatism.[15]

In the 1870's, a rather unique group of Harvard scholars came together to consider the epistemological implications of evolutionary theory. It was there, in the Metaphysical Club—as Peirce called it—that the name and doctrine of pragmatism were established. Provoked by the "unevolutionary character" of both British empiricism and German idealism, all effort was directed toward a reconsideration of reason and experience.[16] Kant had used the term *pragmatisch* to stand for contingent beliefs which formed the basis for choice in a means-end situation, and Peirce, for whom all reasoning was hypothetical, stripped it of its transcendental cover and assigned the term as the name of the new philosophy. The philosophy itself constituted a new "rule of method" to make ideas clear and to test claims to truth. To reach this goal, emphasis was shifted from antecedents to consequences, from the origin of ideas to their verification. First causes were set aside as the *how* of life was stressed rather than the *why*. Along with a primary concern for the process of development, there came a rejection of the characteristic monism of the grand philosophies. No single formula was deemed capable of comprehending the rich complexity of life, and the acceptance of this position led to a pluralism that not only sustained specialization

---

[14] Quoted in Wiener, op. cit., p. 94.

[15] I make no effort to consider Social or Spencerian Darwinism, which were brands of "moral Darwinism" that transformed evolution into dogma. Though these obviously influenced Woolsey and Burgess, they are of negligible importance to our discussion here. See R. Hofstadter, *Social Darwinism in American Thought* (rev. ed., Boston: Beacon Press, 1955).

[16] See Wiener, op. cit., Chapter 2, for a full discussion of the problem before the club.

but permitted methodology to be adapted to the problem at hand. The pragmatic attitude was experimental in nature; all ideas, all theories, all hypotheses were to be subjected to empirical test: only those proposals that could be verified and only those maxims that could be shown to influence behavior were to be deemed significant.

These were the pegs upon which pragmatism hung, and out of the welter of its thought came the emphasis on practical results and possibilities for action. When James popularized the philosophy, it had already come to mean "looking away from first things, principles, 'categories,' supposed necessities; and of looking toward last things, fruits, consequences, facts." This is the essence of James' *practicalism*—the form by which pragmatism first took root in American social science. The pragmatic worker, James wrote, "turns away from abstraction . . . from bad a priori reasons, from fixed principles, closed systems and pretended absolutes. . . . He turns toward concreteness and adequacy, towards facts, towards action, towards power."[17]

This is the tough-minded attitude that overthrew the hegemony of the moral philosopher. Ranging over the entire gamut of social life in the broadest and most comprehensive strokes, his criteria of relevance seemed unlimited and his reference class unbounded. Nor was it that the principle of specialization eluded him or that the concept of a "field" escaped him. It was, rather, that his epistemology did not require the close and intensive empirical description that sustains a specialized field of observation. For the moral philosopher, knowledge was deemed a function of reason; the empirical fact was minimized and evidence meant logical truth.

For the new social science, in almost direct contrast, knowledge became a function of experience, the fact became crucial and warrant was to be based upon the rule of observation. To follow the

[17] William James, *Pragmatism* (New York: Longmans, Green & Co., 1907), p. 51.

Hyperfactualism in the Study of American Politics

pragmatic mode meant to look at social life as it really was, to attend to social institutions as they *really worked,* to find the *how* of things—not the why. And to find out, pragmatism rejected the ways of the moral philosopher, carved his whole world into special parts, and began to institutionalize the process of "selective" or "disciplined" observation. By the turn of the century, the specialized pursuit of knowledge, that is, the establishment of specific fields, had become a characteristic feature of social science. For each domain, a distinctive profession had emerged to assume the control and direction of inquiry. By 1886 economists moved to strengthen their claims by forming the American Economic Association; in 1892 the American Psychological Association followed suit; and in 1903 the American Sociological Society and the American Political Science Association were established.

It does not do, therefore, to say that the new political science merely passed over legal forms to the study of actual government. For this passage followed an epistemological route that was of revolutionary consequence. No longer to be contained by the a priori framework of their predecessors, this generation effected the "revolt against formalism." It took the "givens" of its teachers and transformed them into problematic features of life. It shifted from a mechanical model to an evolutionary model, from the logic of geometry to that of induction—and thereby built an empirical discipline. This is the difference which obtained between the *juristic* and *realistic* frameworks of thought.

III

Were it now to be said that "in the beginning was Woodrow Wilson," it would not be too much of an exaggeration. The point here is not that Wilson was *sui generis,* that he arrived as a complete novelty; on the contrary, who can minimize the circumstances of the time and such powerful influences as that, say, of Walter Bagehot. It is, rather, that Wilson's pioneering efforts present so striking a fusion of image and method as to be taken as the first clear instance of the new pragmatic politics.

The prologue to his work is more than a demand for the reform of government; if it directs itself to the excesses of *Congressional Government,* it also turns our attention to the fact that the American system "has *never* received complete and competent treatment at the hands of *any,* even the most acute, of our constitutional writers." Directing his thrust at the moral Newtonianism[18] that had controlled for so long, Wilson rejected a scholarship born of paper pictures, of long-accepted but erroneous formulas, a scholarship that had transformed the Constitution into an object of worship as it had shielded it from examination and criticism. Any observer, he quotes Bagehot, who looks at the living reality will wonder at the contrast to the paper descriptions. He will see in life much that is not in books and he will not find the many refinements of literary theory in the rough practice of government.

In a remarkable passage, Wilson warns us of the power of language and the confusions it may engender when one does not distinguish between a sign and its referent, a model and reality, a name and a thing. Names, he cautioned,

> are much more persistent than the functions upon which they were originally bestowed; . . . institutions constantly undergo essential alterations of character, whilst retaining the names conferred upon them in their first estate; and the history of our own Constitution is but another illustration of this universal principle of institutional change.

There has been a constant process of growth, a vast alteration of the conditions of government, and so radical a change in the function of government as to be "no longer conformable with its original pattern." Yet all of this has happened "without perceptibly affecting the vocabulary of our constitutional language." It is this language that forms the "literary theory" that has obscured

---

18 See Chapter 3 of this book.

Hyperfactualism in the Study of American Politics

the realities of government. If we are to understand government, if we are to exercise control over its movements, we shall have to lay aside the niceties of the theory of balance in the search for the facts of its operations. These "do not obtrude [themselves] upon the observation of the world." They run through the undercurrents of government and take shape "only in the inner channels of legislation and administration which are not open to the common view." It is, therefore, "the difficult task of one who would now write at once practically and critically of our national government to *escape from theory and attach himself to facts . . .* striving to catch the delicate *organism* in all of its characteristic parts exactly as it is today." This is an undertaking all the more arduous and doubtful of issue *"because it has to be entered upon without guidance from writers of acknowledged authority."*[19] Such was Wilson's evaluation of the political science that had come before.

This, with all its implications, presents the shift in metaphor that was to direct the course of inquiry for succeeding generations to follow. Where once the language of mechanics had reigned, now it was to be the language of biology. A political system, Lowell writes, is not a mere machine that can be adjusted to the fancy of its designer. "It is an organism, and in order to appreciate its possible forms and the causes of its development, stability, or decay, it is necessary to investigate the laws of its organic life."[20] Investigation, however, was to proceed in accordance with James's rule; the "thin abstraction" would yield to the "thick particular fact." For Bryce, the "temptations of the deductive method" were to be resisted. And for Goodnow, only a policy of "opportunism" was likely to achieve desirable results; adherence to fixed general theories was productive of harm, not good, and

---

19 Wilson, *Congressional Government*, op. cit., especially pp. 28–32, from which these quotations are drawn. Emphasis added.

20 A. Lawrence Lowell, *Essays on Government* (New York: Houghton Mifflin, 1890), pp. 2–3.

the postulation of universal principles was "mere useless opprobrious theory."[21]

This was the "fresh and original approach" that was to provide the escape from a political science which "thinks, argues and dogmatizes only about a constitution, about the nature of the state, the essence of sovereignty,"[22] but which fails to realize that "the growth of a nation ... would snap asunder a constitution which could not adapt to new conditions."[23] Government, Wilson was later to declare, falls under the theory of organic life: "It is modified by its environment, necessitated by its tasks, shaped to its function by the sheer pressure of life."[24]

This is the formulation that mandated realism. "A knowledge of the actual workings of a political system," Lowell wrote, "is an essential." And there issued forth a spate of volumes on "Actual Government as Applied under American Conditions" (which was the title of A. B. Hart's text in 1903). "How it grew, what it does, and how it does it" (which was the subtitle of another volume) became the primary concern of the discipline. But this, Lowell cautioned, "is the first step in the study of government; ... only the first step." It would do no violence to present concepts to call this first step "functional analysis."

IV

We now return to hyperfactualism as Easton originally defined it:[25] a method that elevates fact as it depreciates theory and is productive of random collections of factual researches, each of which seems to stand alone. It is an apparent plausibility to assign

[21] Frank J. Goodnow, *Social Reform and the Constitution* (New York: Macmillan, 1911), pp. 3–4.
[22] Woodrow Wilson, "The Study of Administration," *Political Science Quarterly*, Vol. 2 (1884), p. 482. I have changed tenses.
[23] *Congressional Government*, op. cit., p. 30.
[24] Woodrow Wilson, *Constitutional Government in the United States* (New York: Columbia University Press, 1908), p. 56.
[25] Ibid., pp. 67–78.

Hyperfactualism in the Study of American Politics

this property to the early realists and I have done so myself.[26] There is no doubt, of course, that to the early pragmatic workers observation was to come first; the fact stood paramount and the secondary—even dangerous—character of theory was stressed. And there is no doubt as to the lack of effort to codify researches explicitly and organize findings into systems. Had this occurred, however, our institutionally oriented forebears would not have been institutionalists, which is to state that the foundations of the modern discipline would have been theoretical to begin with—a situation that would have been an inversion of the development of every other science, physical or social.

Yet hyperfactualism in this instance is a somewhat misleading[27] and certainly an incomplete description of their approach. The fact is that there were codes, there was a logic of relationships, and there was a distinctive methodology—all of which was made operative by the entrance of the Darwinian metaphor into political science. Once the transfer took hold—and it dominated the discipline by 1900—inquiry was directed by the rules of biological analysis as they were then understood. Indeed, such was the power of the metaphor that its hypothetical character was virtually lost. So firmly were the rules of biology established that few if any questions obtained. It was a natural logic to follow, sustained as it was by the Zeitgeist, and before too long to follow it was to "speak prose."

The resultant analysis was far less formal than one would expect when research is a matter of conscious theoretical develop-

---

26 See Chapters 3 and 6 of this book.

27 It is really misleading in every instance. Strictly speaking, there is no such thing as a fact pure and simple, chaste and inviolate. The doctrine of immaculate perception (Nietzsche's phrase), which we may know better as the *tabula rasa,* has long been put to rest by researchers in language, perception, and cognition. Observation presupposes cognition and cognition supplies the stereotypes, images, maps, belief systems, categories, types, or whatever, which direct our observation. These may be taken as *learned dispositions* to see, and they range all the way from hallucinatory images to scientific models. See Chapter 2 of this book for a discussion of categorization and observation.

Political Theory and Political Science

ment. But the line of inquiry was nevertheless set by such concepts as structure, function, process, and adaptation. It presupposed an "open system" and therefore "boundary exchange." It assumed the principle of "self-regulation" and therefore "steady state." It did not use this vocabulary, but when it turned to its object of interest, it saw a governmental *system* (it did use *this* term, however) as a set of functionally interrelated processes. And here we must call attention to Lowell's statement of procedure; written in 1889, it has a familiar form:

A government is an organism whose various parts act and react upon one another; and it follows that a change in any one of them will cause changes more or less great in all the others until the system settles down with a new balance of forces. In order to understand the organic laws of a political system, it is necessary to examine it as a whole, and seek to discover not only the true functions of each part, but also its influence upon every other part, and its relation to the equilibrium of the complete organism.[28]

Intended as a preface, it turns out to be a summary of the methodology of the time.

Lowell's formulations clearly exhibit the "central orientation of functionalism." Recall that in Merton's statement functionalism is the practice of interpreting data by establishing their consequences for the larger structures in which they are implicated.[29] And this is the method that Wilson, Lowell, Goodnow, and company pursued. They even employed the concept "latent function" (which is another way of expressing "adaptation"), as when Wilson, having described the disintegrative (we would now say dysfunctional) effects of the committee system on the total governmental structure, interprets the caucus as an "antidote to the committees." Where the "multiplicity and mutual independence" of the committees tend to destroy the cohesion necessary for a stable government, where there is in Congress "no *visible*

28 Lowell, op. cit., p. 4.
29 Merton, op. cit., pp. 46–47. And see Chapter 4 of this book.

Hyperfactualism in the Study of American Politics

and . . . no *controllable* party organization," it is the caucus that supplies cohesion, "the only bond of cohesion." Or, at another point, this time by implication, in a fragmented party system the function of log-rolling is to secure a majority vote. Fifteen years later, always sensitive to the "constant subtle modifications . . . of form and function" in living systems, Wilson is quick to note the adaptation of the Speaker and the House Rules Committee so as to *function* as a "steering ministry," as the integrating agency of the House. And, he adds with complete consistency, as this function has evolved, the congressional caucus has fallen into the background.[30]

But it is the work of Henry Jones Ford that serves to suggest that if we had not forgotten our founders so soon, functional analysis in political science might well have advanced beyond its present ambiguous state.

V

In his now classic statement of the latent function of the political machine, Merton asks the following question: "In view of the manifold respects in which political machines, in varying degrees, run counter to the mores and at times to the law . . . how [do] they manage to continue in operation?" The theorem that warrants this question states that persistent social patterns and social structures (however negatively they are perceived) perform positive functions which, at the time of their operation, are not adequately fulfilled by other existing structures. Historically, the political machine has exhibited a remarkable vitality in the face of extraordinary attack, and Merton suggests that the continuity of the organization may be explained by the fact that it satisfies basic latent functions.[31]

---

30 Wilson, *Congressional Government,* op. cit., see Preface to fifteenth printing, Chapters 2, 3, 6. Emphasis in the original. They did not name "latent function," however.

31 Merton, op. cit., pp. 71–72.

Political Theory and Political Science

Basing himself on Sait,[32] Merton notes that the constitutional framework of American political organization precludes the legal possibility of highly centralized power and thus discourages effective and responsible leadership:

> The key structural function of the boss is to organize, centralize, and maintain in good working condition "the scattered fragments of power" which are at present dispersed through our political organization. By this centralized organization of political power, the boss and his apparatus can satisfy the needs of diverse subgroups in the larger community which are not adequately satisfied by legally devised and culturally approved social structures.[33]

Two variables are involved here, as Merton indicates—the "structural context" which makes it difficult, "if not impossible," for morally approved agencies to fulfill necessary functions, and the community "subgroups" whose needs are not met save through the latent function of the machine.

With respect to the first, the political machine may be taken as an administrative agency par excellence and the boss as its general manager or chief administrator; with respect to the second, it appears as a broker, a connection or coupling device which eases community strain and tensions in any number of ways (from humanizing the provision of public services to easing social mobility), thereby contributing to its integration.

Sait's analysis, some twenty years earlier, comprehends all of this. The theorem remains informal and the variables are not named, but the analysis is of the same form. One quotation makes this clear:

> The rise of the machine must be connected also with a feature of American government which discourages the growth of effective and responsible leadership. The framers of the Constitution, ... distrusted

---

[32] Edward M. Sait, "Machine, Political," *Encyclopedia of the Social Sciences,* Vol. 9 (1930), pp. 657–661.

[33] Merton, op. cit., p. 72.

Hyperfactualism in the Study of American Politics

power as dangerous to liberty; and therefore they spread it thin and erected barriers against its concentration. In our state governments, where the principal executive officers were elected and thus made independent of one another, this fatal weakness was still more pronounced; and these officers had been deprived by minute and specific statutory directions of all latitude in the discharge of their official duties. A similar dispersion of power marked local areas. As a consequence, when people or particular groups among them demanded positive action, no one had adequate authority to act. The machine provided an antidote. There was built up, in the words of Herbert Croly, "a much more human system of partisan government, whose chief object soon became the circumvention of government by Law. . . . The lawlessness of the extra-official democracy was merely the counterpoise of the legalism of the official democracy. The lawyer having been permitted to subordinate democracy to the Law, the Boss had to be called in to extricate the victim, which he did after a fashion and for a 'consideration.'" (*Progressive Democracy* [New York: 1914] 254).

The boss is the kind of leader that the machine develops. He typifies its efficiency as an instrument of power, which in contrast to the arrangements in American states and municipalities objectifies the principle of concentration. His operations are facilitated, it is true, by certain more or less accidental conditions of American democracy: the existence of the spoils system, the overelaboration of electoral processes, the indifference of "good citizens," the pliability of the ignorant masses; and his opportunities for aggrandizement have been vastly enlarged during the past half century by his traffic with big business—he has become the broker, the indispensable intermediary in the purchase and sale of political privileges. But these various factors hardly make clear his essential function. The boss is the man who, like the prime minister abroad, brings together the scattered fragments of power. Leadership is necessary; and since it does not develop readily within the constitutional framework, the boss provides it in a crude and irresponsible form from the outside.[34]

The last sentence of this passage is characterized by Merton as "rigorously functional," and it is of interest that Sait is even

[34] Sait, op. cit., p. 658.

more precise in distinguishing state and local structural contexts from the national. Despite the principle of separation, the national system provided for a central executive and over time it was the Presidency that evolved to meet the "need of a unifying agency," often with "a big stick and a contempt for legal restraints." Thus, "there has never been a national boss." Bosses and machines, then, derived from the functional deficiencies produced by the scattered powers of state and local governments. As Merton generalized this, "the functional deficiencies of the official structure generate an alternative (unofficial) structure to fulfill existing needs somewhat more effectively." And all of this stems from the axiom that "structure affects function and function affects structure."[35]

If the calendar is now moved back to 1900, we shall find Professor Ford instructing that "structure and function are correlative." The use of this language is not a mere coincidence, nor does similarity end with phraseology. Expressed in a review of Goodnow's celebrated *Politics and Administration*,[36] this principle was the axiomatic foundation of all of Ford's work. One needs only to examine that remarkable book on *The Rise and Growth of American Politics* to realize the grip of the Darwinian metaphor and its consequences for analysis.[37] Here everything is taken as in flux; everything changes, adapts, has meaning for the system—that is, performs functions, even latent functions. An institution, or practice, or procedure is to be interpreted "by establishing its consequence for the larger system" and it is—whether it be the electoral college or the press or the political

---

35 Merton, op. cit., p. 82.
36 Henry Jones Ford, "Politics and Administration," *Annals of the American Academy of Political and Social Science*, Vol. 16 (1900), p. 185.
37 (New York: Macmillan, 1898). Resort to Darwinian formulas was quite conscious in Ford's case. It can be said, thus, that for him evolutionary theory was more a model than a metaphor. Following this line, Ford concluded that it was a necessary corollary of Darwinian theory that the state (whether taken to cover every polity or only a particular type) has a "natural history"—that it is "a phase of development." For Ford's analysis of this proposition, see *The Natural History of the State* (Princeton: Princeton University Press, 1915).

party. And its function changes over time and circumstance. During the Adams administration, the function of party was to prevent the second American revolution; its formation was "the great unconscious [we may say 'latent'] achievement of Thomas Jefferson [serving] to open constitutional channels of political agitation, to start the processes by which the development of our Constitution is carried on." Had this not occurred "the government would have blown up."[38] Once secured, however, so inflexible was the organization of the American governmental system that "political change had to take the form of functional development." Divergent processes evolve, a multiplicity of forms develop, characteristics vary widely and all these various species have American politics as their habitat.[39] But they do not come apart because "party organization acts as [serves the function of] a connective tissue, enfolding the separate organs of government, and tending to establish a unity of control...."[40] Adaptation is still incomplete, still imperfect, which is to say that "American politics are in a transition state."[41] Government will continue to develop but it cannot "be tinkered into some sort of mechanical excellence." Those who see only mischief in politics and seek to eliminate *the mischief of politics* would only do greater mischief, for the elimination of party organization would remove that which maintains union, establishes stability, and prevents the anarchy which is so disastrous to all social interests.[42] Here the second variable enters the discussion and it may suffice to call attention to the shattering pressures imposed upon the "national community" in the 1840's and 1850's. "But still party organization continued to bear the strain, and it was the last bond of union to give way." Once it broke, there went that crucial "nationalizing" force and war became inevitable. After the war it was "the powerful agency

38 Ibid., pp. 125–126.
39 Ford, "Politics," op. cit., p. 182.
40 *Rise and Growth*, op. cit., p. 215.
41 Ibid.
42 Ibid., pp. 354–357.

of party" which reincorporated the South into the life of the nation.[43]

So, too, did the boss and machine (party organization) act in city politics. It is, after all, the machine that is our reference point and we shall have to allow Ford to speak to this problem. But first we may note, as Ford did, Lord Bryce's puzzlement over a system which multiplies elective executives and diffuses authority and responsibility amongst a myriad of offices. Will not such a scheme, Bryce asked, "want every condition needed for harmonies and efficient action? ... Such a system seems the negation of a system, and more akin to chaos." To Ford, however, the mystery existed only because of the failure to comprehend the processes of evolution and adaptation. The mystery vanishes when one comes to understand that the "scattered powers of government are resumed by party organization." It is, to use Merton's phrase, "the functional deficiencies of the official structure" which generated the boss and which maintained his function.

In language which is again familiar to us, but which came so long ago, Ford wrote:

The city boss is the nexus of municipal administration,—a center of control outside of the partitions of authority which public prejudice and traditional opinion insist upon in the formal constitution of city government. ... The state boss is the natural complement of the situation produced by the dissolution of executive authority in state government. The office restores outside of the formal constitution what is lost inside of it—*effective control*. In the national government no such dissolution having taken place, the case is different. There is no national boss but the President. ... *Thus by a perfectly natural process of evolution, the structure and functions of party organizations have been elaborated*, so as to comprehend the political activity of American citizenship from the minutest subdivision of local government up to the formation of a national administration.[44]

43 Ibid., p. 303. See all of Chapters 23, 24, 25.
44 Ibid., pp. 300–302. Emphasis added.

Hyperfactualism in the Study of American Politics

When Ford turns to Goodnow's work, there is much to please him. Where Goodnow finds that but for the office of party in connecting divisive political structures "we should have anarchy instead of government"; where he holds that party supplies the "administrative connection among the scattered powers of government"; that party is changing our governmental system; that one characteristic of this change is "the integration of administrative authority within party itself"; that the boss is a stage in the process of integration; and that his role is attributable to the marked divergence between the national and local governments as regards the progressive centralization of administrative authority[45]—Ford is quick to appreciate his work.

And why not? As Sait followed Goodnow, Goodnow followed Ford. But there was something wrong in Goodnow's case: if Sait met Merton's standards of "rigorous functionalism," Goodnow did not meet Ford's. For Ford, the logic of his line of analysis had to extend as well to social organization.

It is a necessary implication of functional analysis that proposals for social reform take due account of the manifest and latent functions performed by the social institutions at issue. To seek change without such knowledge is "to indulge in social ritual rather than social engineering."[46] Clear understanding of this principle is what impelled Ford to reject Goodnow's scheme for democratizing party (including such classic reform devices as the primary) as exactly that kind of proposal which fails to see that "wholesale disintegration" of party control would bring disorder (dysfunction), not government. To Ford, Goodnow's program is a "strange nonsequitur" which in no way follows the logic of his analysis. The proper method of reform is not direct popular supervision of government, nor is it the diffusion of party control. The true method is that of "administrative centralization,"

---

[45] Frank Goodnow, *Politics and Administration* (New York: Macmillan, 1900), Chapters 8, 9, 10.
[46] Merton, op. cit., p. 81.

of strong executives, of the short ballot, of transferring the functions of the boss to the mayor.[47]

Here we can observe Ford's recognition of another functionalist theorem: "any attempt to eliminate an existing social structure without providing adequate alternative structures for fulfilling the functions previously fulfilled by the abolished organization is doomed to failure."[48] So, upon the introduction of his own program, he is careful to state that reform should take due account of the institutions that exist and the functions they perform and therefore must be as simple as possible and innovate as little as possible. It should utilize existing political material and avoid the wholesale displacement of existing political interests. If proposals are functionally sound, their ordinary operation will, over time, "gradually purge conditions and supplant irresponsible boss rule by responsible leadership."[49] The documentation of the inverse relationship between boss rule and strong executives may be left to a Ph.D. dissertation.

VI

This was not conservatism, this was "actual workings" analysis. This was the realism of the pragmatist (now so necessary in developmental administration). Never formal, eschewing theory, concerned with fact, it nevertheless possessed a logic of its own —the practice of functional analysis. In our time, we have tended to dismiss the pragmatic realism of these early scholars as a historic episode, as a moment in our development which did not count for too much. Theirs, after all, was a "traditional" political science, narrowly confined as it were, failing to make contact with psychology, economics, and sociology. What we have for-

---

47 Ford, "Politics," op. cit., pp. 184–188.
48 Merton, op. cit., p. 81.
49 Henry Jones Ford, "Principles of Municipal Organization," *Annals of the American Academy of Political and Social Science*, Vol. 23 (1904), p. 216.

gotten, however, is the simple fact that the model they employed informed much of the work of the next half century. When the political scientist asked: what is the role of the Supreme Court; what is the role of the regulatory agency; of delegation of legislative authority; of conventions, committees, patronage, and the like?—in the context of this tradition he was seeking to find the functional consequence of each for the whole governmental system. When T. V. Smith cautioned Leonard White not to displace patronage by the merit system too abruptly,[50] was he not referring to its "latent function"? When Dean Landis referred to the independent regulatory agency as our generation's response to the inadequacy of the separation of powers, was he not aware of functional adaptation?[51] Presently, one may note, the search for a viable role for Congress founders on the inability to establish, as Lowell would say, "its true function."

Perhaps if we had been aware of this model we would have moved earlier to effect a more formal justification of its hypotheses. In the process of making these more explicit, we would have had to reduce ambiguity, probe the range of application, and thereby provide for that precious element of science—"continuity of theoretically directed research." I wonder if this is not what Lowell called for in that sixth presidential address to "political science" when he lamented the lack of a "barbarous vocabulary" —namely, an exact vocabulary, incomprehensible to laymen, remote from ordinary usage, and therefore devoid of the very richness of the vernacular which makes only for an absence of precision. But there is no doubt that then, in 1910, he asked for a second step—the careful study of "the Physiology of Politics," by which he meant "not the functions which the organs are intended, or supposed, to perform, but those which they actually do perform." If I take this as the distinction between manifest and

---

[50] Leonard White and T. V. Smith, *Politics and the Public Service* (New York: Harper, 1939), Chapters 3, 5, 8.

[51] James M. Landis, *The Administrative Process* (New Haven: Yale University Press, 1938).

Political Theory and Political Science

latent function, I do not think I propound an error. For it was Lowell's basic hypothesis, shared by so many pragmatists, that "the functions of an organ at work may in reality be quite different from what they appear."[52]

Thus, at the genesis of empirical political science we find what Flanigan and Fogelman now call empirical functional analysis writ large in its studies. The basic model was that of an energy-transfer system expressed directly in terms of a biologic system. By the nature of this logic, a general skepticism was directed at the appearance of institutions: their manifest or stated functions were held in brackets as investigators sought their "real" functions, i.e., the contributions they made to a system then in transition. Fully immersed in the doctrine of evolution, they turned their eyes to "seeming irrationalities" or to anomalous situations and inquired into their regulative (adaptive) contribution to American politics. And they—Wilson, Lowell, and Ford—made this a rule of procedure.

Conclusion

When we return to the contemporary scene, there are very few instances of this type of analysis. Beyond Merton, one is hard-pressed to find illustrations of an explicit search for specific self-regulating aspects of the American political system. There is, to be sure, a marked usage of the labels "manifest and latent," or "system," or "integration," but attaching a label to a study does not necessarily mean that the line of analysis it denotes is being pursued. Before me now is a volume of readings that is directed to the structural-functional concept of a political party. In the first chapter there is an elaborate statement, in rather general terms, of the concept itself. It moves from the abstract formulations of Parsons through Merton to eclectic functionalism. And its final caution notes that because of the different perspectives of

---

[52] *American Political Science Review*, Vol. 4 (1910), p. 2.

the authors, "function" is used variously.[53] In fact, the correct description of the collection is that it is *eclectic*. For the readings vary so widely that only this term can make sense of them.

Much of this difficulty arises because of the widespread misunderstanding that functional analysis mandates the question, "What functions are performed by a given institution, and how?" As we have indicated earlier, no analysis can proceed without this question, and everyone must ask it. Nor does it help to say "Look for unintended and/or unrecognized consequences," for we are often in the position where we would not even know them if we did see them precisely *because* we have no clear basis for identifying them. Moreover, if they are fulfilling basic latent (necessary) functions, the moment we identify them they begin to cease to be latent and become quite manifest. The transformation of the boss into the strong mayor is but one illustration and is seen most clearly when we state the problem in terms of "administrative centralization."

If, however, Merton's functionalism is directed toward "seemingly irrational" patterns of political behavior that persist over time, or the appearance of anomalous or unexpected political practices, then it may indeed serve the heuristic function of directing us toward theoretically fruitful fields of inquiry.[54] For, given the acknowledged difficulties that attend the a priori postulations of requisite functional analysis (i.e., general functional theory), it may allow us to *discover* what is necessary to a system at a particular stage of development, what must be "maintained" and how and by what types of institutions (structures) this is done. Such descriptions must perforce strengthen general functional theory.

Insofar as the middle range (empirical functionalism) is concerned, we can observe one of those historic discontinuities that make it necessary to relearn a procedure that served as the

---

53 Charles G. Mayo and Beryl L. Crowe (eds.), *American Political Parties* (New York: Harper & Row, 1967), p. 35.

54 Merton, op. cit., p. 65.

foundation stone of the discipline itself. Perhaps if we had followed Lowell's advice, functional analysis would not have had to be rediscovered. In any case, recognition of such discontinuities commends a greater concern for the logic and procedure of analysis. For those who are interested in science, this is a "functional requisite."

CHAPTER 6
Development Theory: Some Methodological Problems

Names and Concepts

IN the initial stages of any inquiry, concepts are rarely defined so as to permit a determination of their extension with any appreciable degree of precision. What this means is that we are often not sure of what it is we are talking about, looking at, or looking for. Ominous as this may sound, it is not necessarily a cause for alarm. If we had certainty with respect to the object at issue, there would be no reason to enter upon its study. Inquiry always begins with vague notions which, by a process of successive definition, sometimes lead to formulations of great power.

But it is to be emphasized that in its early stages, systematic investigation must employ lexical terms—those with conventional meanings. These frequently, if not always, result in paradox: their denotations are much clearer than their designations. By custom and convention, that which they point to is recognizable, the things they denote are relatively clear, but the *grounds* upon which identification is made remain quite implicit. Once the ground itself is opened to question, the process of redefinition has begun.

With this in mind, I wish to discuss the matter of naming and conceptualization as it emerges in the work of Fred Riggs.[1]

[1] My remarks here are primarily addressed to Fred W. Riggs, "The Structures of Government and Administrative Reform," in Ralph Brai-

---

Reprinted, with modifications, by permission of Duke University Press from Martin Landau, "Theoretical Analysis and Persuasive Discourse," from *Political and Administrative Development*, pp. 334–349.

Political Theory and Political Science

I shall be direct in my comment if only because Riggs is, in my view, one of the foremost theoreticians in the area of political and administrative development. No one in this domain is without obligation to him—which is the same as saying that the entire field is in his intellectual debt. What troubles me, however, is that his formulations have not generated the research they warrant.

It may well be that this is the result of a rather large volume of writing, which appears sprawling and unorganized. And, to be sure, the theoretical output of Riggs is in need of some codification if its basic structure is to be properly explicated. While this is a weakness, the major problem turns on the use of vocabulary that is at once esoteric and alien and which, contrary to its intention, obscures the theory. The continuous, almost relentless, introduction of new names makes it extremely difficult to order Riggs's work and serves, in addition, as an obstacle to the development of a standardized vocabulary. Accordingly, I want to offer some comment on names and concepts.

There is appended to Riggs's essay a glossary of some fifty-odd terms, each of which is defined by stipulation; that is, each is assigned a definite meaning by Riggs. A general exposition in a technical domain often carries a similar glossary, but the definitions are lexical: i.e., the glossary is a list of the names of important concepts in the field and the more or less standardized meanings of these concepts as they are used in that field.[2] The glossary itself is a convenient reference for readers because they can always turn to it should they be puzzled about the meaning of a term. It is especially helpful to the lay reader or the untrained student, who, not too familiar with the usual or standard terms of discourse, can thereby ease his difficulties. For the professional reader no such glossary is necessary, for it is assumed that he

---

banti (ed.), *Political and Administrative Development* (Durham, N.C.: Duke University Press, 1969).

[2] See, for example, Colin Cherry, *On Human Communication* (New York: John Wiley, Science editions, 1957).

Development Theory: Some Methodological Problems

possesses the same working vocabulary. On occasion, of course, a new term will be introduced and its author will both explain and demonstrate its need.

But the fact that a new concept is offered does not mean that it will be accepted. Standard vocabularies are marks of considerable development in any field and are built, as all knowledge is built, rather slowly and carefully. In this process, a great many terms are volunteered but only a few are retained. Some, presented with the appearance of authority—say, from a highly reputed scholar—may enter a technical vocabulary easily, only to be discarded as their promise fails to materialize. Those that do remain, that become standard terms of discourse, are not and cannot be legislated from on high. They are employed because they do their job—they name concepts that possess a demonstrated power. In such a field, research is organized on the basis of these concepts.

One can, therefore, understand Riggs's effort to provide a technical vocabulary. In a rather fundamental sense it is quite salutary. For it is true that our locutions in this field vary widely, that many of our key terms are ambiguous, that we often use the same name for different concepts and different names for the same concept. With a considerable integrity, Riggs seeks to avoid such confusions by making his usage as exact as he can. In this effort, he invents a large number of new concepts, so many in fact that any reader is transformed into a novice. The glossary is really necessary.

It is one thing, however, to seek to clarify an existing concept, and another to invent one. Moreover, it is often not clear whether we are inventing a new concept or a new name, a neologism. For a name and a concept are by no means identical. A concept is a class term and it consists of a set of properties or attributes. The set of characteristics which define the concept (its intension) provide the criteria by which we assign things to the class (its extension). The name of the concept is a tag we append to it for purposes of convenience.

Political Theory and Political Science

In the essay under review, Riggs employs the term "tonic" polity. Originally, this was presented in a discussion of "whole political systems," but there it was subordinate to a naming system based upon the root form "cephal" which was used to tag such systems.[3] Here the focus is more restricted and tonic anchors the analysis.

Tonic polity is given a formal definition—one which is stipulated. Such definitions are crucial, absolutely necessary, when a new term is introduced; otherwise one is lost as to its meaning. Nor is it required that the definition be wholly original. It suffices that it be novel in the domain of discourse in which it is introduced. But once presented, it constitutes no more than a proposal for adoption. The receiver may accept or reject the proposal. If we find that it has advantage, that it reduces surplus meaning, eliminates emotive connotations, and organizes the intended sphere of application more effectively than any other concept, we will undoubtedly accept it. We may do so on any one of these grounds, depending upon the nature of the problem that confronts us. If there are too many sets of meanings assigned to one name, we may find it helpful to narrow this down by using a specific term for each set. If the name has persuasive force where we wish a purely cognitive construct, we may again create a new term for the concept. But if none of these factors weighs heavily, and if it cannot be shown that they do interfere with our understanding of the problem, then the new terms may confuse more than enlighten. Coining new words cannot be wholly arbitrary; the minter must take due account of existing linguistic practice and the problem at hand. It suffices to note that many of the fundamental terms in physics—force, field, wave, particle, mass, friction—were drawn from the vernacular.

---

[3] Fred W. Riggs, "The Comparison of Whole Political Systems," in Robert T. Holt and John Turner (eds.), *The Methodology of Comparative Research* (New York: Free Press, 1970). Here the classification system includes such terms as metacephalies, heterocephalies, orthocephalies, procephalies, acephalies, and supracephaly.

Development Theory: Some Methodological Problems

To return to tonic polity, we find that it consists of an executive, a complex bureaucracy, and a constitutive system. To proceed further, a polity is a political system at the societal level. Riggs does not define political and allows it to remain primitive. An executive is an office (used interchangeably with role) which asserts authority (undefined) over a polity. A complex bureaucracy (bureaucracy itself is defined as a hierarchy of offices subject to the authority of an executive) is one in which there is a multiplicity of command as represented by a line-staff type organization. And a constitutive system consists of an elected assembly, an electoral system, and one or more political parties. In turn, an elected assembly is a collegial organization most of whose members are elected, and an electoral system (elections) is a procedure whereby voters cast ballots for one or more candidates for public offices. And finally, a party is an organization which nominates candidates for election to public office. Needless to say, all definitions are Riggs's.

We can now say that a tonic polity is one that consists of an office which asserts authority over a political system, a hierarchy of subordinate offices, a collegial organization most of whose members are elected, a procedure whereby voters cast ballots for such public offices, and an organization which nominates candidates for these offices. Alternatively, we may say that a tonic polity is one which possesses an executive, a bureaucracy, an assembly, an election system, and parties—what we usually refer to as a governmental system. Indeed, we even have terms (concepts) which indicate the logic of relations (structure) which obtain among these components, as when we say *separation of powers, presidential system, party government,* and the like. To be sure, this form of address is not very exact but it may nevertheless be superior to the notion of tonic with all its "precision." It is, after all, a relational (and, therefore, a structural) construct, while tonic is merely a collection of components.

In any case, it is difficult if not impossible to determine or to appreciate what is new about this concept. Ordinarily, the appearance of a new term in the analysis of a problem signals a new concept, a new category of analysis, a new system of classification. But this is not so here. A tonic polity is a very familiar notion to me. I just did not know its name.

There is, however, a special utility in fixing a name on a concept, even an old one. Frequently we allow concepts to slip by us because they are not labeled.[4] When they are named, they can more easily be called to mind and put to use. It may, therefore, be helpful to accept the name *tonic*. If I hesitate, my doubt has to do with the fact that Riggs uses the three major properties of a tonic polity to form a vast classification system—further complicated by the fact that each of these properties is itself subdivided. The result is a bewildering number of names, each standing for a particular subclass: orthotonic polity, homotonic, syntonic, anatonic, antetonic, antitonic, protonic, paratonic, heterotonic, neotonic, montonic, isotonic, hypotonic, hypertonic, atonic, and nontonic. Interestingly enough, the intention of this effort is very well placed. In establishing a set of constant reference points, a typology of formal structures, a basis for charting change is set down: by distinguishing between formal structures and the functions they perform we can see what has happened.

It follows, then, that the tonic formula is not simply "a mnemonic and heuristic device," as Riggs suggests,[5] designed simply to help keep the basic concepts in view. Far more is involved: a theory is involved. Riggs may see his formulations as only a framework for the treatment of "developmental change" and may look to enlarge it by means of what he calls "ecological" factors.[6] But his definitions are all within a stated theoretical context, informed by the basic concept of structure. What he is

---

[4] It is likely that the discontinuities which characterize the history of functionalism in political science would not have occurred had the founding fathers of the discipline named their concepts. See Chapter 5 of this book.

[5] Ibid., p. 249.

[6] Ibid., p. 317.

Development Theory: Some Methodological Problems

saying is that his concepts, all presented as sets of structural properties, will permit us to predict the behavior of those polities which the class term covers. Thus, the level of development in orthotonic polities is generally higher than in heterotonic systems, and the degree of concentration of power is generally greater in anatonic than in isotonic polities.[7]

To fix the point, let us look at the latter hypothesis somewhat more carefully. Both classes are tonic (having an executive, a complex bureaucracy, and a constitutive system). Both have accountable executives and a compensated bureaucracy, but the isotonic polity has a competitive but not assembly-oriented constitutive system, and the anatonic has a noncompetitive system. A competitive system is one in which opposition parties nominate candidates for election.[8]

Now I am not sure whether we have a hypothesis before us or a tautology, but let us assume the former. The distinguishing feature here, as nearly as I can follow, seems to be opposition politics or party competition. Suppose, then, that we have two countries, A and B. A falls into the class isotonic and B is anatonic. In placing them in their respective classes, we are stating that each possesses the requisite class properties. Suppose, again, that while I knew Riggs's classification system well, I had never encountered these countries in any way. All that I knew was that one, B, was anatonic and the other was isotonic. Would I not then claim (predict) that B would evidence in its operations a much greater degree of concentration of power? In fact, I would go further and state categorically that A has at least two parties and B has only one. Were I to find the opposite, I would immediately wonder whether we have classified these countries properly. And if I had a classification system, the extension of which permitted the prediction of only the most obvious behaviors, its value would be quite debatable.

But I do not wish to question the value of Riggs's system. The

---

7 Ibid., p. 265
8 Ibid., p. 322

more immediate trouble is that the typology itself is elusive. It is so hard to work with. It would be one thing if it consisted of a few well-chosen basic properties divided into a few subclasses, each with a name. Logically speaking, Riggs's system could be easily reduced without any damage and with much profit. A reader could keep in mind four or five simple terms and follow the discussion with relative ease, even to the point of internal consistency. With fifteen or more neologisms, all rather tortuous, it becomes almost impossible to read his formulations. The names get in the way. To check the proposal about anatonic and isotonic polities, I had to swing back and forth: first to tonic, then to isotonic and anatonic, then to orthotonic, to anatonic again, and then to neotonic, to compensated bureaucracy, back to isotonic and anatonic, and I am still not sure I have it. One has the double task of keeping track of the name of each type and what it stands for, and the result is simply the loss of the line of analysis. The central question—the relationship between types of governmental structures and administrative operations—is all but obscured. One concludes Riggs's essay not with a clear set of concepts, not with a clear statement of their interrelationships, but with a long list of names. And names do not provide any basis for research.

Finally, I wish also to point to one special irony revealed by Riggs's essay. If there is any concept that we have tried to move to the point of standardization, it is bureaucracy. As La Palombara points out, the "classical formulation of the distinguishing features" (defining properties) of bureaucracy is Max Weber's.[9] And elsewhere I have suggested that the formulation is so classic as to have reached the status of a paradigm, in Kuhn's sense.[10] Apparently, although I may misread Riggs, he does not wish to

9 Joseph La Palombara, "Values and Ideologies in the Administrative Evolution of Western Constitution Systems" in Braibanti, op. cit., pp. 171 ff.

10 See "Sociology and the Study of Formal Organization" in Dwight Waldo and Martin Landau, *The Study of Organizational Behavior,* Special Series No. 8 (Washington: American Society for Public Administration, 1966). But see Chapter 2 of this book.

use this concept because it contains functional properties.[11] Instead, he selects "hierarchy of offices" under an executive and proceeds to call this bureaucracy. Since this usage is different from the usual, and is in fact a different concept, why retain the original name?

By way of contrast, Braibanti's procedure in the introduction of new terms and the assignment of new meanings to old terms is rather modest. Seeking to identify characteristics of political development that are germane to administrative reform, he transfers the term "architectonic" to stand for "an overarching purpose which gives form, cohesion, and direction to all public action within a sensed community." In doing so, he reviews the usage of several terms which roughly express the whole or parts of this concept. In one case, the instance of "polity," he states that earlier published formulations of his paper employed this term but with its meaning changed—narrowed from its original Aristotelian usage. This now appears "to be somewhat of an impertinence as well as perplexing, since 'polity,' so ancient a term and with little change in connotation, fulfills an important expository and conceptual need, and is comfortably seated in the literature."[12] Hence the need for a different term.

In not following this rule, which is so sensible precisely because it is economic, Riggs, despite an expressed doubt as to the wisdom of using bureaucracy to name hierarchy of offices,[13] contributes much to the ambiguity he strives to reduce. One patent illustration should suffice: employing the usual or classical formulation, La Palombara recognizes bureaucracy as a product of the West, not to be found before the seventeenth century; whereas Riggs denies that it can be taken as a Western invention.[14]

It might seem to the uninitiated reader that this is an empirical

---

11 Riggs, op. cit., pp. 221, 227.
12 Braibanti, op. cit., p. 37.
13 Riggs, op. cit., p. 221.
14 La Palombara, op. cit., pp. 170 ff, and Riggs, op. cit., p. 223.

difference, to be resolved by further research. In fact, it constitutes only a semantic difference—there are two distinct concepts involved and each denotes a different institution.

Terminology is thus a problem of telling proportions in any empirical domain. If we seek a knowledge that is publicly accessible to all, then our working vocabularies must possess clear and standard meanings. It is worth emphasizing that this rule is at the base of proposals which call for operational definitions, the goal of which is to develop concepts (and terms) that have identical meanings for all who use them. If standard vocabularies can be had, the power of our theories and concepts can be put to effective test. But if we employ vocabularies that are idiosyncratic, that disregard conventional disciplinary usage, the net effect must be a semantic confusion that restricts effective exchange of experience as it promotes unnecessary research. It behooves all of us at work in an empirical domain to treat our language with great care.

Theoretical Analysis and Persuasive Discourse

Among the many methodological problems that beset students of politics, none is more vexing than the subtle but powerful tendency to employ "persuasive" definitions in theoretical discourse. The significance of this difficulty is to be seen in the fact that such definitions are essentially evocative in character and are to be distinguished from other types of definitions by their appeal to interests, to dearly held values, and to emotion.[15]

The presence of persuasive definitions is always to be observed when there is a conflict of interest or a difference in ideology. An election campaign, a protest meeting, the summation of a trial attorney, a legislative debate, a session of the Security Council—all these situations will be replete with the familiar device of

---

15 Charles L. Stevenson, "Persuasive Definitions," *Mind*, Vol. 47 (1938). See also Irving M. Copi, *Introduction to Logic* (New York: Macmillan, 1961), pp. 99–107.

Development Theory: Some Methodological Problems

shifting the cognitive meaning of a term without in any way changing its subjective connotation, i.e. its emotive content. In such circumstances, this may be a sensible propagandist procedure; for the special purpose or rhetorical function of a persuasive definition is to move people, to effect a change in their attitudes, not to classify, delimit, or differentiate. But it is not to be assumed that their appearance is limited to exhortation. Any definition—theoretical, stipulative, lexical—can become persuasive: it does so the moment evocative elements override cognitive elements. There is always the risk, then, that persuasive definitions will intrude quite implicitly—an intrusion that is traceable to the value-laden connotations of the definiendum. And there is the further risk that such intrusion will not be recognized for what it is, thereby contributing to considerable confusion. Needless to say, as we have noted earlier, this is a primary ground for the introduction of neologisms in scientific discourse.

In political science, we have an additional difficulty. As an empirical discipline, our concern is with matters of fact and the relations that obtain among them. I trust, of course, that it is not necessary to defend this statement—a trust, incidentally, that is sustained by the efforts of both Carl J. Friedrich and Henry S. Kariel to ground their discussion of ends on empirical foundations.[16]

Yet many of our terms, those in widest use, are patently ethical constructs. They are, as Friedrich says, elements that the world "goes on bitterly fighting over." To be sure, such concepts as freedom, justice, democracy, representation, responsibility, and participation have considerable cognitive content. But they carry enormous valuational connotations. This is immediately to be seen when we couch them in the negative, for their negation is not simply a contrary cognitive assertion. It is far more. What, for example, is the character of the meaning involved when we say

[16] See Henry Kariel, "Goals for Administrative Reform in Developing States," and Carl J. Friedrich, "Political Development and the Objectives of Modern Government," in Braibanti, op. cit.

Political Theory and Political Science

of something that it is undemocratic, or unrepresentative, or irresponsible? Responsible government, democratic government, representative government—is it not clear that these are good governments and the contrary are bad?

Now, in using terms like responsible or representative, we assume that because we have stipulated definitions that are in nowise preferential, we have transformd them into cold, precise, and technical concepts.[17] It is as if this process has automatically neutralized their ethical, valuational, or subjective connotations. But the plain fact seems to be that for all our efforts to establish these terms as descriptive concepts, their meaning contains a large emotive or evocative component. If so, theoretical analysis that turns on such concepts will oscillate between the demands of theory and those of preference. The net result is bound to be a confusion which helps neither. I suspect that this is one difficulty that confounds us in the analysis of political development. Perhaps I can demonstrate this, but a few comments on the concept itself may be in order before doing so.

Political development is, as we all know, neither a new concept nor a distinctive one from the standpoint of program. It was absorbed into American political science at the very time that the empirical discipline was established.[18] No one who reads the work of Woodrow Wilson, A. Lawrence Lowell, Frank Goodnow, or Henry Jones Ford can escape the fact that the evolutionary (functional) thrust of their analysis prompted their revolt against the existing vocabulary of constitutional language because it had obscured the reality of political development.

What, then, is distinctive about the contemporary effort? The

---

[17] Philip Weiner quotes the Newtonian psychologist Chadbourne stating in 1771, "When a writer introduces terms with new meanings—he should realize that the older connotations of these terms will persist in the mind of the reader and will interfere with the process of grasping new meanings." *Evolution and the Founders of Pragmatism* (Cambridge: Harvard University Press, 1949), p. 14.

[18] See Chapter 5 of this book.

Development Theory: Some Methodological Problems

answer lies in the difference between a metaphor and a model.[19] Whereas the early pragmatists proclaimed an atheoretic bias, we have reversed this procedure, eschewing ad hoc formulations as we seek, deliberately and consciously, to build appropriate and effective models.

Partly, this is a product of our intellectual climate. But it may also be said that the exasperating problem of the new states has assigned a priority to theory-building. Interest in these countries was originally stimulated by matters of practical concern, which is the way most inquiry begins. Quite apart from practical considerations—or rather because of our early involvements—it has become obvious that such countries actually constitute a new set of phenomena for us: they defied our usual category systems and presented, therefore, a vast uncharted area. Hence we have been prompted to review our formulas and have been forced into the construction of models by which to represent these phenomena. Moreover, the opening of a vast new research area which provides a laboratory-like setting for the study of institutional change permits us to raise formulations whose range of application can be tested against the universe of states. This is one time, as George Washington Plunkett might say, that "we seen our opportunity and took it."

Thus, we have become preoccupied with our first major theoretical problem—the invention of a classification system that would simplify (order) our object of inquiry. Heretofore, our basic class terms, many of which are contained in the Constitution where they appear as state descriptions that are to last indefinitely, were largely employed on the assumption that the data they organized were discrete in character. And a good deal of it is. But we have met with increasing difficulty in assigning behavior to a particular class. There are too many borderline cases, there is a vast "twilight zone" or "penumbra"—which terms are employed because we cannot precisely distinguish a

[19] See Chapter 3 of this book.

strong executive, a party government, a responsible bureaucracy, or a developed polity.[20] This inability to clearly mark off the class of behavior involved may be the result of faulty definition in the first place. But it is more likely that this difficulty will be greeted with a firm declaration that politics does not lend itself to clean, precise, and mutually exclusive boundary markers. This has often been used as an excuse to avoid the arduous task of definition— leaving us with a set of disjunctive classes (either/or) which we use as we violate them.

These difficulties may very well suggest that "those characteristics of the subject matter which are to provide the defining basis of classification cannot fruitfully be construed as simple property concepts determining, as their extensions, classes with neatly demarcated boundaries."[21] That is, our subject matter is continuous in character, and we had best approach it in terms of more or less, not either/or, on the basis of gradations, not inclusion and exclusion. In the area of political development, this posture is mandated by definition.

Accordingly, the sphere of comparative politics and administration has been struggling to create a classification system that forces recognition of the continuous character of its problem area. It is in this context that Riggs's original formulations are so impressive. Tackling the difficult problem of traditional, transitional, or modern systems, Riggs's point of departure is the principle of structural differentiation and functional specialization which he has coupled to several Parsonian pattern variables. These dichotomous variables, interestingly enough, provide the polar points of a scale of differentiation that marks the range of variation within which societies can be ordered in terms of degree. It is thus possible, in principle, to plot (describe) any society on

20 For discussion of the problem of classification as it relates to difficulties in comparison, see Ralph Braibanti, "Comparative Political Analytics Reconsidered," *Journal of Politics,* Vol. 30 (1968).

21 Carl G. Hempel, "Typological Methods in the Social Sciences," in Maurice A. Natanson (ed.), *Philosophy of the Social Sciences: A Reader* (New York: Random House, 1963), p. 213.

Development Theory: Some Methodological Problems

this scale, thereby permitting movement "from the classificatory, qualitative level of concept formation to the quantitative one."[22] In this respect Riggs's work is truly comparative; not because of its coverage of numerous countries but because it provides an orderly framework for both diachronic and synchronic analysis.

This venture is not unique. It can be observed that the concept of development, defined in terms of structural differentiation and functional specificity, seems to have attained pre-eminent status in this sphere of interest. There are some variations on the theme, but these are either minor or derivative.

Pye, in one estimate of the state of inquiry, distinguishes some ten basic formulations and then proceeds to extract a "developmental syndrome" consisting of three basic properties: equality, capacity, and differentiation. Equality as a definitive factor is immediately persuasive, but I do not wish to dwell upon it. It involves participation ("active citizens or at least the pretense of popular rule are necessary"), laws that are universalistic (the rule of law), and recruitment on the basis of achievement (the well-known merit principle). Capacity, a more neutral term, has to do with the ability of the government to affect society and economy and thus is associated with performance and scale of operations. Differentiation, of course, refers to the specialization of structures: distinct offices, limited functions, and division of labor within government. There is an added note here that differentiation entails an ultimate integration.[23]

Upon analysis, differentiation emerges as the critical property of development, if not the only one. That is, capacity is conjoined to differentiation so closely that it may be no more than a logical extension thereof. Structural differentiation means an increase in the scale of performance, an observation that we may make more

---

[22] Ibid., p. 216. In the interest of continuity, I am here iterating some material presented in Chapter 4 in the context of functional analysis. This presentation is somewhat more extensive, however.

[23] Lucian W. Pye, "The Concept of Political Development," *Annals of the American Academy of Political and Social Science,* Vol. 358 (1965).

Political Theory and Political Science

easily by noting that Pye states, "with differentiation there is also, of course, increased functional specificity of the various political roles in the system."[24] Specification of role, needless to say, entails a fixed domain of operations. So far as equality is concerned, universalistic law is implicit in functional specificity; otherwise neither the merit system (the achievement principle) nor the substitutability of actors could obtain. As regards participation—mass participation, that is—it seems to me to be theoretically irrelevant. If Pye were to suggest pluralism as we usually understand it, it could be shown that this too is entailed by differentiation and specialization. It does appear that we will not find differentiation and capacity as defined here to vary inversely anywhere. But one always remains open to correction.

To continue, La Palombara marks out four major properties: structural differentiation, magnitude, achievement, and secularization.[25] Magnitude is not defined with any appreciable clarity and is therefore a difficult variable to work with. But it seems to be employed in a manner similar to Pye's use of capacity. It stands as a "ratio of political activity to all other activity that takes place in a society." By definition, then, it can only be observed upon the appearance of differentiation and, as La Palombara notes, "will increase as greater structural specialization evolves." We need not deal with "achievement orientation" again, and with respect to secularization, it too is implicit in differentiation.[26] If we turn to Almond's work,[27] he also builds upon differentiation and specificity. For Eisenstadt, "the first

24 Ibid., p. 12.
25 Joseph La Palombara, "An Overview of Bureaucracy and Political Development," in La Palombara (ed.), *Bureaucracy and Political Development* (Princeton: Princeton University Press, 1963).
26 For a discussion of secularization in this context see Martin Landau, "Decision Theory and Development Administration," in Edward Weidner (ed.), *Development Administration in Asia* (Durham, N.C.: Duke University Press, 1970).
27 Gabriel A. Almond and G. Bingham Powell, *Comparative Politics* (Boston: Little, Brown, 1966), and Fred W. Riggs, *Administration in Developing Countries* (Boston: Houghton Mifflin, 1964).

Development Theory: Some Methodological Problems

characteristic of political modernization is a high degree of differentiation. . . ."[28] The list could be extended at great length.

From this brief exercise, it should be clear that scholars have assumed the defining property of development to be structural differentiation and functional specificity. Those additional properties which are usually stipulated are either redundant or they have the status of accompanying characteristics. What remains in bold relief is the proposal that rates and levels of development are to be addressed as rates and levels of differentiation.

It is well to remember, however, that what we have been puzzling over is the concept of "development," not that of "political." In the latter case, the variety of locutions to be found in the literature does not obscure the fact that this term is taken as a primitive. There are occasional references to something like the authoritative allocation of values, but the concept itself invariably remains nonproblematical. Its meaning is intuitive, that is to say, it is employed quite conventionally. Its denotation, therefore, presents no mystery since it is *known by custom and usage.* We all know that it refers to a system of government.

Now it would appear that our line of reasoning from this point on should be rather simple. To determine the extent of development, all we need to do is treat governmental systems in accordance with the rule of differentiation. To be sure, there are some difficult technical problems to be overcome, but these do not in principle bar us from plotting governmental systems in terms of the dimension specified. Just as economists employ per capita income as a rough indicator of economic development, so we might use, in Max Weber's phrasing, "the quantitative extension of administrative tasks." This, or the extension of the merit system (recruitment on the basis of skill qualifications) may in fact provide us with a "simple and generalizable index of political development," but it is a fair suggestion that such a pro-

[28] S. N. Eisenstadt, "Bureaucracy and Political Development," in La Palombara, op. cit., p. 99.

posal would be opposed by the comment, "*That* isn't political development."

Such objection may be offered because it is felt that the index itself (contained in the principle of structural differentiation and functional specificity) is faulty. But it is more likely that the objection is more *persuasive* than otherwise. For, as can be seen in the essays by Braibanti, Friedrich, Kariel, and La Palombara,[29] politics is a term that is richly laden in value and emotion. Mixed emotion, more precisely, because the emotive meaning of this word varies in accordance with the approved value system of different groups. I cannot extend upon this here, but to contemporary scholars, politics does not connote graft, cynicism, chicane, and sheer opportunism as it may for the man in the street when he declares, "That's politics." It was so in the days when political scientists joined with civic movements to take politics out of government, but in our time it is, rather, the goodness of democracy, constitutionalism, participation, and the sharing of power that is meant.

Hence it is that in retaining "political" as a primitive term to be understood conventionally, its fairly stable emotive meaning is maintained even when its conceptual elements are rearranged (by means of a stipulative definition) in the interests of purity. As a result, the tacit element of persuasion works to transform analysis and argument into advocacy and debate. The process is subtle but is to be observed in the widespread tendency to react negatively to formulations that do not include such "good" attributes. On the positive side, Braibanti's brief review of prevailing definitions serves to illustrate conceptualizations that are quite evocative.[30] Or better still, we need only note the following: "Political development is in quintessence the ordering of the affairs of men into a polity more or less commonly agreed upon, clearly known, capable of rational adjustment, the whole being infused with qualities of freedom ennobling the puny lives of

29 Braibanti, op. cit.
30 Ibid., pp. 34–36.

those who have formed the state." Moreover, it "can be viewed as a series of ultimate progressions (with periodic regressions and even oscillations) from ascription to personal achievement, from ambiguity to certainty in the use of public power, from alienation and withdrawal to enlightened participation . . . , from coarseness and coercion to refinement and sensitivity in public action, from contraction to expansion of free choice." This moving language need now only be reinforced by the magnificent statement from the encyclical *Populorum Progressio* "to do more, know more and have more in order to be more."[31] Against such persuasive rhetoric who can stand? I, for one, am ready to toss my index to the fires below.

Before doing so, let me illustrate this phenomenon another way. The institutional manifestation of the index is, of course, bureaucracy. We can, therefore, return to Max Weber's original proposals, as we invariably do. What is interesting here is the way we repeat them and the way we resist them.

We repeat them because we have to. But frequently discussions of the bureaucratic paradigm transform it into a checklist of simple class properties, against which "bureaucracies" themselves are measured. What emerges is the "finding" that it has much less than universal application, that there are rather sharp variations in administrative agencies, many of which are quite irrational. One case after another is produced to demonstrate the weakness of the model.

What is often lost sight of, and we owe this observation to Carl Hempel, is the fact that Weber was not defining bureaucracy by genus and difference, under which specific cases could be covered.[32] On the contrary, Weber thought it was "nonsense" to even try, and he used this word.[33] What he thought he was

[31] Ibid., p. 34.
[32] "Typological Methods in the Social Sciences," in Natanson, op. cit., p. 211.
[33] Max Weber, "Objectivity in Social Science and Social Policy," in Natanson, op. cit., p. 399.

Political Theory and Political Science

constructing was a genuinely comparative typology—a limiting concept—against which one could determine the *extent* to which a given concrete situation "approximates to or diverges from" the model.[34] This is entirely consistent with his fundamental formulas, built upon painstaking analysis of historical change, which establish a direction of movement from Kadi-justice to a legal rational order. The latter is to be understood as a system founded upon the *principle of substantiation* where "the presentation of facts is decisive." Hence the preeminence of the trained expert, the informing principle of differentiation, which not only establishes bureaucracy as the major institutional form of modern society and government but makes the latter "absolutely dependent upon a bureaucratic basis." Indeed, "the larger the state, and the more it is or the more it becomes a great power state, the more unconditionally is this the case."[35] The proposal here is not for a classification *bureaucracy* which permits sharp and precise coverage of discrete cases but for a polar point *bureaucracy,* which permits concrete institutions to be ordered in terms of "the extent to which." The closer a system approaches this point, the more is it "modern."

If we understand this logic, it is pointless to suggest that systems are mixed no matter how modern. Nor need we be surprised that particularism, spontaneity, ascription, traditionalism, nepotism, are also to be found; on the contrary, they should be anticipated. But it is also to be anticipated that as institutions assume a bureaucratic form, "action orientations" based on kinship, tradition, and personal sympathy weaken to the point of displacement. Not without great tension, however. For in this process, one cultural mode is being replaced by another—sometimes quite abruptly.

Nevertheless, Weber is unequivocal in the statement that the "peculiarities" of modern society demand an absolute and uncon-

---

[34] Ibid., p. 396.
[35] *From Max Weber,* trans. and ed. H. H. Gerth and C. Wright Mills (New York: Oxford University Press, 1958), p. 211.

Development Theory: Some Methodological Problems

ditional dependence upon bureaucracy. These transform the "quantitative extension of administrative tasks" into "qualitive changes of administrative tasks." Rules, matter-of-factness, and the means-end calculus, "dominate the bearing" of the mature bureaucracy. It is rational, precise, technical, and ordered, and the "more complicated and specialized [we would say structurally differentiated and functionally specific] modern culture becomes, the more its external supporting apparatus demands the personally detached and strictly 'objective' *expert*."[36]

A new order of social relations is predicted here, a new "style of life," a new set of cultural rules for the pursuit of any social objective. These give rise to an action orientation unlike any known in the past, the summation of which Ilchman refers to as "rational productivity bureaucracy."[37] So powerful is this phenomenon that it tends increasingly to characterize the whole of governmental operations, let alone those of the external sectors. All we need do is to look about us to see its penetrating effects. There is little doubt that the primary institutional characteristic of highly complex and differentiated societies is bureaucracy.

Yet such a conclusion is troubling: not because of any logical or empirical weakness but because, as Merton put it, bureaucracy is a *Schimpfwort*.[38] It is pertinent to note that the word *bureaucracy* entered the English language about 1848 and soon after was stamped by Carlyle as that "continental nuisance." It is invariably tied to the rise of Prussia and Germany, enabling the caution that it was the product of a set of values and an ideology that were anything but democratic. If we follow Laski, it is more: it is a profound threat to public liberty. And from Kariel, after Marcuse, we learn that it is a breeder of "one-dimensional man."

---

36 Ibid., pp. 212–219, 244. Emphasis in original.

37 Warren Ilchman, "Productivity, Administrative Reform, and Anti-Politics," in Braibanti, op. cit.

38 Robert K. Merton, "Bureaucratic Structure and Personality," in Merton et al., *Reader in Bureaucracy* (Glencoe, Ill.: The Free Press, 1952), p. 364.

Political Theory and Political Science

Such men may be "ritualists," exhibit the "insolence of office," and if not this, then a "trained incapacity to think." We have a long way to go in purifying this concept of its persuasive power, and it should be clear that a large part of its meaning is emotive.

But it is one thing to evaluate the phenomena a theoretical proposal directs us to and quite another to evaluate the proposal itself. In the former case a value judgment is expressed, and in the latter the worth of the proposal depends upon empirical demonstration. It appears, however, that many of our criticisms of Weber are not so much directed to his theory as to the phenomenon which he predicted. By a subtle stroke, antipathy to the phenomenon of bureaucracy is transferred to the theory itself. There is then a tendency to inquire into the motivation of the theorist, the values that prompt—so to speak—the theory itself. Thereafter, the test of the theory can easily become the ethics of its father. When this occurs, the theory has been transformed into ideology and the universe of discourse has changed.[39]

With respect to Max Weber, this has been done in many ways, two of which are immediately relevant—the assignment of a "metaphysical pathos" and the selective use of rhetoric. Originally, it was Alvin Gouldner who urged that the metaphysical pathos of the theory of bureaucracy was "pessimism and fatalism."[40] And it is on the foundation of this pathos that both Kariel and La Palombara erect their caveats, warning us about the dangers inherent in the acceptance of Weber's theories. But when Arthur O. Lovejoy introduced this term, his primary concern was to establish "the ultimate objects" of interest for the historian of ideas. "Of what sort . . . are the elements, the primary and persistent or recurrent dynamic units, of the history of thought, of which he is in quest?" Among these elements, Lovejoy included metaphysical pathos—"exemplified in any description of the nature of things, any characterization of the world to which

---

39 See Chapter I of this book for an extended discussion of this.
40 "Metaphysical Pathos and the Theory of Bureaucracy," *American Political Science Review,* Vol. 49 (1955).

Development Theory: Some Methodological Problems

one belongs, *in terms which, like the words of a poem, awaken through their associations, and through a sort of empathy which they engender, a congenial mood or tone of feeling* on the part of the philosopher or his readers."[41] The point of this was not to assert, as Gouldner does, that "those who have committed themselves to a theory always get more than they have bargained for."[42] Rather, Lovejoy suggests, there exist susceptibilities to various types of pathos, and these play a part both in the formation of "philosophical systems" and in their public reception. And this he adds, "has nothing to do with philosophy as a science." We may say with theory as theory; it has "to do with philosophy as a factor in history."[43]

Nevertheless, suppose that we allow for a metaphysical pathos in the case of a theory. It would still have nothing to do with the power of the theory, or with its range of application. The test of a theory must always stand independent of the personality, the values, the motives of the theorist. Otherwise, criticism reduces to the *ad hominem,* and we have blocked the way of inquiry.

Assume, further, that we cannot escape a metaphysical susceptibility and that Weber's theory is bathed in pathos of necessity. Then it follows that Friedrich, Kariel, and La Palombara must respond in accordance with their own moods. For the metaphysical pathos that they exhibit is most pronounced and rarely disguised, and it is not at all congenial to such proposals as those which Weber offers. This, in good measure, accounts for the tendency to transform theoretical problems into ideological contests. But even more, it begets a selective use of rhetoric that is frankly persuasive and designed to elicit an emotive response.

Thus Friedrich, in commenting on Weber's discussion of election and appointment, hierarchy, control, and discipline, writes: "The very words vibrate with something of the Prussian enthusi-

---

41 Arthur O. Lovejoy, *The Great Chain of Being* (New York: Harper Torchbook, 1960), pp. 7, 11. Emphasis added.
42 "Metaphysical Pathos," op. cit., p. 498.
43 Lovejoy, op. cit., pp. 13–14.

asm for the military type organization." I have never felt such vibration despite the fact that I have been told this many times. Should I persist in my position, there may be added to the discussion the assertion that "Weber's fully developed bureaucracy is most nearly represented by three modern organizations: (1) an army, (2) a business concern without any sort of employee or labor participation in management, (3) a totalitarian party and its bureaucratic administration." With this imagery, the conclusion is inescapable that the more fully developed a bureaucracy, the less responsible it is.[44] But if one notes that "precision, speed, unambiguity, knowledge of the files, continuity, discretion, unity, strict subordination [read strict accountability]";[45] that "specializing administrative functions according to purely objective considerations"; that calculable rules and the "personally detached and strictly objective expert"—that all these are the marks of full development,[46] then it is a fair hypothesis that it is "most nearly represented" by a perfect problem-solving system.

Such, then, are the devices by which we tend to transform theoretical questions into ideological problems. By resorting to persuasive definitions, by allowing the implicit ethical connotations of so fundamental a concept as "political" to intrude, by assigning a metaphysical pathos, and by using a directive rhetoric, we all fall prey to this tendency. When this happens we are more likely to legislate preferred ends than engage in systematic analysis, and to opt for political solutions to problems as against bureaucratic solutions. We will, of necessity, seek to enlarge the ratio of political activity to administrative activity on the assumption that politics is intrinsically superior to administration. This is so fundamental an ethic that we do not hesitate to export it. It appears to me that this is one reason why, as Montgomery

---

[44] Carl J. Friedrich, "Some Observations on Weber's Analysis of Bureaucracy," in Merton et al., *Reader in Bureaucracy,* op. cit., p. 31. See also La Palombara, op. cit., pp. 175ff.
[45] Gerth and Mills (eds.), op. cit., p. 214.
[46] Ibid., pp. 214–216.

puts it, "administrative reform has lost its grip on the imagination of political scientists."[47]

There was a time, however, when American political scientists —fully cognizant of the German experience—were not all that fearful of bureaucracy. This was a time when the ratio of political activity to administrative activity was very large. It was the time of the long ballot, the Black Horse Cavalry, and the "shame of the cities." Bosses, rings, courthouse and gashouse gangs, nepotism, favoritism, and chicane—this was "politics." It was all very personal, and if there were protected islands of objectivity, it was always possible to buy personal attention. This, incidentally, is the function of a bribe.

When, in this circumstance, the pragmatic political scientist came to offer solutions, it was bureaucracy that was to provide the correction. Along with a host of devices to depoliticize many of the affairs of government, i.e., to reduce the ratio, the bureaucratic mode of operation—objective, efficient, technical, and achievement-oriented—became a paramount preferred end. Constitutions and charters were rewritten, the short ballot was introduced, the system of public administration was extended, and its organizational form, under a strong executive, became monocratic. The highest priorities were assigned to the minimization of "political" interference, the establishment of technical qualifications for appointment, and the assignment of increasing authority, as Weber would say, to the personally detached and strictly objective expert. And all of this was under the banner of "democracy": *for it was then assumed that the primary tension derived from the relationship between democracy and "politics," not democracy and "bureaucracy."* There were, to be sure, cries of "administrative absolutism," resistance to an "administrative law," and dire predictions that the constitutional system was itself being undone. But again, as Weber would say, the external

---

[47] John Montgomery, "Sources of Bureaucratic Reform" in Braibanti, op. cit., p. 427.

Political Theory and Political Science

apparatus of an emerging industrial society demanded the action orientation most favorably offered by bureaucracy. It is not often observed that Frank Goodnow's celebrated *Politics and Administration* provides a theoretical basis for the "structural differentiation and functional specificity" which informed the praexiology of this period.

None of this is to suggest that there is no strain between politics and bureaucracy at the present time. But if the implicit ethical connotations of politics are as favorable as they seem to be, then this attitude may be attributed to the remarkable achievements of the American passion for administrative reform. The ideological implications of this page in history merit fully as much attention as does the German or the English experience. Theoretically, however, these variations serve to sustain Montgomery's general rule that bureaucracy is not to be presented as a constant surrounded by a set of dependent variables, but is itself a variable factor.[48]

Ends and Means

This rule can be stated alternatively, following La Palombara: an organization "exists within a particular cultural setting and will be influenced by and in turn influence that setting."[49] When phrased this way, we can recognize it as an expression of the familiar principle of "mutual interdependence." Drawn from the classic model of an energy-transfer system, it specifies that a statement about a system, or any part of it, takes in the environment as well.

There are several implications of this rule, but the most immediate instructs that an organization will influence and be influenced to the extent that its distinguishing properties are distributed throughout the system of which it is a member. In the social

---

48 Ibid., p. 470.
49 La Palombara, in Braibanti, op. cit., pp. 166–170.

Development Theory: Some Methodological Problems

sphere such properties are, in their fundamental form, existential and evaluative premises. When they are widely distributed, when there is a congruence between the organization and its task environment, the situation is rendered less uncertain; when there is not, it is fraught with hazard. Recognition that some degree of congruence is necessary lies at the base of the caveat that Western canons of public administration cannot be automatically or uncritically applied in developing states.

Existential and evaluative premises are another way of speaking of fact and value and, thus, of means and ends.[50] Means-end relationships are problem-solving devices, and all societies have their own trusted recipes for meeting trouble. But trouble is precisely the loss of correlation between means and ends. When there is a good fit between the two, things run smoothly or at least predictably. If there should arise anomalies, discrepancies between normal expectations and actual outcomes, the fit has been broken. If the break persists, an ordered situation has become random and a reassessment of some kind must occur. The usual things (means) do not work anymore and there is trouble. Whatever conflict and tension ensue, the stage has been set for the deliberate introduction of a change agent. For the overwhelming tendency of the twentieth century is not to leave such conditions to chance.

In general, and *a fortiori* as regards developing states, governments are brought into play in these troublesome situations. Their task, regardless of whether their jurisdictions are total or partial, is to act upon a set of conditions that are deemed unsatisfactory, and their goal is to produce outcomes that alter the existent condition in such manner as to constitute a solution to those problems that originally called forth their deployment. Hence, all governments are instrumental in character; they are, in Dewey's words, "intermediate between an existing situation and a situa-

[50] See Landau, "Decision Theory and Development Administration," op. cit.

tion that is to be brought into existence" by their own actions.[51]

This does not mean that specific governmental or administrative or political arrangements cannot be valued. In fact, they must be. As Dewey puts it: "For every condition that has to be brought into existence in order to serve as a means is, *in that connection,* an object of desire and an end-in-view, while the end actually reached is a means to future ends as well as a test of valuations previously held."[52]

Now it should be clear that the principle of "mutual interdependence" mandates the *field-determined* character of the instruments we choose to solve problems with. And we have come to understand this; which is why we are insistent in pointing to the transactional relationship between culture and instrument. For example, we no longer rush to apply the formidable technology of Western administration to developing states without considerable modification. We know full well that the epistemological premises that sustain technology are not widely enough distributed in the environment and that any indiscriminate application is foolhardy. If we hesitate, it is because we recognize that the choice of means in any problem-solving situation is a crucial factor and is *to be valued only to the extent that it contributes to a solution.* And when a means arrangement continuously contributes the solution to a problem, we elevate it to the status of a process law and adopt it as the *best* means at our disposal. But the word "best" is to be understood as such only in a strictly defined field.

But what of ends? How are they to be regarded? The answer is partly given to us by Friedrich, in voicing his complaint that ends, objectives, and purposes are rarely discussed in terms of their content by students of development. In illustrating such ends, Friedrich asks, "Should economic development have prior-

---

[51] John Dewey, "Theory of Validation," *International Encyclopedia of Unified Science* (Chicago: University of Chicago Press, 1939), Vol. 2, Part IV, pp. 27–33.

[52] Ibid., p. 43. Emphasis in the original. See also Herbert Simon, *Administrative Behavior* (New York: Macmillan, 1947).

Development Theory: Some Methodological Problems

ity . . . should it be agricultural or industrial, should capitalism or socialism be developed . . . should the development of democracy be given preference . . . or should strong, sizeable national states with a powerful bureaucracy (administration) be developed first."[53] Each of these alternatives, however, can easily be viewed not as *ends* but as *means,* for whether a condition is to be regarded as an end or a means can be determined only by the place it occupies in a means-ends chain. This is the essence of Dewey's quotation. Such alternatives are not ends in themselves for they presuppose even further ends—as the very form of Friedrich's question indicates. They are neither final nor ultimate and can only be regarded as intermediate. As intermediates, they necessarily become *means*. In this regard, our difficulties arise because we simply do not know which alternative is best and which, accordingly, to value. There may come a time when the state of our knowledge is such that we will be able to establish on empirical grounds that one or another of these alternatives is to be valued. What this will mean is that we have established a particular program of operation as the *means* that contributes most to the solution of the relevant problem. In the absence of such knowledge, what we invariably do, what we have to do, is to cut the continuum at some point and establish this point as an *end*. Thereafter, we may quarrel over these ends on ideological grounds. But it should be clear that along the length of a means-ends chain, *knowledge and ideology bear an inverse relationship to each other.*

Where, however, should we cut the chain? Here again the decision must be field-determined. Relevant, important, valued, ends are only relevant, important, and valued in a cultural context. Ends are never "independent of the structure and requirements of some concrete empirical situation"[54] and cannot be treated as such. The logic that applies to a consideration of means applies to ends as well; for ends as outcomes can be anticipated

---

53 Friedrich, in Braibanti, op. cit., p. 110.
54 Dewey, "Theory of Validation," op. cit., p. 55.

Political Theory and Political Science

"only in terms of the conditions by which they are brought into existence."[55] It follows, then, that an indiscriminate legislation of ends is as foolhardy as the indiscriminate application of means. Unless we understand the field-determined character of both means and ends we run the risk of maintaining a dreamworld even as we watch it collapse. It must be remembered that a means-ends relationship is a proposition, a hypothesis. If we break its contextual limits, we not only transform a hypothesis into sheer speculation, but we rob ourselves of the opportunity to observe consequences and to build knowledge. Effective development strategies depend upon accurate appraisal of systemic conditions and upon the construction of means-ends continua that are contextually or systemically revelant. Thus, the existence of a one-dimensional bureaucrat may be a problem in the United States. Elsewhere, the problem may be to bring him into existence.

---

55 Ibid., p. 35.

CHAPTER 7
Political Science and Public Administration: "Field" and the Concept of Decision-Making

THE final paragraph of Dwight Waldo's *Perspectives on Administration* (University of Alabama Press, 1956) provides the point of departure for this chapter. Waldo speaks of the fears of Fritz Morstein Marx that public administration, grown so broad, and so involved at its periphery with a multitude of other activities and disciplines, stands "in danger of disappearing completely as a recognizable focus of study." At first this struck him "as misplaced." But, he added, "I have a nagging worry of late, a fear that all is not as healthy as it should be at the center of the discipline."[1]

To establish the center of a discipline is a problem in definition; but discussions of definition, as of methodology, are often received with irritation and impatience, and frequently minimized, if not as fad, as esoteric ventures that serve only to divert from, and even confuse, the ongoing study of important problems. Yet

[1] Contrast this with Waldo's earlier optimism in *The Administrative State* (New York: Ronald Press, 1948), p. 206. Also see John C. Honey, "Research in the Public Administration: A Further Note," *Public Administration Review,* Vol. 17 (Autumn 1957).

Martin Landau, "The Concept of Decision-Making in the Field of Public Administration" in Sidney Mailick and Edward H. Van Ness, Eds., *Concepts and Issues in Administrative Behavior,* © 1962. Modified and reprinted by permission of Prentice-Hall, Inc., Englewood Cliffs, N.J.

methodology, in its basic sense, has to do with the organizing assumptions, the concepts and definitions that underlie any systematic inquiry. These are the elements that provide a field with coherence and relevance. Hence a close and continuing concern with the logic and procedure of analysis remains a prime necessity for any discipline if it to locate its center and clarify its principal points of reference. A healthy discipline, stated Waldo, "has a solid center as well as an active circumference." Indeed, without a center, it has no circumference: a condition usually to be associated with unstructured, unsystematic, and undisciplined effort. And this, perhaps, is the basis of the present fear that public administration, that lusty young giant of a decade ago, may now "evaporate" as a field.

In "The Study of Administration" (1887),[2] Woodrow Wilson cautioned that in entering upon investigation "it is needful:

To take some account of ... the history of the study
To ascertain just what is its subject matter
To determine just what are the best methods by which to develop it...."

In somewhat modified form, these are the instructions which I shall follow.

The Concept of "Field"

With respect to this concept there are two factors to be considered before turning directly to public administration: (1) the instrumental character of a field, and (2) the way in which modern social science has tended to constitute its fields.

1. The Field As an Analytic Tool

Human behavior in its totality is far too complex and bewildering to be perceived or studied as such. From a purely observa-

---

[2] Reprinted in *Political Science Quarterly*, Vol. 56 (December 1941), pp. 481–482.

tional standpoint, if this were possible, all we could see would be a mass of confusion—an undifferentiated, unwieldy stream of activity. Unless we construct 'categories,' 'types,' and 'forms,' it is doubtful that we would see any "thing." Without such categories, it would be virtually impossible to distinguish one behavior from another, one object from another. Special aspects of behavior have to be abstracted from the whole if any sense is to be made. It is this "abstractive differentiation" that enables us to group together, to classify certain activities, to make sense of them, and, thereby, to impose a measure of order.

This is the process of categorization,[3] the process that enables specialization. As the architectural principle of society, it is embodied in our language. We need only to recall that most of the words we use are terms of class power. Our culture, largely through language, provides us with sets of categories, with the necessary preconceptions and selecting devices, which are designed to enable us to come to terms with everyday experience. From birth onward we take our place in an ordered world that has a history and structure. We are taught how to "look at it" on the basis of the experiences and interpretations of others who came before. We learn "general types" that enable us to anticipate the experiences of others who have lived in and are living in our sociocultural context. The striking feature of these categories is that they have directly observable referents. They refer to named things and events, they denote the objects of everyday life; but these are so close and familiar to us that we often forget that they typify only the "common features" of these objects. That is, the categories of the common-sense world are generally employed as reified categories in which no distinction obtains between the construct and the thing.[4]

[3] I take this phrase from Arthur Pap, *Elements of Analytic Philosophy* (New York: Macmillan, 1949), p. 2. And see Chapter 2 of this book for a discussion of "categorization."

[4] See Alfred Schutz, "Common-Sense and Scientific Interpretation of Human Action," *Philosophy and Phenomenological Research* (September 1953) Vol. 14.

Political Theory and Political Science

For other purposes and other goals, however, we may construct an entirely different set of categories. To the social scientist, the significance of this process is to be found in its ability to provide for a disciplined empirical study; to make possible a close and intensive focus, to render a knowledge of careful observation and record. To this end certain behaviors are abstracted from the mass, isolated for close and continuing study, and these constitute the subject matter of a field. The "field," then, is a category of analysis; it is an artificial construction, manmade and made quite deliberately. It constitutes an instrument or tool that, in modern dress, aims at providing empirically valid data. Through a process of 'selective perception' we construct special fields, fence them off; we do so not to come to terms with the real world but in order to control our observation.

Fields, therefore, must be treated as tentative and provisional; they are not "given" as the concrete categories of the real world are given. By their nature they are bound to undergo continuing reconsideration: properly employed, they provide the basis for their own alteration and modification, even for their replacement. And this is a measure of their success. If specialized analysis is initially productive, we are able to discover new variables, perceive new relationships, and construct new categories of analysis. Our focus shifts acordingly, our subject matter changes and leads again, we hope, to concepts that explain more than we were originally able to. This is the logic and perspective of specialization.

2. The Fields of Social Science: "Real Types"

We have earlier indicated that insofar as the field of political science is concerned, its categorical framework was established under the press of pragmatism at the turn of the century.[5]

To constitute a field, however, means that some principle of selection is operative. And, whatever the proclaimed atheoretic

---

[5] See Chapters 3 and 5 of this book.

bias of the new pragmatic science, it could in no way transcend this requirement. Its movers may not have dealt with principles of selection explicitly, nor were their categories matters of deliberate conceptualization, but that they classified is beyond doubt. What they did was to organize their fields in terms of the typifications and conceptualizations of the common-sense world.

The political concepts current after the Civil War present themselves on two levels. There were, first, such abstract general concepts—in the tradition of *Staatslehre*—as sovereignty, state, natural law, and the like; and, second, the more specific terms, such as legislative, executive, and judicial. The former were the "pretended absolutes" to be abandoned. They were constructs which bore little visible relation to the process of government as it was generally observed. But the latter were not invisible; they appeared as real. They were concrete; they could be pointed to, observed, and touched. They could be examined for their operations. They were, after all, names of ongoing and working institutions that everyone knew existed. And in the context of pragmatism, what could be more logical, more natural, than to turn toward the *concreteness* of institutions, the *facts* of their existence, the character of their *actions,* and the *exercise* of their power. This was James's instruction to the pragmatic worker, and "institutionalism"—institutional economics, institutional sociology, institutional political science—was its product.

Perhaps this was a necessary beginning; it was an effort to offset the excesses of moral philosophy. But its consequences are especially important. To construct a field in terms of categories conceived of as concrete is immediately to congeal the field. Its tentative character is lost, and its form becomes rigid. The discipline itself, which guides those students who are professionally engaged in a continuing and more or less systematic study, tends to lose what it must be built upon—flexibility and initiative. Instead of consciously controlling its own efforts, it becomes imprisoned in the institutional activity it presumes to study. By establishing its categories as synonymous with real institutions,

Political Theory and Political Science

the practical problems of the institutions become the problems of the discipline. It is the institution which then sets the terms of inquiry; the discipline remains passively bound to its experiences, to the claims it imposes, and to the behavior it manifests. Under such circumstances the ordering process is already done for us.[6] We follow familiar forms as they appear to us, as they seemingly are. We accept their outlines and we are left to pile fact upon fact and case upon case. We do this quite carefully, footnoting, documenting, exercising great care in our observation; we pay close heed to all save the categories that structure our observation. These, in typical common-sense fashion, we take for granted, as we do the field itself. It exists as a matter of convention and its domain becomes more a problem of jurisdiction than of theoretic construction.

A field so constituted lends itself to ready fragmentation. When conceptual categories are reified, they are endowed with an objective character. They become concrete things, with a completeness that enables them to exist in their own right.[7] The executive becomes an entity wholly separate from the legislature or the party. Fragmentation is almost automatic, because each of the specialities that arises can also be deemed to have a separate existence. Although we are prone to bestir ourselves these days over the "fractionization" of our fields, we should note that in their origins few presented any theoretical center. Political science, for instance, can be represented as an association of concrete categories tied together by custom and metaphor.[8] The first presidential address to the American Political

---

[6] Robert Merton, *Social Theory and Social Structure* (Glencoe: Free Press, 1957), Ch. 1. See Merton's suggestion as to the use of "latent functional analysis" in this respect (p. 65).

[7] See W. Donald Oliver, *Theory of Order* (Yellow Springs, Ohio: Antioch Press, 1951), Ch. 13.

[8] On the use of the term *metaphor* see Chapter 3 of this book. See also Richard C. Sheldon, "Some Observations on Theory in the Social Sciences" in Talcott Parsons and Edward A. Shils (eds.), *Toward a General Theory of Action* (Cambridge: Harvard University Press, 1951).

Science Association by Frank Goodnow presents a statement of purpose, but no theoretic stipulation as to the nature of the politics. Politics, on the contrary, was defined through pointing operations; beyond political philosophy and jurisprudence, it consisted of law (constitutional, administrative, international), legislation, the executive, the party, and the like. This system of organization, necessary as a beginning, invites separatism; it warrants the rise of many subspecialities, each corresponding to an institution, and makes it entirely logical for any specialty to claim an independent status.

Some twenty-five years later John Fairlie, again in a presidential address, summed up intervening developments as to the scope of the field by noting the establishment of public administration as a branch of political science.[9] As might be expected, the claim to independence has been asserted for a number of decades. And although it may be regarded by tradition as a division of political science, Waldo has described public administration as a general academic discipline which bears a semi-autonomous relationship to political science. Ironically enough, public administration as a general academic discipline has had to resist a strong splintering tendency that derives from its component elements.[10]

The Subject Matter

"Public administration," then, is a concept that must be presumed to possess a set of defining characteristics. It is also the name of an academic-professional field of inquiry whose whole reason for being, logically speaking, is to engage in a disciplined study of that subject matter specified by the concept itself. What,

[9] John Fairlie, "Political Developments and Tendencies," *American Political Science Review*, Vol. 24 (February 1930). Fairlie refers to Goodnow's address in his statement.

[10] Dwight Waldo, *Political Science in the United States of America* (Paris: UNESCO, 1956), p. 68. See also Roscoe Martin, "Political Science and Public Administration," *American Political Science Review*, Vol. 46 (September 1952).

Political Theory and Political Science

one may ask, is the definition of public administration? What is the nature of its subject matter? How is it distinguished from other fields? How, for example, is it to be differentiated from political science?

The analytic function of a definition is to expose the principal features of a concept (or a field), thereby making it definite and precise; in this manner we delimit it from other concepts and make possible a systematic exploration of the subject matter with which it is to deal. Concepts structure our field of observation. When defined adequately they provide an immediate standard of relevance that permits a controlled and selective focus. Without such standards, it is obvious, no subject matter can be identified. Without a subject matter, no empirical field exists Accordingly, our definitions must be taken seriously.[11] But are they?

A classical text tells us that, generally speaking, "among those who have written basic treatises in the field, there is a substantial agreement on what public administration is." The text cites in support the definitions of such leading scholars as W. F. Willoughby, Luther Gulick, Marshall Dimock, Leonard White, and John Pfiffner.[12] Aside from the technical adequacy of these defi-

---

[11] Morris R. Cohen and Ernest Nagel, *An Introduction to Logic and Scientific Method* (New York: Harcourt, Brace & World, 1934), pp. 231–232. See also Chapter 12. And see John Hospers, *An Introduction to Philosophic Analysis* (Englewood Cliffs, N.J.: Prentice-Hall, 1953), Chapter 1, for an excellent discussion of lexical and stipulative definitions. With respect to the use of the latter in scientific inquiry, see Marion J. Levy, Jr., "Methodological Difficulties in Social Science," *Journal of the Philosophy of Science*, Vol. 17 (October 1950), and Gustav Bergmann, *Philosophy of Science* (Madison: University of Wisconsin Press, 1957), pp. 48–67.

[12] Marshall E. Dimock, Gladys O. Dimock, and Louis W. Koenig, *Public Administration* (New York: Holt, Rinehart & Winston, 1958), pp. 11–12. As the text quotes them, (1) for Willoughby, the "administrative function is the function of actually administering the law as declared by the legislative and interpreted by the judicial branches of government"; (2) for Gulick, it "has to do with getting things done; with the accomplishment of defined objectives"; (3) for Dimock, it "is concerned with the 'what' and the 'how' of government. The 'what' is the subject-matter, the

nitions, the matter of time alone should give pause. They reflect the history of public administration in its three major stages, each distinguishable by a difference in scope and content.[13] Willoughby's statement was written when an emerging field was confined, quite narrowly, to management practice and procedure.[14] Dimock and Gulick wrote in 1937 when the field had been set firm on the politics-administration dichotomy and had structured itself in terms of POSDCORB. The postwar formulations of White and Pfiffner (both were written in the 1950's) reflect the new "public policy" orientation—the conception of administration as a political process. In each case the range and type of data varies, the sharpest change to be seen between the definitions of the 1930's and those of the 1950's; a change easily visible when one contrasts the earlier texts of White and Pfiffner with their postwar revisions.

Public Policy: The Disintegration of a Field

The postwar definitions have given rise to a set of problems that challenge the integrity of the "field." These, designed to counteract the rigidities of the politics-administration dichotomy, are so extensive as to provide little meaning. They make it virtually impossible to specify an area of activity that cannot be considered within the scope of administration. Yet, in context, it is quite clear that White and Pfiffner restrict their reference to government. We are then presented, however, with an area of interest that embraces the entire range of governmental activity.

---

technical knowledge of a field which enables an administrator to perform his tasks. The 'how' is the techniques of management, the principles according to which cooperative programs are carried through to success. . . . Together they form the synthesis called administration . . ."; (4) for White, "public administration consists of all those operations having for their purpose the fulfillment or enforcement of public policy"; (5) and for Pfiffner, public administration is "the coordination of collective efforts to implement public policy."

13 See Waldo, UNESCO, op. cit., pp. 67–70, and Martin, op. cit., pp. 666–672.

14 The Dimock text uses the 1936 edition. The first edition was published in 1919. The formulations are the same in both.

Political Theory and Political Science

Legislatures, executives, courts, parties, and the bureaucracy all "perform operations having for their purpose the fulfillment or enforcement of public policy." It is their "collective efforts" that are to be coordinated; and this constitutes one of the traditional problems of political science. Such definitions, therefore, make it impossible to fix the center of the field—the core of subject matter that is to be of primary concern. The field of public administration is left with an imprecise and shifting base, indistinguishable from political science. By these definitions, public administration is neither a subfield of political science, nor does it comprehend it; it simply becomes a synonym. In the effort to define the field, to make it "definite," the field evaporates.

The Dimock-Koenig text provides further illustration of this. It too rests on the postwar conception of the administrative process as an integral part of the political process. Whether the administrative is a part of the political, or vice versa, depends on definition, but there can be no question that the behaviors which these concepts specify, whatever they may be, are empirically related. Our task, however, is to differentiate these classes of behavior for purposes of analysis. How, in other words, does this text establish the focal points of difference between two concepts which are in current use as the names of academic fields, politics and administration. The text is, after all, a work in *public administration;* it addresses itself to a special subject matter; and it attempts to present the cumulative product of the field.

But we should note, as a matter of caution, that textbooks are quite unsystematic and this one is no exception. It does, however, attempt some definitional clarity, and scattered throughout the introductory chapters are a series of formulations that serve to highlight our problem. We are told that

> by politics is meant everything government does in the way of determining public policy, largely by gauging the pressure of interest groups upon the whole of government, administration included.

Political Science and Public Administration

. . . .

Public policy is the reconciliation and crystallization of the views and wants of many people and groups in the body social. . . . The reconciliation of diverse interests in the public interest is a joint undertaking by both legislative and executive branches, and the crystallization occurs when a law is passed. . . . Then when the law is executed, it is the public administrator who is primarily involved, . . . [but] in a complex age such as ours, legislation cannot be sufficiently detailed to cover every contingency; hence government officials must exercise a considerable discretion, not only in the execution of a law but also in its interpretation.

. . . .

laws now also increasingly originate in the executive departments, many of which have established formal administrative machinery for that purpose.

. . . .

the administrator has a continuing interest in legislative policy. He must sponsor the legislation he needs, . . . and follow and try to influence all other legislation that might affect his own program. In addition, much modern legislation is merely general and permissive, leaving the details to be filled in by the administrator. . . . This gives rise to sublegislation . . . having the force and effect of law. Many modern statutes require the administrator to act as a kind of judge, to hear and decide cases.

and finally,

Administration makes policy, initiates legislation, amplifies legislation, represents pressure groups, acts as a pressure group itself, and is caught up in many ways in the tug of war between the two major parties.[15]

This position is dwelt upon not for its empirical validity but because of its logical consequences. It establishes the Presidency and the bureaucracy as the unifying agencies of government; it

---

15 See Dimock, Dimock, and Koenig, op. cit., pp. 36; 3-4; 37; 38; 36 respectively.

confirms the "presidential system" as it refutes "separation of powers." It does away with the politics-administration dichotomy. But it also serves to depreciate any claim to independence that public administration may advance; i.e., it drains public administration of any distinctive subject matter and moves it right back to the center of political science. The images it evokes have a long history in political science, the relationships drawn involve its traditional categories of analysis, and the subject matter denoted has been particular to political science since its inception. The definition which the text offers—"as a study, public administration examines every aspect of government's efforts to discharge the laws and to give effect to public policy"[16]—leads in this context directly to the executive. Logically enough, Dimock, Dimock and Koenig have written a text on the executive; on the role and function of the presidency, its organization, and the organization, operation, and management of the bureaucracy. It is no inaccuracy to suggest that this is a text on American government that takes its form in terms of the centrality of the presidency in matters of public policy. This, apparently, is the public administration approach to government.

Public Administration and the Executive

The suggestion that the field of public administration has now been constituted in terms of the executive would probably meet initially with considerable protest. Yet if we define the field operationally there is substantial basis for this conclusion. That is, if we simply assume that public administration is what students of public administration study, the executive is clearly the solid center of their special concern. In constructing a field of study, students of public administration have appropriated the executive from political science. It is, of course, entirely consistent with the institutional base, the concrete categories, of political science to make the executive a separate field. But if we think of the

---

16 Ibid., p. 12.

legislature, the judiciary, the executive, or the party as "political" institutions, it is because each of these shares the defining characteristics of the larger concept (political) which subsumes them. To withdraw the executive from the political without a reconceptualization of the latter, and to establish it as the distinctive domain of public administration, will have to be explained on other than logical or intellectual grounds. Nevertheless, this has happened.

We might, in this respect, consider the Committee on Public Administration Cases. In preparing its program it had to set limits; hence it had to be concerned with definition. Definition, it stated, is an act of exclusion, it delimits the area under investigation. And,

> the area selected for investigation by the CPAC is approximately the area *conventionally denoted by "public administration"* as the phrase is used within, and applied to, the United States; it is the area roughly coterminous with the executive branches of the federal, state, and local governments in the United States.[17]

What is interesting here is that this definition, given its timing, rests upon the principle of separation of powers. The case studies themselves clearly reflect the general repudiation of the politics-administration dichotomy. They are constructed in terms of the policy aspects of administration, that is, of the executive branch. But to delineate a field in terms of the executive can provide a "disciplined" focus only as long as a sharp separation of power and function exists. As long as each of the branches of government has a sufficiently clear-cut set of operations of its own, a field can be delimited. Stein has noted that

> in studies dealing with local governments . . . where the formal separation of powers has been subjected to overt modification or abandonment, the area for inquiry lacks precise delimitation; and the spheres

---

[17] Harold Stein, "Preparation of Case Studies," *American Political Science Review*, Vol. 45 (June 1951), pp. 479–480. Emphasis added.

of the executive and legislative branches in international organizations are even more amorphous.[18]

But the formal separation of power has little descriptive validity even at the national level. Dimock reminds us that the executive branch is characterized by legislative and judicial functions as well. The consequence, therefore, of a public administration constructed in terms of the executive is that it must spill over all of the traditional categories of politics. To follow the executive may be a matter of practical concern, but it cannot lay down a basis for a disciplined field of inquiry. The field of public administration is just as amorphous at the national level as in the international area.

Public Administration: Interest or Field?

The definition of public administration and its status as a field has also occupied Frederick C. Mosher. Is there a field of public administration,[19] he has asked; is there such a discipline? If so, what is its scope, its rubric, its method? Consider Mosher's statement:

I am not sure that either question can be answered. Public administration has a genetic, still a logical, and in most academic places an organizational relationship to political science. It is always vaguely and sometimes intimately related to business administration. It has cross-interests with virtually all the other social sciences. . . . Public administration cannot demark any subcontinent as its exclusive province—unless it consists of such mundane matters as classifying budget expenditures, drawing organization charts, and mapping procedures. In fact, it would appear that any definition of this field would be either so encompassing as to call forth the wrath or ridicule

---

18 Ibid.
19 It is most instructive to note John C. Honey's observation that at the 1957 meetings of the American Society for Public Administration "a common pool of understanding was lacking with regard to what public administration is and whether it is a separate field. . . ." (op. cit.).

Political Science and Public Administration

of others, or so limiting as to stultify its own disciples. *Perhaps it is best that it not be defined. It is more an area of interest than a discipline, more a focus than a separate science.* Like administration itself, the study of administration must employ a variety of methods and approaches. It is necessarily cross-disciplinary. The overlapping and vague boundaries should be viewed as a resource, even though they are irritating to some with orderly minds.[20]

Irritating orderly minds is of minor concern. Rather, it is the domain of public administration that is at issue. Mosher himself has expressed fear that "the field" is in danger. He too states that its scope is so broad as almost to defy classification, that its research is random and scattered, that it can boast few correlations, syntheses, or summaries of findings. But the lack of cumulative findings is a result of unchanneled research, a condition that readily occurs when the scope of interest is so broad as to be undisciplined. To suggest, then, that administration is more an area of interest than a discipline is difficult to comprehend. To state that it is best not to define not only begs the issue but implies waiving claim to the status of a disciplined field—a move which Mosher is obviously not ready to make. On the contrary, he proposes to avoid a "senescence into mere dilettantism" through "premises and hypotheses that are in some degree ordered and tested." But this can be achieved only by conceiving of public administration as a disciplined area of interest, as a field of scientific focus. The great creative effort, then, is to provide public administration with the kind of structured relevance that enables sustained and disciplined analysis. If, as Mosher has indicated, the profession does not exhibit continuity in research, a rigorous methodology, or paradigms, theorems, and theoretical systems, it is precisely because, in his phrase, it has been "pretty blasé about definitions." It is by definition that we initially fix a field of inquiry and structure a domain. Not to meet this problem squarely,

[20] "Research in Public Administration," *Public Administration Review,* Vol. 16 (Summer 1956), p. 177. Emphasis added.

Political Theory and Political Science

difficult as it is, can only result in a scope of interest so unlimited as to produce a subject matter that defies discipline and order as it reflects babel and confusion.

It may be asserted that, by their nature, fields cannot be constructed without overlap; that boundaries cannot be cut with hard and fast precision. Completeness, or formalization, is indeed a characteristic of theories, not of fields. Nevertheless, it is not only possible but it is a requirement of systematic and disciplined inquiry that a common unifying center be established. Unlike such formal disciplines as logic and mathematics which consist of analytic or nonfactual statements, public administration is empirical in character; as a field it must rest on a body of factual knowledge which is distinctive though not exclusive. Our problem, then, is to fix the common center—the primitive facts that the field is all about. It is the center of a field that is most crucial and, in Waldo's phrase, requires the hardest sort of intellectual work.

At the present time, if we follow Sayre, a consensus seems to be developing around the following themes: that public administration is a major political process; that organization theory is a problem in political strategy; that public administration, bound to sets of cultural values, is ultimately a problem in political (democratic) theory.[21] If these are the central premises of the discipline, and the strength of the "public policy" approach indicates that they are, then it is clear that public administration now "finds its chief satisfaction in providing a way of looking at government."[22]

Simon, the Field, and the Dichotomies

In the first flush of enthusiasm for "public policy," we may recall that Herbert Simon cautioned that by this path public

---

21 Wallace S. Sayre, "Premises of Public Administration," *Public Administration Review*, Vol. 17 (Spring 1958), pp. 102–105.

22 Martin, op. cit., p. 672.

administration must lose its identity as a separate field. Because its goal is the solution of practical problems, it cannot recognize the limits of a field established for purposes of academic specialization. It must range as far as its problems take it. It cannot ignore anything that is relevant to public policy, be it the theory of sovereignty or of representation: "nor can it stop when it has swallowed the whole of political science; it must attempt to absorb economics and sociology, as well." The public policy approach stands as applied social science.[23]

Contrary to some rather mistaken impressions, Simon did not reject this movement as inconsequential. But he did urge the possibility and the desirability of a scientific field which focused upon behavior in organization, and in government organization in particular. Here the goal is to understand the nature of this behavior and not to prescribe for public policy. With respect to the latter, applied social scientists might well find the resultant propositions of an administrative science to be quite useful to their purposes. The two developments may proceed side by side, but one must keep clearly in mind the area he proposes to work in, and the set of goals which govern his work.

Simon's efforts have met with a curious reception. Few books in administration have aroused as much passion as *Administrative Behavior* (Macmillan, 1947). A review of the second edition spoke of the "straining and the pretense," and concluded that it "was a better book ten years ago than it is now."[24] Although the reactions to this volume have been mixed, it is evident that Simon's work has been talked about and thought about; perhaps more talked about than thought about. In my own view, it represents a powerful contribution to a "field" of public administration —a contribution all the more significant in the face of the general disorganization which has occurred. Simon was trying to redefine

---

[23] Herbert Simon, "A Comment on 'The Science of Public Administration'," *Public Administration Review*, Vol. 7 (Summer 1947), p. 202.

[24] Edward C. Banfield, "The Decision-Making Scheme," *Public Administration Review*, Vol. 17 (Autumn 1957).

Political Theory and Political Science

public administration so as to give it a "solid center," a standard of relevance, a set of operating concepts—to make it, in short, a "field" of inquiry. This was the function of the decision-making scheme.

The crux of the objection to Simon's work, aside from the usual criticisms of logical positivism,[25] is that by separating fact and value in decision-making he has produced "a new and subtle version of the earlier formulation of the separation of policy from administration."[26] Actually, Simon was trying to clarify these concepts, but in any case we would do well to review this ancient dichotomy. I quite agree with Fesler[27] that one cannot now make a useful career of harassing the ghosts of Wilson and Goodnow: there is still too much to be learned from them.

The Politics-Administration Dichotomy: Another Look

The original formulation was introduced into academic political science by Frank Goodnow, although it is to be found in the writings of Thomas Paine.[28] Goodnow, along with Woodrow Wilson, represents the first clear break with the a priori rationalism of late nineteenth-century political science. In typical pragmatic style, they resorted to the test of experience and plunged into the study of how government actually worked. This is the

[25] Most of these references are quite unfortunate; aside from the question of competence, they serve to impute to Simon more than is the case. But, even more importantly, they have diverted attention from the substantial contributions of Simon's work.

[26] Wallace S. Sayre, "Trends of a Decade in Administrative Values," *Public Administration Review,* Vol. 11 (Winter 1951), p. 5.

[27] James Fesler, "Administrative Literature and the Second Hoover Commission Reports," *American Political Science Review,* Vol. 51 (March 1957), p. 139.

[28] Paine, in the *Rights of Man,* objected to the classical separation of powers as an effective principle of government. His classification rested on what we now call politics and administration. In government there were two primary functions—legislating or enacting law and executing or administering law. The judicial function was to be classified as executive. See Raymond G. Getell, *History of American Political Thought* (New York: Appleton-Century, 1928), pp. 102–103.

Political Science and Public Administration

meaning of Wilson's famous paper on administration.[29] Such study led Goodnow to reject the descriptive validity of separation of powers. The activities of government could not be accurately classified under the traditional triad; rather, there were in all governments two primary or ultimate functions—politics and administration. Politics consisted of those operations necessary to express the will of the state, administration of those necessary to execute that will.

This was the reformulation that provided the logical foundations for a "field" of public administration. What we tend to forget is that Goodnow was engaged in "abstractive differentiation." He was not making concrete distinctions; i.e., he was not distinguishing branches of government nor was he equating a given operation with a given agency—as Willoughby and so many others have done. He was differentiating behavior. His original formulations cut across the concrete institutions of government, abstracted certain sets of behavior, and made them the basis for study. He stated quite clearly that although the operations or functions which government performed could be conceptualized (differentiated) in terms of policy and administration, the authorities (concrete agencies) to which such operations were entrusted could not be completely separated: the empirical processes of politics were far too complex to be discharged by any single governmental body and, similarly, administrative functions could not be deemed exclusive to any specific agency. Though not too clear, perhaps, Goodnow's distinctions were conceptual in character.[30] Each concept referred to a different class of behavior and each presented a different set of problems. A field of administration could be distinguished from political science because it focused upon a different subject matter. If, as did happen, the abstract character of Goodnow's distinction was

---

29 Wilson, op. cit., *Political Science Quarterly*, Vol. 56.
30 Frank Goodnow, *Politics and Administration* (New York: Macmillan, 1900), see Chapters 1, 2, and 4.

Political Theory and Political Science

lost, this still does not negate the fact that the founder of the field maintained a logically consistent position in contrast to contemporary movements which have repudiated this distinction, returned administration to politics, yet still insist on maintaining it as a separate domain of inquiry.

I am not arguing now in defense of the old dichotomy, or even for the retention of the two terms. But the greater portion of discussion devoted to these concepts has not had to do with their effectiveness as analytic tools. If, as Sayre suggests, the most orthodox texts have had to yield ground on the separability of politics and administration, it is precisely because these terms have been employed not as concepts but as the names of institutions. In concretizing the concept of administration, equating it with a given branch or agency of government, a dichotomy was formed that was inevitably to be repudiated. That is, if the original concepts were only partially adequate, and if they were retained at all, even implicitly, it was only a matter of time for it to be observed that *the* administration (the executive departments) also exhibited behavior presumed to be political. Hence the sharp swing away, not from the concept "administration," but from the effects of "misplaced concreteness." Had careful consideration been given to the analytic character of these concepts in the first place, had they not been confused with "real types," the sharp swing which has occurred would probably not have been necessary. The concepts would have been tested consistently; modified, qualified, and perhaps replaced as more effective analytic instruments were developed. As it is, the general repudiation has not helped much: politics and administration are still key terms, they remain in wide use as the names of things, and we stumble over them fully as much as before.

In fact, the notion of repudiation is somewhat misleading. Because both the orthodox and the public policy advocates work with real types, they employ the same institution as the prime category of analysis—the executive. The differences, therefore, are not so sharp as is ordinarily thought. In both cases the executive has been divided into an internal (technical-instrumental) sector and an external (political) sector. This, historically, is the classic separation of the orthodox. But it is also the essence of the distinction that Harold Stein has made in attempting to differentiate a "process" administration from a "politics" administration. After arduous effort to clarify these terms, Stein concludes that "process is more manageable if it is applied only to the internal functioning of public administration," while "public administration as politics . . . is given an external orientation."[31] The differences between the old and the new, then, are primarily geographical, not conceptual. Whereas the domain of the orthodox was restricted to the internal operations of the executive branch, the public policy advocates have conceived of the field as embracing both the internal and external sectors; i.e., "the whole contribution of the executive branch."[32] The essential categories of the orthodox, politics and administration, have been retained. What has been repudiated is the notion that they are empirically separable. In the context of public policy they have now been placed in some kind of interrelationship—one which Goodnow observed some sixty years ago! And it was only a quarter of a century ago that Luther Gulick described the politics-administration dichotomy as a matter of specialization, of "division of labor" in the interest of "better results."[33] Although this statement was made in the context of the practical world of everyday affairs, its principle holds here: if we had kept clear the distinction between a disciplined, scientific inquiry and the sphere of public policy, the concepts of politics and administration would have been more readily understood "as the appli-

[31] Stein, op. cit., pp. xiii–xv.

[32] See Paul Appleby, *Big Democracy* (New York: Knopf, 1945), p. viii.

[33] Luther Gulick, "Politics, Administration and the New Deal," *Annals,* Vol. 169 (September 1933), p. 63.

cation of the principle of specialization. . . ." The two concepts would not have been reified and there would have been no need to "repudiate" them.

The Fact-Value Business

To return to Simon's treatment of this problem, we must emphasize again that to employ these terms, politics and administration, or process and politics, is to refer to two conceptually distinct sets of behavior. Moreover, as long as we use them, we suggest that they are either different aspects of the same system of action, or different systems. If we state, therefore, that politics and administration are related, we mean to indicate the existence of an empirical relationship between the referents of both concepts. The trouble is, as Simon has put it (and he is one of the few who has actually subjected these concepts to careful scrutiny), that their referents are not clear enough to be useful for purposes of inquiry. They have never been defined, either by Goodnow or anyone else, so as to present clear-cut criteria that would enable a policy question to be distinguished from an administrative question. "Apparently it has been assumed that the distinction is self-evident—so self-evident as hardly to require discussion."[34]

In Simon's scheme, decision-making is the heart of administration. A decision is defined as a conclusion drawn from a set of premises. Premises are of two kinds: factual and ethical. Because factual statements are empirical propositions, they are testable against experience. But ethical (value) statements make no such claims and cannot be empirically validated. They are neither true nor untrue in any empirical sense.

Simon's purpose in stressing this distinction was to make clear the "different criteria of 'correctness' that must be applied to the ethical and factual elements in a decision."[35] The rules of scien-

34 *Administrative Behavior*, op. cit., p. 54.
35 Ibid., p. 53.

Political Science and Public Administration

tific procedure, most particularly the rule of observation, cannot warrant ethical judgments. If we follow Felix Kaufman,[36] value judgments are analytic propositions. If they are deemed correct, it is because they are in accord with a set of presupposed axiological rules.[37] "Oughts" are derived in terms of such rules, and are not deducible from the "is." Different criteria of correctness apply in each case.

Simon employs this distinction to clarify policy and administration. In Goodnow's usage, as well as today, politics has to do with the expression of goals or ends, with the basic question of social policy and, thus, with value judgments. There is, says Simon, no scientific way of making such judgments. But with respect to administration, Goodnow referred to a class of activities that differed in character from politics and could be freed very largely from the control of political bodies. This class "is unconnected with politics because it embraces fields of semiscientific, quasi-judicial, quasi-business or commercial activity—work which has little if any influence on the expression of the true state will." In this formulation, Simon notes, there is an attempt by Goodnow "to segregate a class of decisions which do not require external control *because they possess an internal criterion of correctness.*"[38] The difference in the criteria of correctness, in the grounds for judgment, forms the basis of the line usually drawn between questions of policy and of administration. If, states Simon, it is desired to retain the terms "policy" and "ad-

36 Felix Kaufman, *Methodology of the Social Sciences* (New York: Oxford University Press, 1944), Chapters 9 and 15.

37 For those who have followed the Waldo-Simon debates, I would suggest that this is the basis of Simon's statement that "Democratic institutions find their principal justification as a procedure for the validation of value judgments." Ibid., p. 56. See also Waldo's reply to Simon in *American Political Science Review*, Vol. 46 (June 1952), pp. 501–503.

38 Ibid., p. 55. Emphasis added. Goodnow's quotation is also cited by Simon.

ministration," they can best be applied to a division of the decisional functions along these lines.[39]

This is the "separation" that has met with continued objection and which has given rise to the statement that Simon's position is empirically unsound; in the real-life process of decision-making fact and value are organically related and thus incapable of separation. But, again, failure to recognize the analytic character of Simon's formulations is responsible for such interpretations. Simon was not defying reality, but trying to distinguish its various and essential components—in much the same manner as Goodnow before him. Certain characteristics of the decision process were isolated and made central for *purposes of analysis* only. *Administrative Behavior* itself represents an attempt to construct a rational model of decision-making, to develop a set of concepts that would permit empirically valid descriptions of administrative situations.

Whether Simon's model will prove adequate to its task—a theory of administration—is an empirical question. There can be, however, no doubt as to his treatment of fact and value, and to its purpose. They were, as concepts must be, defined and delimited; the ground upon which this was done was made quite explicit. Their relationship to a decision was also made clear: decisions have both an ethical and factual component. The relevance of this formulation to administration is to be seen in the purposive character of organization which functions to permit groups of individuals to achieve goals ordinarily beyond their individual reach. The concept of purposiveness involves the concept of a "hierarchy of decisions," a means-ends chain. Behavior in organization (a complex network of decision processes) is, therefore, "intendedly rational" in character, adjusted to the goals that have been erected. "Each decision involves the selection of a goal, and a behavior relevant to it; this goal may in turn be mediate to a somewhat more distant goal; and so on, until

[39] Ibid., pp. 58–60.

Political Science and Public Administration

a relatively final aim is reached." The relationship between means-ends and fact-value is this: insofar as decisions lead to the selection of final goals, they may be treated as "value judgments"—i.e., the value component predominates; insofar as they implement such goals, they may be treated as "factual judgments" —i.e., the factual component dominates.[40] The relationship of a decision to a set of ends remains, necessarily, a factual question.

In no case does Simon refer to "value decisions" and "factual decisions";[41] there are only premises and components. The essence of his system is the analysis of the premises upon which decisions are founded, and the sources from which these premises derive—a scheme which, if applied and developed, promises much scientific increment. Had Simon used these terms, his position would have been empirically unsound and tantamount to the old concrete separation of politics and administration. To admit of "value decisions" and "factual decisions" is to congeal two worlds, each having an independent existence of its own. It is a short march to equate each with a concrete branch of government; we would then be back to the old institutional separation. But this type of error is more to be associated with those whose work is characterized by "real" types, whose categories of analysis are "real" institutions, and whose problems are institutional problems—in short, with those who work in practical common-sense terms. The concretization of abstractions is a key feature of the common-sense world, and the ease with which this transformation is made is quite visible.

Simon's system of analysis, far from banishing values, makes it abundantly clear that in the practical, operating system of administration both value and factual elements are involved. Indeed, it is tautological to state that values are involved, because

---

[40] For further clarification, see Simon, op. cit., Chapter 3 and pp. 4–5, 52–53, 74–75 in particular.

[41] See Dwight Waldo, "Development of Theory of Democratic Administration," *American Political Science Review*, Vol. 46 (March 1952), pp. 97–98.

Political Theory and Political Science

administration is purposive by definition. In any event, throughout *Administrative Behavior* one finds the constant caution that in any system of action problems do not come wrapped in bundles with the value elements and the factual elements neatly sorted. On the contrary, "strict separation in practice is not possible." Finally, Simon holds that his analysis "exposes the fallacy of an argument that declares all [administrative] decisions to be factual as it refutes an argument that declares them all to be ethical."[42] If the first part of this statement refers to the weakness of an earlier period, the latter portion may well be pondered by the public policy advocates who, in their concern with values, frequently run the risk of pressing their position to this extent.

The Field of Public Administration

Any discussion of Simon, and of his contribution to a field, prompts a reference to that ubiquitous phenomenon in social science—the science-art controversy. On one hand, it is asserted that public administration is an art[43] and, as with Simon, that it may be a science. Moreover, this controversy, and its attendant confusions, has led to a good deal of acrimonious debate ("quarreling" is perhaps more accurate) which has more to do with the problem of professional status and self-identity than with the intellectual issues involved. In public administration the attempt to resolve this controversy has been through the assertion that the field has aspects of both.[44] But constant reference to the

---

42 Op. cit. See respectively pp. 5, 52, 57, and 56.
43 See Honey, op. cit.
44 But the "artistic" position not only commands the greatest following but continues to resist a "science." Thus Sayre writes of the "prophets" (Simon is their leader) who have "presented a new administrative science" and whose "claims of a new science . . . have not been widely accepted." *Premises,* op. cit., p. 104. It should be clear from the above discussion that no "claims" are involved. What is involved is a difference in perspective and goal—a difference I try to clarify in this section.

Political Science and Public Administration

"art and science of . . .," as Waldo puts it, can only serve confusion because it reflects "a desire to bypass the definitional problems, to compromise the issues by yielding to both sides. . . ." This controversy, however, does not constitute a real issue. It arises because of the usual failure to distinguish the "systematic study" of public administration from the actual "practice of public administration."[45] The problem is more appropriately stated in terms of practical (applied) versus theoretical (scientific) goals of inquiry.

Practical and Theoretical Inquiry

Logically speaking, there is no reason to consider these pursuits to be in conflict. On the contrary, they may proceed side by side to their mutual advantage, provided the ends involved are kept clear and separate. But this condition has not been met; as a result, practical inquiry (which equates with the public policy approach) and theoretical inquiry (which equates with a "science" of administration) have been placed in opposition to each other, most frequently by the public policy advocates. On the assumption that inquiry which remains closest to practical problems will do more for the solution of these problems than inquiry which remains at a distance, scientific analysis is often depreciated because of its lack of immediate social relevance; hence the

---

45 Dwight Waldo, *The Study of Administration* (New York: Doubleday, 1955), pp. 2–4. Waldo is very clear on this distinction. To illustrate the failure to make this distinction, note the following from Dimock, Dimock and Koenig: "Public administration is part of the larger field of general administration, which is a study of how all kinds of institutions are organized, staffed, financed, motivated, and managed. But public administration is also part of the political process in that administration in government is related to political parties and their programs, and shares in the methods by which public policy is determined. As the offspring of these two parent subjects—management and politics—the study of public administration is complicated but enlivened by the fact that the administrative process is an integral part of the political process of the nation." Op. cit., p. 4. See also Sayre, *Premises,* op. cit.

prevailing "suspicion that the purer a science of administration, the less will it be socially relevant."[46] Given the primacy of practical goals, discussion also takes the form, if obliquely, that practical inquiry is morally superior to that of scientific inquiry. Historically, practical needs have doubtless stimulated scientific inquiry; nor should the latter be divorced from practice. On the contrary, "this world of everyday life is indeed the . . . questionable matrix within which all our inquiries start and end."[47]

Once scientific inquiry is begun, however, practical goals recede into the background. Such inquiry develops a logic of its own, a specific methodology and its own standards of relevance. The more it expands, "the more it strives toward autonomy in the setting of its problems."[48] What may be stated, then, is that these are two different but related types of inquiry; they differ in their goals, in the questions they ask, and in the problems they pose. Nor need it be the case that the closer we stay to the practical world, the better we serve its needs. History is replete with illustrations of the impact of the results of scientific inquiry on this world. Without placing the two in any causal sequence, we may note, with Kaufman, that practical-applied inquiry logically presupposes scientific inquiry: in the attainment of a practical goal it is the results (findings) of scientific inquiry that are *applied*.

Further, as has been the case in public administration, a "practical" type of inquiry cannot constitute a field with any degree of

---

46 F. M. Marx, "A Closer View of Organization," *Public Administration Review*, Vol. 8 (Winter 1948), p. 65. See also Sayre, *Trends*, op. cit., p. 5; and Banfield, op. cit. The object in point in each case is Simon's work.

47 Alfred Shutz, "Symbol, Reality and Society" in L. Bryson, L. Finkelstein, H. Hoagland, and R. M. Maciver (eds.), *Symbols and Society* (New York: Harper & Row, 1955), p. 173.

48 See Kaufman, op. cit., p. 206. My discussion of this problem draws largely from Kaufman's formulations; see Chapter 15. Kaufman also suggests that given the present state of social science, it is unlikely that social scientists will pose their problems with as little attention to practical considerations as do astronomers for example. But by 1959, astronomical knowledge has created a new set of practical problems for the commonsense world.

Political Science and Public Administration

coherence and control. Such inquiry restricts itself to those considerations, immediate in nature, which have relevance and meaning only in terms of the common-sense world; i.e., that world which is common to our senses. In addition to the fact that it cannot be bound by the limits of a scientific field in the solution of its problems, its organizing premises are taken for granted, its assumptions remain implicit. I have already indicated the function of language in this respect. Our lexical vocabulary is not only ambiguous—perhaps a necessary condition for communication in the common-sense world—but it contains a host of unconscious assumptions about nature, society, behavior, and so forth. The language of ordinary life reflects the approved relevance system of the linguistic group. Hence it predetermines to a considerable extent what features of the world are important, what qualities of these features and what relations among them are deserving of attention, and what typifications, conceptualizations, and generalizations are relevant for achieving its purposes.[49] There is a "givenness" about the practical world that must pass into practical inquiry and that structures its observational categories. These categories are taken as real because they are deemed to be real; but their reality is that of daily life. In this system of relevance the reality of "the executive" cannot be denied; hence, the term itself, a "typical" term in that it refers to a set of properties, becomes the name of a thing (an office or institution) vested with all the implicitness, ambiguity, and complexity that is characteristic of "real" systems of action.

However adequate Harold Stein's statement that the administrative world is so complex, replete with so many variables and intangibles, as to offer "an incorrigible resistance to any highly systematic categorization," it must be understood in the relevance system of the common-sense world. If it is further suggested that administrative situations are so unique, so inherently disorderly that "every man is his own codifier and categorizer, and the

---

49 Shutz, *Symbols,* op. cit., pp. 194–195.

categories adopted must be looked on as relatively evanescent,"[50] one must conclude that thinking this way makes it pointless to talk of a field.

The Field and the Scientific Situation

But the problem of science cannot be dispatched in this fashion, and to try to do so is to confuse the two systems of goals, the practical and the scientific. Moreover, such assertions constitute a counsel of defeat to social scientists, "who by their very choice of profession are committed to persistent efforts to unravel the tangled skein of social relations."[51] The present categorical organization of social science reflected in its origin the epistemological foundations of modern sciences: it is a part of this movement and rests upon its presuppositions. The continued use of the concept "administration" as an ordering principle is indicative of our efforts to simplify the complexities of human behavior. Properly treated, it identifies a set of behaviors that constitute a fit subject for careful, systematic study. Hence, the development of a field. If not too large a measure of success has been achieved in public administration, this is primarily due to the failure to recognize that a field is a part of the scientific situation. It presupposes order and system. It is an instrumental construct which, through a process of selective perception, enables certain phases of human behavior to be isolated for scientific study.

Such abstractions are, as Shutz has put it, constructs of the second degree; constructs of the constructs made by the actors

---

[50] Stein, op. cit., pp. xx–xxvi. This is essentially the classic position of those who hold that the subjective, indeterminate character of human behavior establishes a qualitative difference between the social and natural sciences that does not permit scientific inquiry. For an effective reply to this position see Adolf Grunbaum, "Causality and the Science of Human Behavior" in Herbert Feigl and May Brodbeck (eds.), *Readings in the Philosophy of Science* (New York: Appleton-Century-Crofts, 1953). And see Chapter 1 of this book.

[51] Fesler, op. cit., pp. 139–140.

on the scene.[52] They are used not simply to learn more about the experiences of the actor, but in an attempt to reorganize this experience within a structure that enables their interconnections to be understood. These concepts are not to be locked into the vise of practicality; they are relevant to an enterprise which has as its goal a scientific knowledge of human behavior. With respect to the diversity and complexity of the real world, they enable us systematically to attack it—to disentangle the tangled skein. The concept remains, in Max Weber's phrase, "one of the great tools of scientific knowledge."

To construct a field in theoretic (as distinguished from practical) terms, to define it conceptually, as Simon has done, is entirely consistent with the presuppositions of a field. The effort to provide adequate linguistic and conceptual tools is more than an exercise in semantics; on the contrary, the existence of a language of administration that has been so vague and ambiguous as to make a mystery of its referents (and thus of its field of focus) makes it a necessary condition for any systematic analysis. If Simon has developed a grammar of administrative language, we should remember that the grammar of any language "is itself the shaper of ideas, the program and guide for the individual's mental activity, for his analysis of impressions, for his synthesis of his mental stock in trade."[53] To set the concept of decision-making at the center of administration, to define it with care and precision (as much precision as is possible at the moment), is to provide explicit principles of selection on the basis of which a subject matter is constituted and studied. A concept may be more or less general, more or less distant from a given set of empirical phenomena, but to be analytically useful it must be properly defined; there must be concrete phenomena or aspects of these phenomena which, whatever the level of abstraction, the criteria of definition

---

52 Shutz, *Common-Sense,* op. cit., p. 3.
53 Benjamin Lee Whorf, "Science and Linguistics" in John B. Carroll (ed.), *Language, Thought, and Reality* (New York: Wiley and the Technology Press, 1956), p. 212.

identify.[54] However else one may differ with Simon (his model is provisional and subject to much refinement), his system of analysis meets this condition and sets forth a basis for cumulative findings.

For this reason we may pause over Banfield's comment, on reviewing Simon, that "conceptual clarity, like other virtues, can be carried too far for this world."[55] I assume that "this world" is the common-sense world, but if the reference is to the field of public administration, then an excess of clear thinking need not concern us at the present stage of its development. To be sure, concepts are limiting devices. Care must always be exercised that they do not harden and rigidify—a danger that always results when we forget that an analytic construction is not a thing in a material sense. But if it is objected that a careful and precise delimitation deprives it of the surplus meanings of our lexical vocabulary—it is just such vocabularies that contain the greatest number of unconscious assumptions. The exploitation of Simon's model would contribute considerably to a structured field of inquiry.

Cooperative Rational Behavior and the Reconstruction of the Field

For these reasons, it is encouraging to observe the recent work of Dwight Waldo, in which administration is distinguished abstractively through the concept of "rational action." Waldo defines administration as cooperative human action marked by a high degree of rationality. Rational action is action designed to maximize the realization of goals. In this context, organization, by analogy, may be represented as the anatomical structure; management as the physiological process. Organization is "the structure of authoritative and habitual personal interrelations in an administrative system," and management is "action intended to

---

[54] Marion J. Levy, *The Structure of Society* (Princeton: Princeton University Press, 1952), p. 35. See Chapter 2 and pp. 226–237.

[55] Banfield, op. cit., p. 285.

Political Science and Public Administration

achieve rational cooperation" in the system. Public administration, thus, is a part of the larger field of cooperative human action, to be distinguished, if at all, by the special character of its goals (public), which Waldo attempts to clarify through structural-functional analysis and the culture concept.[56]

That Waldo's formulations share much with Simon, despite past differences, should be clear enough. In Simon's terms, administration has to do with complex interdependent systems of human behavior that exhibit a high degree of rational direction of behavior toward goals that are objects of common acknowledgment and expectation.[57] The similarity between the two extends even to the use of biological metaphor. Simon also speaks of anatomy and physiology; the former as the system of distribution and allocation of decision-making functions, the latter as the processes whereby the decisions of members are influenced, that is, supplied with decisional premises. Although there is some difference here as to formulation, their proximate nature remain clear; i.e., the formal distribution and allocation of decision-making functions constitutes a structure of sanctioned and regularized patterns of response, whereas the action intended to achieve rational behavior consists of influencing or supplying the necessary decisional premises. This is somewhat oversimplified; there are significant distinctions to be made in considering both.

But my point is to gloss over these differences in order to fix on two positions that seek, in similar terms, to reconstruct a field of public administration. In this respect, we may also call attention to Fred Riggs's work, the root of which is Chester Barnard's concept of "conscious coordinated activities."[58] Here is a striking

---

56 Waldo, *Study of Public Administration,* op. cit., Chapter 1.

57 See also Herbert A. Simon, "Comment on the Theory of Organizations," *American Political Science Review,* Vol. 46 (December 1952), and "Recent Advances in Organization Theory" in *Research Frontiers in Politics and Government* (Washington, D.C.: Brookings Institution, 1955).

58 "Agraria and Industria—Toward a Typology of Comparative Administration" in W. J. Siffin (ed.), *Toward the Comparative Study of Public Administration* (Bloomington: Indiana University Press, 1957). Note

convergence: a series of statements, developed over a twenty-year period, which set the concept of "cooperative rational behavior" at the center of the field.

It may now be said that this is a new field, with a different focus, and one that requires a rather profound shift in orientation and training. No doubt. It arises, however, because its organizing concepts are deemed to be of greater power. If it promises to eliminate the older conventions—this, in the logic of scientific inquiry, is as it should be. A field remains an instrument; its transformation into an end makes our efforts pointless.

We are, finally, still faced with the problem of clarifying the "public" nature of administration. This classification may turn out to be of limited effectiveness as far as its yield is concerned. The traditional distinction between a public and private sector— again an institutional distinction—might well be erased. In such an event, the field of public administration will evaporate—and that system of behavior which we usually refer to as public or governmental will be no more than a particular problem in administrative theory. One may hope so at any rate. For such a development will mean that we have advanced to "higher-order constructions" that explain far more than we were originally able to. In science, Max Weber tells us,

each of us knows that what he has accomplished will be antiquated in ten, twenty, fifty years. That is the fate to which science is subjected; it is the very *meaning* of scientific work. . . . Every scientific "fulfilment" raises new "questions"; it *asks* to be "surpassed" and outdated. Whoever wishes to serve science has to resign himself to this fact.[59]

---

also that Chester Barnard's book, *The Functions of the Executive,* was a major influence on Herbert Simon, and that Riggs in employing structural-functional analysis was following Waldo's suggestion.

59 Max Weber, "Science as a Vocation" in Logan Wilson and William L. Kolb (eds.), *Sociological Analysis* (New York: Harcourt, Brace & World, 1949), p. 7. Emphasis in original.

CHAPTER 8
Due Process of Inquiry

A Mere Matter of Words*

THE existence of a high degree of ambiguity in the ever expanding vocabularies of "natural languages" tends to obscure the fact that a linguistic system possesses a definite logic. It has a grammar, a syntax, and may be conceived of as a program—a set of rules that one is obliged to follow.

This formulation lies at the base of the Whorf-Sapir hypothesis—the principle of linguistice relativity. In capsule form, it states "that users of markedly different grammars are pointed by their grammars toward different types of observations and different evaluations of externally similar acts of observation . . ."[1] Whorf's principle refers to natural languages which carry the patterns of their respective cultures and as such contain the unconscious assumptions and concealed premises through which their users make contact with nature: the categories and concepts, the images and models of a natural language are the unquestioned "givens" that hold throughout a speech community. A natural

---

* As is generally the case in political science, I have taken "model" as a synonym for "theory" (although in a formal sense a model serves as the interpretation of a theory). My comment is directed to all types of models but I have chosen to bypass a discussion of mathematical models so as not to unduly complicate this chapter. For similar reasons, I have not extended discussion to include "idealized research models."

1 Benjamin Lee Whorf, *Collected Papers on Metalinguistics* (Washington, D.C.: U.S. Department of State, Foreign Service Institute, 1952), p. 11.

Reprinted, with modifications, by permission from Martin Landau, "Due Process of Inquiry," *American Behavioral Scientist*, Vol. 9, No. 2 (October 1965).

language lays down a "network of tracks"—a system of organization that fixes upon specified phases and features of reality as it ignores others (which may be featured by other languages). This system resists change: social and technological development will yield an enlarged and expanding vocabulary, rapid development will yield rapid expansions, but the basic structure of a linguistic system (which Sapir described as being self-contained) changes very slowly.[2] It thus permits a body of conventional and customary forms to be carried from one generation to another.

So, to Whorf, a linguistic system is not a simple reproducing instrument but "is itself the shaper of ideas, the program and guide for the individual's mental activity, for his analysis of impressions, for his synthesis of his mental stock in trade."[3] When we approach nature, "we organize it into concepts, and ascribe significances as we do" because we are parties to an agreement that pervades a speech community (culture) and which is codified in the language of that community. To speak a language is to follow the system of organization and classification of data which the language itself decrees. No member of a speech community is, therefore, free to describe nature as he pleases since he is constrained by the modes of interpretation impressed upon him by the language he uses.[4]

Technical and scientific languages are also programmatic. To be sure, they are deliberate constructions, ad hoc in the sense that they are designed for special purposes, and their categories and concepts, images and models are much more prone to conscious and deliberate evaluation, manipulation, revision, and rejection. They also constitute agreements, but they are not, as natural

[2] See Morris Swadesh, "Diffusional Cumulation and Archaic Residue as Historical Explanation," *Southwestern Journal of Anthropology*, Vol. 7 (1951), pp. 1–3.

[3] *Language, Thought and Reality, Selected Writings of Benjamin Lee Whorf*, J. B. Carroll (ed.) (New York: John Wiley & Sons, 1956), p. 212.

[4] Ibid., pp. 213–214. For a full discussion of the Whorf-Sapir hypothesis, including some relevant researches, see *Language in Culture*, Harry Hoijer (ed.) (Chicago: University of Chicago Press, 1958).

Due Process of Inquiry

languages, implicit and unstated agreements into which a person is born. Those who become parties to this "contract" elect to do so and when they are taught the language they learn a vocabulary, a set of formal rules that make up its grammar, and the ground upon which these rules are warranted. Such languages are less resistant to change: indeed, both their vocabulary and structure are always in a state of revision—sometimes quite radical, depending on the pace and extent of change in the science. Some languages have very precise vocabularies and very strict rules. Others have a more ambiguous vocabulary and less formal sets of rules. Whatever the case, the user of a scientific language is bound to its terms and conditions in fully as obligatory a manner as is the member of a natural speech community. Perhaps more so. Because the rules of a scientific language are explicitly formulated, the obligations they impose are relatively clear. And where they are not, the members of this linguistic community will make every effort to clarify them. It is a clear statement of the grammatical rules of a scientific language which, upon any reflection, sanctions the use of the language. A sometime violation of a rule constitutes an error: but a general disregard of its rules and regulations transforms the language into nonsense. To use a mathematical language, for example, is to abide by its rules: not to abide by its rules is not to use mathematics.

Scientific languages free us from the restraints of the vernacular. They uncover the concealed premises and unconscious assumptions of a natural language. They transform the "givens" of the common-sense world into problematical questions. They allow for a much greater autonomy in the selection of observational categories. And they provide new concepts, new images, and new models. But they also impose their own constraints. They are ordered systems which fix upon selected features of reality as they ignore others.

With this in mind, we may turn to the problem of theory and research in political science—an adventure that cannot be contemplated with any sense of ease.

The Languages of Politics

Consider now some of the language of political science. One may read, as follows:

Congress is inevitably the Old Frontier. Congress is the defensive stockade, not the pioneering scout. It is an old stockade, under the command of seasoned veterans. Its manual of arms is traditional and wily. Its defensive capacity is impressive. And this defensive capacity is directly related to the age, experience, and continuity of the institution and its commanding officers.[5]

And what is it that the Congressional stockade is defending? Well, it defends itself, it defends freedom, and it "defends a set of interests, institutions, and individuals which are frequently alien to the national interest as viewed by the President."[6] It defends against the Presidency.

We like to use military metaphor these days and this language evokes some vivid imagery. It reminds us of scenes we have often observed on television: a frontier stockade under attack and able to defend itself against enemies on all sides. Sometimes the stockade falls, however. But the point of this representation seems clear: the Congress is a defensive agency, neither aggressive nor pioneering, and it stands against the press of the Presidency.

Yet if we turn to another writer, the Presidency is "truly a fortress perpetually under siege."[7] And it is besieged by administrative subordinates, seekers after patronage, pressure groups, and—here we pause—legislators. The metaphor is still military but the relationship has been reversed. Now it is the legislator who

[5] Stephen K. Bailey, "Is Congress the Old Frontier" in *Continuing Crisis in American Politics,* Marian D. Irish (ed.) (Englewood Cliffs, N.J.: Prentice-Hall, 1963), p. 68.

[6] Ibid., p. 71.

[7] Louis W. Koenig, "Foreign Aid to Spain and Yugoslavia" in *The Uses of Power,* Alan F. Westin (ed.) (New York: Harcourt, Brace & World, 1962), p. 75.

Due Process of Inquiry

presses against the Presidency and it is the Presidency that resists attack.[8]

Such representations are not novel. We have all had occasion to speak of this situation as "friction" between the President and Congress. And if our sentences are completed they will usually refer to the "balance" which must be established. Others will talk of a "pendulum of checks and balances," which is supposed to suggest that power alternates between one branch of government and another over time. And when it comes to a consideration of federalism, it appears natural to represent this aspect of American government as one of "centrifugal and centripetal forces." This, of course, is the language of mechanics—a language we use very freely. After all, did not "the Constitution provide for the meshing of the wheels of government in such a way that the government machine could function as an integrated mechanism."[9]

Function and integration are suggestive of another language—that of biology. And those who speak it are legion. They have produced hundreds of studies of the "evolution" of this and that. They are, as Woodrow Wilson put it so long ago, "accountable to Darwin, not to Newton."[10] They see institutions as living things, as "growing and evolving organisms" which "must be adapted to changing conditions" and they teach their students accordingly.[11] Their vocabulary is one of process and function, growth and development, alteration and adaptation. For this community, all politics "is modified by its environment, necessitated by its tasks, shaped to its functions by the sheer pressure of life." The Presidency is not a fortress; it is an organism which has been formed by its environment. So the vast increase in the authority and

8 Ibid., p. 113.
9 Carl B. Swisher, *The Growth of Constitutional Power in the United States* (Chicago: Phoenix Books, 1963), p. 51.
10 *Constitutional Government* (New York: Columbia University Press, 1908), p. 56.
11 J. M. Burns and J. W. Peltason, *Government By the People* (Englewood Cliffs, N.J.: Prentice-Hall, 1957), pp. 33, 88.

prestige of this office is explained quite simply: "the political evolution of the last forty years has shown that the modern state requires a strong executive."[12] There is no pendulum in this language, there are no rhythmical swings—there is only a steady process of growth and development, of alteration and adaptation. From here one may proceed to structural-functionalism, to ecological analysis, to the representation of politics as one institutional factor in an "ecology of games."[13]

A game is something we usually think of in terms of recreation or amusement. Conventionally defined, it is a diversion in the form of a contest which is played in accordance with a specified set of rules and which is decided on the basis of skill, strength, or chance. Where a game possesses only chance factors, it has now come to be known as *nonstrategic* in character. Where the players possess discretion, where they may choose courses of action in the interest of a win, the game is said to be *strategic*. Historically, nonstrategic games (craps, solitaire, slot machine) have been described by the language of probability. For strategic games, however, Von Neumann and Morgenstern invented the language of game theory.[14] A scant twenty years old, it has nevertheless become an increasingly popular form of expression. Mathematical formulations—any system of symbolic notation it seems, carry high prestige and even the nonmathematically oriented make use of the vocabulary of game theory. Who now, at some time or another, does not speak of players, strategies and payoffs, of zero-sum and non-zero-sum games, of minimax, choice points and information sets, and, of course, of the rules of the game. For many persons, n-persons, i.e., no discussion is complete

---

[12] Harold Laski, *The American Presidency* (New York: Harper & Row, 1940). See Chapter 1, p. 21.

[13] Norton Long, "The Local Community as an Ecology of Games," *American Journal of Sociology*, Vol. 44 (1958).

[14] The literature of game theory is rather extensive. For an excellent collection of essays and an equally excellent bibliography, see Martin Shubik, *Game Theory and Related Approaches to Social Behavior* (New York: John Wiley & Sons, 1964).

Due Process of Inquiry

unless some such reference is made. And if justification is required for the use of this language, one can emphasize that it was designed to describe decision-making behavior in situations of conflict and contest—a type of behavior which falls within the scope of any of the existing definitions of politics.

And there are other languages. To some colleagues, statistics provides the only grammar of politics. Indeed, during the 1920's, political science was marked by the special efforts of Charles Merriam and the National Conference on the Science of Politics to make numbers *the* language of politics.[15] The lexicon of depth psychology has fascinated us from the time of Lasswell's early studies of political pathology.[16] There are those who will try optics[17] and there are those who have begun to absorb the vocabulary of communication theory.[18] Before long, no doubt, we shall add the language of information theory.[19] The popularity of the concept *system* insures this. "Systems theory" deals with the

15 Some of the Conference Reports can be found in *The American Political Science Review*, Vol. 18 (1924), pp. 119–166; Vol. 19 (1925), pp. 104–162, 371–384. And see Charles E. Merriam, *New Aspects of Politics* (Chicago: University of Chicago Press, 1925), esp. Chapters 3 & 4.

16 See James C. Davies, *Human Nature in Politics* (New York: John Wiley & Sons, 1963). And see Appendix I in Morton A. Kaplan, *System and Process in International Politics* (New York: John Wiley & Sons, 1957).

17 F. W. Riggs, "Agraria and Industria" in W. Siffin (ed.), *Toward the Comparative Study of Public Administration* (Bloomington: Indiana University Press, 1957). And see Riggs, *The Ecology of Public Administration* (Bombay: Asia Publishing House, 1961).

18 Karl Deutsch, *Nationalism and Social Communication* (New York: John Wiley & Sons, 1953); and *The Nerves of Government* (New York: Free Press, 1964).

19 Following Charles Morris, communications theory or the theory of signs (semiotics) may be subdivided into three classes of rules: syntactics (relations between signs); semantics (relations between signs and their referents); pragmatics (relations between signs and their users). Information theory treats of the syntactical rules of communication and is expressed mathematically. See "Foundations of the Theory of Signs" in *International Encyclopedia of Unified Science*, Vol. I, Part 1 (Chicago: University of Chicago Press, 1955). And see Colin Cherry, *On Human Communication* (New York: Science Editions, 1961), Chapter 6.

transmission of energy and information and incorporates a good deal of information theory.[20] Information-energy models[21] are bound to increase and it is not amiss to forecast the widespread inclusion of such terms as alphabets, bits, codes, ensembles, redundancy, signals, noise, limiting capacities into the dictionary of politics. These will be added, no doubt, to a vocabulary that already includes the lexicon of a natural language, and of mechanics, biology,[22] psychology, game theory, and so on. On these foundations, it is not too difficult to combine game theory and depth psychology, optics and functionalism, and mechanics and biology. The vocabulary of political science is truly extraordinary: it is rich, eclectic (interdisciplinary), and fashionable. How much Chinese metaphysics it contains, however, is no light question.

"Blessed magic of Charles Dickens," as Horace Kallen put it forty years ago.[23] The scene is an inn. Pickwick and some young friends are dining when Editor Pott comes upon them. Some preliminary chatter of a delightful sort and Pott is convinced that Pickwick's young friends are waverers—they do not follow the blue. To set their opinion on solid foundations, he urges them to read a series of articles that appeared in his paper in the form of a review of Chinese metaphysics. "An abstruse subject," says Pickwick. "Very," says Pott, but my writer "crammed for it . . . he read up for the subject, at my desire, in the *Encyclopaedia Britannica.*" "I was not aware that this valuable work carried anything on Chinese metaphysics," responds Pickwick. "He read, Sir," rejoins Pott, looking round with a smile of intellectual

[20] James G. Miller, "Toward a General Theory for the Behavioral Sciences" in L. D. White, *The State of the Social Sciences* (Chicago: University of Chicago Press, 1956).

[21] John T. Dorsey, Jr., "The Information-Energy Model" in F. Heady and S. Stokes (eds.), *Papers in Comparative Administration* (Ann Arbor, Mich.: Institute of Public Administration, 1962).

[22] For an analysis on the influence of both mechanics and biology on political science, see Chapters 3, 4 and 5 of this book.

[23] Horace M. Kallen, "Political Science as Psychology," *The American Political Science Review,* Vol. 17 (1923), p. 184; and see, of course, Charles Dickens, *Pickwick Papers.*

Due Process of Inquiry

superiority, "He read for metaphysics under the letter M and for China under the letter C, and combined his information, Sir."

To combine the unrelated, to mix irrelevancies, to confuse different grammars, to build a miscellaneous vocabulary—this is to produce a polyglot that invites the disorganization of a discipline. It does not permit of a clear language of politics. Its rules are as ambiguous as its concepts and are often just as contradictory. Nor does it provide any program to follow. Or it provides so many programs at once, it points observation in so many directions at once, as to challenge the integrity of the field. Field ceases to be a part of the "scientific situation"[24] and political science loses its domain. That we do not agree as to our "primitive facts," that we cannot agree on a working definition of politics, that we possess no common criteria by which to recognize a political act, allows us to appear as scientists in search of a field.

Transfer and Due Process of Inquiry

Restless, uncertain of direction, anxious about our status, we continue to reach out to other domains for concepts and images. Any new language suggestive of scientific yield bids fair to be transported into political science. Hence, it is difficult to fathom Dahl's statement that "the impact of the scientific outlook has been to stimulate caution rather than boldness in searching for broad, explanatory theories."[25] On the contrary, in the last fifteen years we have transferred theories with a boldness that defies scientific caution. We have done exactly what Dahl has urged: we have introduced "broad, bold, even highly vulnerable general theories," as well as theories of lesser order Those who embrace scientific perspectives have done this more explicitly; those who don't, more implicitly. Our problem, accordingly, is not a lack

---

[24] See Chapter 7 of this book for a discussion of "field."
[25] R. A. Dahl, "The Behavioral Approach," *American Political Science Review*, Vol. 55 (1961), p. 772.

Political Theory and Political Science

of theory—even general theory—but an abundance of theory. We possess such a vast number of theories, models, paradigms, concepts, schemas, frames of reference (these are the terms we use) as to make one dizzy. But even more, all appear impregnable to the erosions of experience. They have enormous staying power: few, if any, are ever discarded. And when we become impatient over their limited yield, someone is sure to suggest another expedition into "seemingly unrelated disciplines" to bring back "new ways of looking at things"—i.e., a new language.[26]

None of this is to suggest that minds must be kept closed to new ideas. A science must always be open to suggestions that may be productive of knowledge. Nor does it matter where or how such suggestions originate. Scientists speculate and guess, they are intuitive, they have hunches as to similarities between seemingly diverse worlds. All of this, however, belongs in what Reichenbach has called the "context of discovery."[27] In this context, the scientist is sovereign. He has free choice. There are no scientific limits on what he does. He can choose to represent federalism as a marble cake[28] or a government as a cybernetic system.[29]

But once he makes his choice, he is no longer sovereign. He is now constrained by the "language of science," by the set of rules that make up its grammar.[30] He must follow the logic and procedure of analysis (methodology) that define the scientific situation. And he cannot do otherwise: otherwise is not science.

We may speak, then, of a "rule of law" which governs any

[26] H. Kaufman, "Organization Theory and Political Theory," *American Political Science Review,* Vol. 58 (1964), p. 11.

[27] H. Reichenbach, *The Rise of Scientific Philosophy* (Berkeley: University of California Press, 1951), pp. 230–231. And see *Experience and Prediction* (Chicago: University of Chicago Press, 1938).

[28] Morton Grodzins, "Centralization and Decentralization in the American Federal System" in R. A. Goldwin (ed.), *A Nation of States* (Chicago: Rand McNally, 1961).

[29] Karl Deutsch, *Nerves,* op. cit.

[30] See Felix Kaufman, *Methodology of the Social Sciences* (New York: Oxford University Press, 1944).

Due Process of Inquiry

scientific proposal. As distinguished from natural languages, from common sense procedures and products,[31] the scientific situation, "as ideally described and ideally understood," seeks a special type of knowledge which is both defined and warranted by its own system of rules. There are rules which cover the construction of theory and those which sanction the admission of a proposition into the corpus of a science: there are rules of deductive inference, of induction, of observation, of adequate solutions, of purity of method. These are rules of procedure, maxims of correct scientific conduct, which the scientist must strive to abide by. The scientific situation thus legislates its own due-process clause —a "due process of inquiry." Any proposal, any theory, any model or transfer must be treated in accordance with this principle. In rhetorical disciplines, as political science, this is no easy matter. But failure to honor the requirement of due process not only removes a proposal from the scientific domain but is likely to produce and perpetuate myth in the form of loose and vague metaphors. This, in my view, is a problem of formidable proportions in political science, especially to be noted with respect to the use of models.

The Logic of a Model

When models (and metaphors) are urged and defended, their heuristic functions are usually emphasized. A "new way of looking," a "fresh approach," is assigned value because it stimulates a reorganization of thought that can be quite productive. It may lead to interesting insights, be suggestive of more powerful concepts, disclose relationships heretofore overlooked, and generate questions which were neither contemplated nor anticipated.

---

[31] See Alfred Schutz, "Common Sense and Scientific Interpretation of Human Action," *Philosophy and Phenomenological Research,* Vol. 14 (1953). The bulk of Schutz's work has to do with the analysis of common-sense situations and is contained in his *Collected Works,* 3 vols. (The Hague: Nijhoff, 1967). See also Harold Garfinkel, *Studies in Ethnomethodology* (Englewood Cliffs: Prentice-Hall, 1967).

Political Theory and Political Science

None of this is to be doubted. Yet the ability of a model to provide suggestive clues depends upon an understanding of two of its features which, all too often, are overlooked or ignored.

Any model, like any theory, is a linguistic system.[32] Accordingly, it has its own grammar and vocabulary and it points its user toward special types of observations, evaluations, and interpretations. The more developed (formal) the language (model), the clearer are its concepts, the more explicit and certain are its rules. Where undeveloped, it is largely metaphorical but even here (if used as a frame of reference) it structures inquiry and establishes relevance. Models and metaphors are logics: they constitute methodologies—rules by which we analyze, make inferences, and do research. The logic of a model is very strict. It is expressed in the precise vocabulary (operational) of a scientific language. The logic or program of a metaphor is prescientific: it retains the relative ambiguity of the natural language in which it is stated. The transformation of a metaphor into a scientific model requires the elimination of this ambiguity, the formulation of an ordered set of rules, and the clarification of its basic properties and relationships: the movement here is from a natural to a scientific language.

And, second, to employ a model is *always* to propose the existence of analogy. (If this term is not fashionable, we can substitute isomorphism or homology.) When a model (M) is applied to a problem (P), we treat P "as if" it is similar to M: we "liken" P to M. We "re-present" the problem in terms of (in the language of) the model and in so doing we create a hypothesis: namely, that P is similar in structure and form to M, that it possesses the distinguishing properties of M. To apply, for example, mechanics to government involves the proposition that the two are structurally similar: that government is a member of the set called mechanics; that it is a "case" of mechanics; that it behaves as mechanical systems behave. And because mechanics is a formal

---

32 See Deutsch, *Nerves,* op. cit., pp. 10–11.

Due Process of Inquiry

language marked by clarity of concept and rule, we are able to make predictive statements about the behavior of government. *If* government does possess the structural form, the properties and features of a mechanical system, *then* (by the logic of mechanics) certain behaviors must occur. It is by means of such statements that we test the power of the model, i.e., the range of its application. If it applies, if government is analogous, then we are able to use the language of mechanics to describe the behavior of government.

So, too, when we use biological functionalism, cybernetics, game theory. In each instance, an empirical proposal is made—in fact, a whole set of hypotheses may be derived—which can only be verified through careful analysis and research.

Accordingly, the user of a model must understand its characteristics, its formula, its essential concepts and properties before it can serve him. However restrictive it may appear, following our illustration, he must know mechanics. He must know that a system is mechanical if and only if its basic entities are bodies that move in orbit; that the motion of a body is unequivocally determined by the action of external forces; that these forces arise from the action of other bodies in the system; that change in position is always a function of mass and distance. If he knows this, then he also knows that the method of mechanical analysis is to reduce any process to its irreducible elements or bodies and to treat process as the resultant of the separate bodies acting externally upon each other.

But to follow this "network of tracks," the elements of a governmental system must be identified and placed in correspondence with those of mechanics. The difficulties are great but correspondence is not a luxury: it is a necessity—a precondition for the verification of the proposed analogy. It is what makes a model operational. Any user, therefore, must stipulate what in government is to be equated with what in mechanics: What is to be taken as a basic particle, what is to correspond to force, equilibrium, friction, and so on. And he must understand that if

Political Theory and Political Science

he takes the legislature, or the court, or a department, or a group as basic particles of the system, he is constrained by the logic of mechanics to take the action of any one of them as unequivocally determined by the action of the other system members. If he does not do this, he does not follow the model: he is "off the track" and he has lost the hypothesis as originally postulated. By the logic of mechanics, the pressure in "pressure politics" is a vector and the politics is a resultant. If the user introduces teleological elements, say the functions of "pressure" for politics, the language has changed, the model is different, and the original question is no longer there to be answered.

It is only when some measure of correspondence has been established that the predictive power of the model can be checked. When, for example, the model has been made operational, when it has been related empirically to the problem at issue, hypotheses may be drawn from it and subjected to test. And this, too, is no easy task: anyone who has ever attempted to derive propositions from a deductive system is well aware of the logical problems involved. Nor can the technical difficulties that arise in the construction of a hypothesis and the design of effective test instruments be minimized. But we cannot even approach these problems until the model has been clarified and related observationally to the domain of inquiry.

There are, then, several stages in the use of a model:

1. its initial selection, transfer or formulation—which is anyone's guess;
2. the clarification of its logical properties and basic concepts;
3. the stipulation of correspondence between the elements of the model and the problem under scrutiny;
4. the derivation of hypotheses and their check;
5. the acceptance, rejection, modification of the model itself on the basis of the research undertaken, which in turn leads back to stage one.

Due Process of Inquiry

This, ideally speaking, is the due process of inquiry necessitated by the use of a model. It is a course of action which must be carried through to the end: to the point of breakdown or the point of warranty. Whatever name it goes by (it is often referred to as the rule of "purity of method"), it is this rule which requires the kind of disciplined, consistent, and sustained analysis that we call "rigor."

The Present State of Affairs: Some General Observations

There are several observations that I would now like to make.

1. As is to be expected in rhetorical disciplines, the extensive inventory of re-presentation schemes that characterizes political science is largely metaphorical.[33] However suggestive these schemes are, they provide only a vague *apprehension* of similarity. *They intend a hypothesis: but they cannot provide one.* They cannot provide a hypothesis because their ambiguity and vagueness defies a clear statement of their defining properties. Most, therefore, can neither be justified nor invalidated and they remain outside the scientific domain quite impregnable to the tests of experience. Such transfers not only clutter our vocabularies but they are pregnant sources of myth. Metaphors are frequently taken literally and this means that a presumed analogy is allowed to become an identity without any demonstration of evidence— i.e., an assertion of fact that may be and usually is erroneous. One may add that the more familiar and conventional the metaphor, the greater is the danger.

Yet metaphors can be invaluable aids to analysis. They offer first approximations of similarity that are "often starting points for important advances in knowledge."[34] But this potential can be exploited only when they are made a matter of deliberate

---

33 On metaphorical analysis, see Chapter 3 of this book.
34 Ernest Nagel, *The Structure of Science* (New York: Harcourt, Brace & World, 1961), p. 108.

Political Theory and Political Science

conceptualization, when their properties and features are made so clear as to provide the basis for a working hypothesis. When this occurs, a transfer is being moved to stage two, where it can become a carefully formulated instrument of scientific analysis. And if it cannot be so moved, it is best that it be laid aside.

2. There is in political science an ironic reversal of the requirement of due process of inquiry. Where the interests of science requires a movement from natural languages to technical languages, from metaphors to models, we tend to reverse this process. We frequently take a model which is clear in its literal domain and strip it of all clarity as we transfer it into politics. We take a mechanical, or biological, or communication model and render relatively clear concepts as ambiguous as a marble-cake. We go from stage two back to stage one, instead of proceeding to the task of correspondence. Sometimes this is done following the statement that we have neither the language nor the methodology to properly treat, for example, underdeveloped areas in their transition to modernization. So optical concepts like prism and refraction are transferred as potentially effective models[35] but in the transfer their original meaning is lost. In optics, refraction refers to the deflection of a ray of light on passing obliquely from one density to another. It is explained by the fact that the velocity of light is greater in some media (density) than others. Perhaps "development" may be likened to "light rays," "density" to "sets of specified social conditions," and the law of refraction used to predict the angle or direction of development. Probably not, which is to say that I doubt that the two processes are at all analogous. But if they are, the formulations here do not permit of a check.

Or there will be reference to communications models from which "we shall borrow some elementary ideas" such as frequency and level.[36] As they are employed, however, their technical mean-

---

[35] Riggs, *Ecology*, op. cit., see pp. 94–97.
[36] J. A. Robinson, *Congress and Foreign Policy-Making* (Homewood, Ill.: Dorsey Press, 1962).

Due Process of Inquiry

ings have been lost and they bear very little relation to their use in communications theory. Their meaning does not vary from that of the natural lexicon and nothing of the relational structure of a communications model is apparent either as an organizer or a predictor. Terms here are simply metaphorical and the movement has again been backward.

3. Because our representation systems are generally vague it is difficult to avoid a running together of or a confusion of different models. In the vernacular, this is known as mixing metaphors and it not only obscures imagery and confuses meaning but it frequently leads to contradictory results.[37] A model is a set of rules by which we analyze: to combine two models, each of which prescribes a different form of analysis, of making inferences, may lead to nonsense results as well as erroneous conclusions. These dangers are intensified when the models provide procedures that are inconsistent with each other as in the cases of mechanics and biology. Historically, this union is the source of a good deal of our difficulty in sustaining a line of analysis and in developing hypothetical propositions that we can test.

While this is more prone to happen when our schemes of representation are concealed, a good deal of our explicit modeling shows the same defect. Input-output formulations are made central elements in biological systems[38] but as they are presented they appear as problems in mechanical efficiency—which is an input-output ratio. (Parenthetically, mechanical efficiency suggests itself here as a measure of representative democracy.) To say that the emergence of pressure groups produced changes in the party system and in administrative and legislative processes, that the rapid expansion of executive bureaucracy triggered the

---

[37] See M. Landau, "Baker v. Carr and the Ghost of Federalism" in Glendon Schubert (ed.), *Reapportionment* (New York: Scribners, 1964).

[38] D. Easton, "An Approach to the Analysis of Political Systems," *World Politics,* Vol. 9 (April 1957). They are intended, however, as they are used in information theory.

Political Theory and Political Science

development of legislative and pressure-group bureaucracy[39] is not at all indicative of the concept of system which "implies that . . . roles are interdependent and that a significant change in any one role affects changes in the others and thereby changes the system as a whole."[40] What this last statement means is that unlike the elements of a mechanical system, the parts of a biological or functional system do not possess properties independent of each other. But the statement that precedes simply points to the consequences that pressure groups have for parties in much the same way that the movement of a particle has for another. It is not uncommon to state one line of analysis and follow another.

4. There are, in my view, several reasons for this. Strict application of a biological model is rarely undertaken. Most of the time, the transfers into political science come by way of such sociological functionalists as Parsons, Levy, and Merton. But, as Nagel points out, there is no agreement as to the distinctive properties of sociological-functional analysis. Indeed, the ambiguity that surrounds this term permits of several modes of analysis.[41]

Apart from this, the logic dictated by a biological system is very complex and exceedingly difficult to apply. A biological system never *is:* it is always happening. It is in continuous interchange with its environment. Accordingly, as Mainx points out, a statement of the biological form "not only relates to the organism but takes in a part of the environment."[42] Which is to state

---

39 G. Almond, "Comparative Political Systems" in S. S. Uhlmer (ed.), *Introductory Readings in Political Behavior* (Chicago: Rand McNally, 1961). And see G. Almond and J. Coleman, *The Politics of Developing Areas* (Princeton: Princeton University Press, 1960), p. 8.

40 Ibid., p. 150.

41 Nagel, op. cit., see pp. 520–535. And see Chapters 4 and 5 of this book.

42 Felix Mainx, "Foundations of Biology" in *International Encyclopedia of Unified Science,* Vol. I, Part II (Chicago: University of Chicago Press, 1955), p. 593. And see L. von Bertalanffy, *Problems of Life* (New York: Harper Torchbook, 1960).

Due Process of Inquiry

that things and entities, organs and parts are not the essentials of the system: rather, the essentials are specified relationships of a structural-functional nature. Here structure is not a "sum" of the separate parts acting on each other, of the separate organs adding up to a unit, as it is a slow relational process of long duration, the description of which presupposes a stoppage of time and constitutes a momentary glimpse of what is happening. It is only relative to function, a fast process of a short duration, that a structure appears constant. Constancy, thus, is not a matter of material substance as it is a matter of form of relationship—relationships that we know as boundary exchanges, mutual interdependence, self-regulation, adaptation to disturbance, approaches to steady states. And by the logic of the system, to speak of one is to take in the others. That is, boundary exchange is defined in terms of mutual interdependence which is defined in terms of self-regulation which is defined in terms of adaptation which is defined in terms of steady states. One presupposes the other. The logic of this system is of the order of "transactionalism" as Dewey and Bentley formulated it.[43] What it requires is a close attention to relationship, not to things.[44] What it requires is that we minimize nouns. That we see politics as a set of relationships in a stated environment; that a political leader is not a noun, that a leader is defined in terms of a follower, that it presupposes follower, that you cannot conceive of a leader without a follower, that to speak of one is to speak of the other. That there is no noun *federalism,* but there is a federative relationship such that a statement about the central government is a statement about the states. And so on. The unit of analysis is always a relationship of a transactional character and comprehends context and process. The application of a biological model to politics is no easy

---

43 See John Dewey and Arthur F. Bentley, *Knowing and the Known* (Boston: Beacon Press, 1949) esp. Chapters 4 and 5.

44 Parenthetically, a close attention to "relationship" would minimize the extent to which we reify concepts.

task:[45] it is more easily written about than executed.

5. With respect to transfers, the stipulation of correspondence ideally waits upon a clear understanding of their properties and features. That is, the task of clarifying the model is logically prior to that of linking it to the real-life situations it presumes to organize. When this procedure has been followed in considerable measure, a fairly well-developed deductive system has been formulated and research can turn on its products—propositions that are logically derived. Such research is what we usually refer to as theoretically directed. The Parsonian group is illustrative of the effort to translate biological functionalism so as to provide the type of abstract deductive system that is the hallmark of science. But it is some distance away from establishing the type of unambiguous correspondence that would permit a proper scientific judgment of its claims.[46]

Generally, however, either very simplified portions of a model are employed or we restrict ourselves to specially selected concepts which are intuitively attractive or which appear relevant. But here, as in the case of a model, correspondence is crucial. Concepts are terms of class power and their classification, i.e. assignment, is predictive in character. (If, for example, I define the concept "pencil" in terms of the property "writing" and I assert that an object falls into the class "pencil," I am predicting it will write.) Then, too, it is always a sensible procedure to know what one is talking about. As with all transfers, theoretical constructs do us no good until they are somehow related to empirical phenomena. A concept no less than a model directs us to certain observations and interpretations: that is, it will if it is properly defined. The observations we make measure the power of the concept.

---

[45] See Nagel, op. cit. for a discussion of some of the conceptual problems involved.

[46] William C. Mitchell's effort to apply Parsons' functionalism to politics is especially interesting because of its effort to reduce the ambiguity of many of its crucial concepts. *The American Polity* (New York: The Free Press, 1962).

Due Process of Inquiry

When such concepts as homeostasis or steady state, feedback, boundary, input-output, equilibrium, adaptation, integration are used, what meaning do they have for politics? How does one recognize a steady state? What are the typifying features by which one identifies an instance of feedback? By what criteria does one assign a set of behaviors to the class "input?" And what is the mark of a boundary? Lest this be considered a proposal to enter upon idle definitional chatter, it may be suggested that the establishment of criteria by which one identifies the boundaries between the political system and any other social subsystem is to go a long way toward easing "the problem of recognition" as Rapoport put it.[47] To be able to distinguish boundaries is to be able to identify a political act.

6. Not enough of our efforts are devoted to the rules of relationship or correspondence that are a precondition for theoretical research. One can therefore understand both the anarchic state of political research and the discipline's inability to weed out models and concepts that are neither relevant nor powerful. Moreover, we do not seem too interested in (or we do not see the need for) processing those models or sections of models where some degree of clarity exists and some measure of correspondence has been worked out. Major researches are conducted with only passing reference to existing models and yet it is possible to state some of their base conclusions as propositional derivatives of such models.[48] Nor are doctoral dissertations turned in this direction. Yet if the energy and enthusiasm of the doctoral candidate was directed to this purpose, the results might lead to a cleansing of the linguistic polyglot that is the present state of affairs in political science.

7. Finally, we may offer a comment on "system." There is

---

[47] A. Rapoport, "Various Meanings of Theory," *The American Political Science Review,* Vol. 52 (1958).

[48] It is not too difficult to show, for example, how Dahl's major conclusions in *Who Governs* may be deduced from certain aspects of functionalism.

really no mystery attached to this term. What it stands for is a logic, an ordered set of relationships, and its popularity symbolizes our recognition of the theoretical character of science. Any theory or well-developed model constitutes a system. But systems vary: there are as many systems as there are theories. There is communication theory, mechanical theory, learning theory, biological theory, and so on. Apart from a difference in subject matter, in the primitive facts with which they are concerned, each has its own system. Each has its own system even when two of them are sufficiently isomorphic as to enable one to be taken as the model for the other. General references to "systems analysis"[49] or to "system building" is therefore another way of speaking about scientific theory. When, however, we transfer a system, it is always a particular system (or perhaps a particular combination) and at the present state of the discipline it is likely to be drawn from the natural sciences or mathematics. The reason for this is to be seen in the fact that there are so few social science theories sufficiently developed to be able to use as effective models: their deployment is often tantamount to comparing one unknown to another. Natural science models are "known": their logic is clear and their language precise. One can, therefore, effectively deploy them. But effectiveness is a matter of following the rule of due process, of purity of method. In rather simple and striking language, Schutz has spoken of this rule as follows:

Choose the scheme of reference adequate to the problem you are interested in, consider its limits and possibilities, make its terms compatible and consistent with one another, and having once accepted it, *stick to it!* If, on the other hand, the ramifications of your

---

49 This is now an ambiguous term: it not only is used as synonymous with structural-functionalism but refers to computer technology, operations research, information and communication theory, biological theory, and general systems theory. Underlaying this ambiguity is perhaps the fact that biological functionalism and communication information theory possess certain structural similarities.

Due Process of Inquiry

problem lead you . . . to the acceptance of other schemes of reference and interpretation, do not forget that with the change in the scheme *all terms in the formerly used scheme necessarily undergo a shift of meaning.* To preserve the consistency of your thought you have to see to it that the "subscript" of all the terms and concepts you use is the same."[50]

If now one asks why we use models, it is clear that we must. We will either use those concealed in our natural language or those that are explicitly chosen in the interest of scientific language. Besides, as Morris Raphael Cohen once put it, "Wisdom does not come to him who gapes at nature with an empty head."

---

[50] Alfred Schutz, "The Social World and the Theory of Social Action," *Social Research,* Vol. 27 (1960), p. 209. Emphasis added.

Index

A

Abstraction, 20, 22–23, 206–207
Abstractive differentiation, 179
Accountability, principle of, 17–18, 23, 46, 76
Achievement orientation, 118, 161–62
"Actual working" analysis, 142
Ad hominum, 169
Adams, John, 88–89
Adaptation, 115, 134, 139, 229, 231
Administration, *see* Public administration
Almond, Gabriel, 58–59, 65, 72–73, 106, 118
Alternative theory, 26
Ambiguity, 63–65, 104, 222
Analogies, 6, 78, 81, 83
  models and, 222–25
  See also Biology, analogies based on; Mechanism, analogies based on
Anomalies, 40, 57–58, 173
Apter, David, 106
"As if," 82
Ascription, 17, 165, 166
Assertability, warranted, 45
Assignment, 49
Atheoretical approaches to political science, 65
Authoritative allocation of values, 125

B

Bagehot, Walter, 92, 101, 129–30
Balance, metaphor of, 86–87, 89, 215
"Bandwidth," 125n
Banfield, Edward C., 208
Barnard, Chester, 209
Bay, Christian, 10
Beard, Charles, 99
Behavioralism
  criticism of, 4–5
  paradigm of, 58, 60, 65–66, 74
Bentley, Arthur F., 229
Bergmann, Gustav, 37
Biology, analogies based on, 79, 91–94, 98–101, 111, 126–27, 131–33, 138, 144, 209, 215, 228–29, 232
Black, Max, 114
Boss, the, *see* Machines, political
Braibanti, Ralph, 155, 164
Bronowski, J., 81
Bruno, Giordano, 15
Buck, Roger, 33–34
Bureaucracy, 151, 154–56, 165–72, 188, 227–28
Burgess, John W., 97, 99
Burtt, E. A., 95
Bryce, Lord, 19–20, 97, 123, 131, 140

C

Carlyle, Thomas, 167
Categorization
  conceptualization as, 48, 49
  example of, 49–53
  "field" and, 179–83
  language as, 23, 211–12
  paradox of, 47–48, 179
  in public administration, 205–208
  systems for, 23, 39, 81, 159
  See also Classification
"Caucus Papers," 59, 66
Causation, 17, 19, 28, 127
Centralization, 31, 113, 136–37, 141–42
Chesterton, G. K., 29

235

Index

"Chinese Metaphysics," 76, 114, 218–19
Classification, 22–24, 29, 47–48, 81–82, 125, 179, 205, 207, 211–12, 230
    in development theory, 147–56, 159–72
    functionalism as, 104, 118–19
    See also Categorization; Naming
Closed system, *see* Mechanism, analogies based on
Cohen, Morris A., 82
Cohen, Morris R., 27*n*, 233
Cohesion, 134
Coincidence, 29
Common sense, 29, 181–82, 205
Communications theory, 65, 217, 226–27, 232
Conceptualization
    categories and expectations in, 48–49
    clarity in, 208
    conventional, 52, 108, 147
    metaphor and, 84, 211, 225–26
    naming and, 147–56
    observation and, 47–48
    persuasive, 27
    prediction by, 230–31
    in study of public administration, 195–202, 207
    See also Language
Confirmation, 45
Conformism, 71
Connotation of terms, 49, 150, 157–72
Consensus, truth by, 75
Conservatism, political science accused of, 4, 25, 40, 142
Constancy, 29, 229
Constitution, 17, 92
    functional analysis of, 136–37
    mechanical analogies for, 84, 87, 91, 99
Context of discovery, 220
Continuity, theoretical, 110, 121

Control procedures, 45–46
Conventional terms, 52, 108, 147
Conversion experience, 56, 65, 68, 72, 73
Cooperative rational behavior, 208–10
Correctness, criteria of, 198–99
Correspondence, rules of, 223–24, 231–32
Criticism, science as, 12–13, 54–56
Croly, Herbert, 137
Cybernetics, 220, 223

D

Dahl, Robert A., 219
Darwinian system, 18, 92–93, 101, 133, 138, 215
    See also Evolutionism
Davis, Kingsley, 108
Decision-making, 198–202, 217
Definition
    analytic function of, 184
    lexical, 147–48
    operational, 156
    persuasive, 27, 125, 150, 156–72
    by stipulation, 148, 157
    theoretical, 156
    See also Conceptualization; Naming
Denotation of terms, 49, 105, 109, 147
Descartes, René, 95–96
Deutsch, Karl, 46, 58, 65, 111
Development theory, 17, 109, 113
    means and ends in, 172–76
    names and concepts in, 147–56, 226
    persuasive discourse in, 156–72
Dewey, John, 173–75, 229
Diachronic analysis, 116
Dichotomous variables, 160
Dickens, Charles, 218
Differentiation
    abstractive, 179
    structural, 18, 161, 166, 172

Index

Dimock, Gladys O., 184–86, 188, 190
Dimock, Marshall E., 184–86, 188, 190
Discontinuities, 145
Disjunctive classes, 53, 160
D-N mode of explanation, 43
Dogma, science and, 17, 42, 55, 72–73, 75–76
Durkheim, Emile, 108

E

Easton, David, 6, 20–22, 46, 58, 65, 106, 110, 114, 124–26
Ecology, 216
  defined, 111n
Einstein, Albert, 22
Eisenstadt, S. N., 162–63
"Emergent" levels in functional analysis, 115
Empirical conservatism, 25
Empiricism, 17, 99, 127–29
Energy-transfer model, 104, 110–14, 119, 144, 172
"Enforcers," 17, 60, 65–66, 72–73
Enlightenment, the, 17, 84, 90, 126
Epistemology, 34–42
Euben, J. Peter, 35, 59–60
Eulau, Heinz, 58, 72
Evaluative premises, 173
Evidence
  anomalies in, 40, 57–58, 173
  objectivity and, 46
Evolutionism, 79, 92–93, 99–101, 105, 126–29, 140, 144, 215
Executive, public administration and, 188–90
Existential premises, 173
Expectations, conceptualization and, 48–49
Experts, bureaucracy and, 166–67
Extension of terms, 49, 63

F

Fairlie, John, 183

Falsification, 45
Feedback, 231
Fesler, James, 194
Feyerabend, Paul, 43, 55, 62–63, 70–71
"Field"
  as analytic tool, 178–80
  disintegration of, 185–88
  public administration as, 183–210
  "real types" and, 180–83
  reconstruction of, 208–10
  scientific situation and, 206–208, 219
Flanigan, William, 106–108, 120–21, 123, 144
Fogelman, Edwin, 106–108, 120–21, 123, 144
Ford, Henry Jones, 99, 123, 135, 138–42, 144, 158
Formalism, 79, 129
France, Anatole, 11
Free will, 27–34
Friedrich, Carl J., 157, 164, 169, 174–75
Function
  definition of, 112–13
  latent, 107, 115, 120, 134–35, 138, 143–44
  manifest, 107, 120, 141, 143
  specialization of, 18, 113, 116–18, 161, 172
Functional analysis, 99, 123–24, 132–46, 228
  eclectic, 106–109, 132–46
  empirical, 106, 109, 143, 145
  energy-transfer model of, 104
  meaning of, 104, 108, 110
  middle range and discontinuity in, 120–21
  structural, 64, 104, 106–19, 208, 216
Functional interdependence, 107, 119–20
Functional specificity, 18, 161, 172

Index

G

Galileo, 15
Game theory, 65, 216–17, 223
Geertz, Clifford, 35
General systems theory, 110–12, 114–19, 217–18
Generalization, empirical, 31
German Darwinism, 18
German idealism, 18, 98, 127
Geometry as a prototype of reason, 96, 98, 129
Gestalt switch, 56, 65, 67, 69
Gewirth, Alan, 33
Goodnow, Frank, 98–99, 123, 131, 134, 138, 141, 158, 172, 183, 194–95, 197–99
Gouldner, Alvin, 168–69
Grunbaum, Adolf, 33
Gulick, Luther, 184–85, 197

H

Haddow, Anna, 96–97
Hamilton, Alexander, 87, 89, 96
Hart, A. B., 132
Hegel, G. W. H., 98
Hempel, Carl, 120, 165
Herren Doktoren, 98
Hierarchy of decisions, 200
Hinshaw, Virgil, 36–37
Hobbes, Thomas, 90
Holmes, Oliver Wendell, 99
Holt, Robert T., 59, 65, 72
Homeostasis, 112, 134, 229, 231
Honey, John C., 190n
Hume, David, 90
Hyperfactualism, 101, 122–46
Hypotheses, 11, 26, 48, 83
  metaphor and, 225–26
  testing of, 40–42

I

Idealism, German, 18, 98, 127
"Idealized" scientific maxims, 70
Identification, 10–11, 28–29
  See also Classification
Ideology, 25, 170, 175
  social science and, 35, 37, 39–40
Ilchman, Warren, 167
Immaculate perception, 44, 133
Inconsistency, self-referential, 37
Incrementalism, 56–57
Information-energy models, 218
Information transfer, communications model of, 110
Innovation in science, 57
Input-output formulations, 227, 231
Inquiry
  due process of, 221–33
  "by reason," 97
Institutionalism, 133, 181
Integration in social systems, 113, 231
"Intendedly rational," 200
Intension of terms, 49, 63, 105
Interdependence
  functional, 107, 119–20
  mutual, 172, 174, 229
Irrationality
  in science, 17, 56, 66–67, 74
  in social patterns, 120, 144, 145

J

James, William, 99, 128, 181
Jefferson, Thomas, 90
Juristic framework, 125, 129
Justification, 45

K

Kadi-justice, 166
Kallen, Horace, 218
Kant, Immauel, 98, 127
Kaplan, Morton, 106
Kariel, Henry S., 157, 164, 167–69
Kaufman, Felix, 199, 204
Knowledge
  ideology and, 34–35, 175
  sociology of, 39
  veridical, 19, 45

Index

Koenig, Louis W., 186, 188
Kuhn, Thomas S., 43, 56–76, 154

L

Lakatos, Imre, 61, 63, 67, 73
La Mettrie, Julien Offroy de, 90
Language
 as classification system, 23–24, 179, 205, 207, 211–19, 225–33
 models and, 211, 222
 ordinary, 5, 22–23, 82
 political analysis and, 78, 99
 scientific, 23, 150, 212–13, 220
 See also Conceptualization; Metaphors; Naming
Landis, Dean, 143
Lasswell, Harold, 217
La Palombara, Joseph, 35–36, 117, 154–55, 162, 164, 168–69, 172
Laski, Harold, 167
Latency
 concept of, 134, 138, 143–44
 in social systems, 107, 115, 120, 135
Law, scientfic, 28, 220–21
Leibnitz, Baron von, 108
Levinson, Sanford, 59, 73
Levy, Marion J., Jr., 105, 107, 109, 114, 120–21, 228
Lewis, C. I., 22
Lieber, Francis, 97–98
Linear progression in science, 56
Linguistic relativity, 207, 211–13
Lippmann, Walter, 87–88, 93–94
"Literary theory" in social science, 92, 130
Logical positivism, 194
Louch, A. R., 38
Lovejoy, Arthur O., 168–69
Lowell, A. Lawrence, 20, 131–32, 134, 143–46, 158
Lykken, David T., 71

M

Machiavelli, Niccolò, 3–4

Machines, political, 107, 135–38
Madison, James, 89–91
Magnitude in social systems, 117–18, 162
Mainx, Felix, 228
Manifest functions, 107, 120, 141, 143
Mannheim's paradox, 4, 34–42
Marble-cake, 226
Marcuse, Herbert, 167
Marx, Fritz M., 177
Masterman, Margaret, 63–64, 69
Mathematical-experimental method, 96
Maxwell, James Clerk, 63
McCoy, Charles A., 4, 6, 13
Measurement, 9–11
Mechanism, analogies based on, 79, 85–91, 94–100, 126–27, 129, 215, 228, 232
Meehan, Eugene, 106, 111, 120
Meehl, Paul, 13, 71
Meehl's paradox, 13
Meliorism, 123
Merriam, Charles, 217
Merton, Robert, 32–33, 35, 105, 107, 109, 120–22, 134–36, 140, 144–45, 228
Metaphorical transfer, 83–84, 85, 219–21, 225–33
Metaphors
 dominant, 80, 100, 126
 heuristic functions, of, 145, 152, 221
 hypotheses and, 225–26
 logic of, 221–25
 mixing, 227
 models and, 159, 225–33
 in political analysis, 5, 78–102, 133, 182, 209, 214–15
 rigidified, 102
 See also Analogies; Biology, analogies based on; Mechanism, analogies based on
Metaphysical Club, 18, 99, 127

Index

Method, rule of, 99, 127, 131, 225
"Methodism," 4, 65, 74
Methodolgy
   of early political science, 123–24, 127, 131–35
   problems in, 115, 147–76
   scientific, 9–13, 70–71, 204, 220–21
Mitchell, William, 106, 114–15
Mixed types, 118
Models, 81, 92, 130, 159, 224
   correspondence of phenomena with, 223–24, 231–32
   energy-transfer, 104, 110–14, 119, 144, 172
   information-energy, 218
   logic of, 221–25
   in natural language, 211, 222
   See also Metaphors; Paradigms
Modernization, *see* Development theory
Montgomery, John, 170–72
Moral indifference, 46
Moral Newtonianism, 86–87, 130
Moral philosophy, 17, 128, 181
Morgenstern, Oscar, 216
Morgenthau, Hans, 10, 13, 15–16
Morris, G., 91
Mosher, Frederick C., 190–91
Murphy's Law, 44
Multifunctionality, structural, 118–19
Mutual interdependence, 172, 174, 229
Myth, 83

N

Nagel, Ernest, 37–38, 84, 228
Naming, 122, 130
   concepts and, 147–56
   paradox in, 147
   precision in, 151
   semantic differences and, 156–72
   tautology in, 153
   typology of, 154

   See also Classification; Definition
Naturalistic philosophy, 17
Neologism, 149
Neutrality, objectivity compared to, 43–45
Newtonian system, 17, 81, 84–87, 93–96, 126, 215
   See also Moral Newtonianism
Nominal scaling, 10–11

O

Objectivity
   impossibility of, 33–34, 38
   scientific, nature of, 43–46, 55–56
Observation
   fallibility in, 47–48
   field-determined, 44, 174
   Newton's rule of, 96
   in political science, 29, 99, 128, 133
   pragmatic theory of, 55, 99
   theory-laden, 44, 46
   value-free, 4, 43
One-dimensional man, 167
Open system, 111
   See also Biology, analogies based on
Oppenheimer, J. Robert, 84, 91–92, 94–95
Optics, 217, 226
Organicism, 98, 100–101, 131–32
   See also Biology, analogies based on

P

Paine, Thomas, 86, 194
Pap, Arthur, 179*n*
Paradigms
   ambiguity in, 63–65
   conversion and selection of, 65–69
   descriptive accuracy of, 60–63
   in natural science, 56–57

Index

in political science, 58–60, 63–64, 72–75
Paradox
  in conceptualization, 147
  Mannheim's, 4, 34–42
  Meehl's, 13
Pargellis, Stanley, 91
Partial truths, 35
Parrington, Vernon L., 18
Parsons, Talcott, 105, 107, 109, 114–16, 120, 144, 228
Pattern variables, 116
Peirce, Charles S., 6, 18, 99, 126–27
Persuasive definition, 27, 125, 150, 166–72
Persuasive discourse, theoretical analysis and, 156–72
Pfiffner, John, 184–85
Phenomenological description, 29
Philosophy
  as "inquiry by reason," 97
  moral, 17, 128, 181
  naturalistic, 17
  of science, political science and, 43–76
"Physiology of politics," 143
Playford, John, 4, 6, 13
Plunkett, George Washington, 159
Pluralism, 27, 127
  paradigm of, 58, 64–66
  theoretical, 55, 76
Polanyi, Michael, 3, 66, 75
Policy science, *see* Public administration; Public policy
Political science
  atheoretical approaches to, 65
  continuity in, 110
  conservatism of, 4, 25, 40, 142
  development of American, 123–29, 131–35
  due process of inquiry in, 213–33
  "fields" in, 177–210
  functional analysis in, 103–20, 123–24, 132–46
  hyperfactualism in, 101, 122–46
  methodological problems in, 147–76
  normal, 72–73
  scientific method in, 6–27
  See also other specific topics
Politics-administration dichotomy, 185, 192–98
Polity, 150–54
Pope, Alexander, 88
Popper, Karl, 39, 40, 46, 61–62, 68, 70
Populorum Progressio, 165
Positivism, 43, 68, 194
Post-behavioralist revolution, 6, 12
Power in political science, 66, 73
Practicalism, 128
Praexiological proposal, 109
"Pragmatic revolt," 79, 129
Pragmatic theory of observation, 55, 99
Pragmatism, 18, 19, 98–100, 105, 180–81, 194
  development of, 128–29, 133, 159
Prediction, 230–31
  reflexive, 32–34
Presidential system, 188
Pressure politics, metaphor of, 224
Primitive terms, 151, 163, 164
Prismatic society, theory of, 116
Probability, 11–12, 33, 47
Progress, scientific, 56, 76, 210
Property concepts, 160, 165
Psychological approaches to political science, 65, 217
Public administration
  art-science controversy in, 202–203
  politics-administration dichotomy in, 185, 192–98
  practical and theoretical inquiry in, 203–205
  as rational action, 208–10
  scientific situation of, 205–208
  subject matter of, 183–92

Index

Public administration (*cont.*)
   value-fact dichotomy in, 194, 198–202
Public policy, field of, 123, 185–90, 192
   See also Public administration
Pure types, 118
Pye, Lucien, 117, 161–62

Q

Qualitative changes of administrative tasks, 167
Quantification, 9–10
Quantitative extension of administrative tasks, 163, 167

R

Radcliffe-Brown, 108
Range of application, 49, 193
Range of variation, 160
Rapoport, Anatol, 231
Rational action, 208–209
Rationalism, 70, 95–96, 99, 194
   See also Reason
Reaction function, 34
Real types, 123, 180–83, 196
Realism, 18, 64, 92, 123–24, 129–32, 142
Reality theorem, 32
Reason
   inquiry by, 97
   role in science of, 6, 95, 97, 99, 128
   See also Irrationality; Rationalism
Recognition, problem of, 231
Redundancy, 45, 118–19
Reference class, 125, 128
Reflexive prediction, 32–34
Regularity, 28, 30–31
Reichenbach, H., 220
Reification, 50, 179, 208
Relativism, 3, 36, 43, 68, 71
Relevance, 4, 12, 21–27, 203–204

Relevance system, approved, 40, 205
"Revolution in perpetuity," 62
Rhetoric
   selective use of, 168
   See also Metaphors, in political analysis
Richards, I. A., 78
Richardson, John M., 59, 65, 72
Riggs, Fred, 114–16, 147–54, 160–61, 209
Rose, Edward, 108
Rush, Benjamin, 90–91
Russell, Bertrand, 6

S

Sait, Edward M., 136–38, 141
Sapir, Edward, 211–12
Sayre, Wallace S., 192, 196
Scaling, nominal, 10–11
Schaar, John H., 5
Scheffler, Israel, 46–48, 68
Science
   applied, 24, 27, 204
   complexity of, 15
   crises in, 57, 67, 72–73
   definition of, 7–8, 54
   language of, 23, 150, 212–13, 220
   metaphors from, 84–102, 232
   methodology of, 6, 9–13, 70–71, 204, 220–21
   neutrality in, 43–44
   normal, 56–57, 59–60, 62–63, 70–73
   objectivity in, 43–45, 55–56
   philosophy of, political science and, 43–76
   physical, social science compared to, 7–8, 14–15
   progress in, 56, 59, 76, 210
   revolutions in, 57–76
   rule of law in, 28, 220–21
   Russell on outlook of, 6
   unity of doctrine in, 46
   See also Biology, analogies based

Index

on; Political science; Social science
Scope of coverage, 125, 178, 191
Scriven, Michael, 43
Secularization, 118, 162
Selective perception, 180, 206
Self-fulfilling prophecy, 32–33
Self-referential inconsistency, 37
Self-regulation
  concept of, 134, 144
  in social systesms, 107, 111–12, 119, 229
Senatus consultum, 42
Separation of powers, 49, 188–90
Shapere, Dudley, 61, 64, 68–69
Shils, Edward, 121
Shutz, Alfred, 206–207, 232
Simon, Herbert, 34, 46, 192–94, 198–200, 207–208
Smith, J. Allen, 99
Smith, T. V., 144
Social engineering, 141
Social ritual, 141
Social science
  applied, 193, 202–205
  categorical organization of, 17, 206
  development of, 17–19, 126–29
  object of, 15–16
  physical science compared to, 7–8, 14–15
  pragmatism in, 128–29
  See also Political science
Sociology of knowledge, 39
Specialization, 3, 113, 118, 128
  in development theory, 162
  in public administration, 179, 197–98
Specificity, functional, 18, 161, 172
Statistics, 11, 12, 71, 217
Steady state, 112, 134, 229, 231
Stein, Harold, 189, 197, 205
Stereotypes, 24, 48
Stipulation, definition by, 148, 157
Strauss, Leo, 3, 10, 13

Structural differentiation, 18, 161, 166, 172
Structural functionalism, 64–65, 106–109, 208, 216
  as energy-transfer system, 104, 110–14
  political theory of, 114–19
Structural multifunctionality, 118–19
Structure
  concept of, 134–35, 138, 140
  definition of, 112–13, 229
  differentiation of, 113, 116–18
Subjective intention, 52
Subjectivity in science, 37, 56, 66–67
Substantiation, principle of, 166
Surkin, Marvin, 59, 64, 73
Swift, Jonathan, 89
Synchronic analysis, 116
Systematization, 29
Systems
  deductive, 70, 95–96
  in early political science, 134
  functional imperatives of, 115
  functional interdependence of, 112, 172
  general theory of, 110, 114–19, 217–18
  hierarchy in, 113
  metaphors based on, 79, 231–32
  open, 111, 134
  scale of, 116, 117
  self-regulating, 111–12
  structure and function in, 113
Systems analysis, 65, 232

T

Tabula rasa, 91
Tautology, 52, 150
Teleology, 224
Testability, 54, 70, 71, 75
Theology, science and, 15–17, 72
Theoretical analysis, persuasive discourse and, 156–72

Index

"Theory-laden" observation, 44, 46
Thomas, W. I., 32
Thompson, Sir George, 25
Toulmin, Stephen, 43, 61, 68
Traditionalism, 12, 122, 142
Transactionalism, 229
Transfer, metaphorical, 83-85, 219-21, 225-33
Triviality, 4, 9, 24-25, 74
Truman, David, 58, 59, 64, 72, 73
Truth
  by consensus, 75
  partial, 35
  value, 66
Typification, 11, 23, 28-29, 166, 179

U

Uniformity, 28
Unity of science doctrine, 46
"Universal geometry," 96
Universalism, legal, 161
Utilitarianism, 86

V

Value-fact dichotomy, 194, 198-202
Value judgments
  in definitions, 27, 125, 156-72
  disguised, 25
  in public administration, 198-202
Variation, range of, 160
Verification, 45, 69

Verstehen, 29
Vocabulary, standardized, 148-49, 156
  See also Language
Von Neumann, John, 216

W

Waldo, Dwight, 177-78, 183, 192, 203, 208-209
Walter, Benjamin, 38
Warfare, analogies from, 5-6, 15, 73-74, 214
Warranted assertability, 45
Wartofsky, Marx, 68
Watkins, J. W. N., 70, 72, 74
Weber, Max, 46. 54, 154, 163, 165-70, 207, 209
White, Howard B., 3
White, Leonard, 143, 184-85
White, Leslie, 14-15
Whitehead, Alfred N., 122
Whorf, Benjamin L., 5, 211-12
Willoughby, W. F., 184-85, 195
Wilson, Woodrow, 91-95, 101, 123-26, 130-31, 134, 135, 158, 178, 194-95, 215
Wolfe, Alan, 59, 64, 73
Wolin, Sheldon S., 5, 10, 13, 30-31, 60, 64-66, 73-74
Woolsey, Theodore D., 19, 40, 126
Wright, Chauncey, 18, 99

Z

Zeitgeist, 39, 126, 133